DATE DUE

JUL 0 1 2010		
AUG 0 9 2010		
SEP 1 3 2010		
OCT 1 4 2010		
10.7.11		

Demco, Inc. 38-293

BURMESE LESSONS

. . . .

NAN A. TALESE

DOUBLEDAY

New York • London • Toronto • Sydney • Auckland

Burmese Lessons

A T R U E L O V E S T O R Y

· · · ·

K A R E N C O N N E L L Y

Book design by Maria Carella
Title page photograph courtesy Design Pics / Jupiterimages

Library of Congress Cataloging-in-Publication Data
Connelly, Karen, 1969–
Burmese lessons : a true love story / Karen Connelly.—1st U.S. ed.
p.   cm.
(alk. paper)
1. Connelly, Karen, 1969—Travel—Burma.   2. Burma—Description and
travel.   3. Connelly, Karen, 1969—Relations with men.   4. Guerrillas—
Burma—Biography.   5. Dissenters—Burma—History—20th century.
6. Political refugees—Burma—History—20th century.   7. Political violence—
Burma—History—20th century.   8. Burma—Politics and government—
1988–   I. Title.
DS527.7.C66 2010
959.105'3092—dc22
[B]   2009040447

ISBN 978-0-385-52800-9

PRINTED IN THE UNITED STATES OF AMERICA

1 3 5 7 9 10 8 6 4 2

First United States Edition

Looking back on what has gone before, one cannot help but think that each event, each moment, could not have happened any other way. But this confuses an honest accounting of the past with another kind of denial. Each moment of life is filled with choices. Should I keep my hand moving over this page? Should I continue the narration as planned? As it has been written before?

Or am I free to imagine?

—from *A Chorus of Stones* by Susan Griffin

BURMESE LESSONS

. . . .

PROLOGUE: FIRST WORD

. . . .

In a quiet street near Sule Pagoda, a woman smiles at me for no reason. I smile back and stop walking. She whispers to the little boy playing on the ground between us. He hops forward and takes my hand, pulling me up the steps past his mother (his aunt? a neighbor?) toward the entrance of a narrow cement building.

At the threshold, he stops. I stop, too, and crane my neck to look inside. Surrounded by flowers, the Buddha sits at the back of the dark room. The boy does a little faux bow, suggesting that I bow also.

Why not? I slip off my shoes to enter the candlelit place, then kneel and genuflect three times. The woman and the child and a few other children stand behind me, framed in the doorway. After I bow, the little boy claps his hands. The others laugh. At the boy? Or at me? Or with delight that I am willing to pay homage to the Buddha? The boy, then two little girls, two more boys, and a toddler come barefoot into the room, sidling against one another in shyness. I think I've happened upon the neighborhood shrine for children. Soon there are a dozen kids clustered around me in the candlelight. As flowers surround the Buddha, I am encircled by thin brown limbs, open faces, an assortment of wide or cautious smiles.

Thus I learn my destiny. I will never leave Rangoon. I will return to this street and find a house here and adopt children as beautiful as these ones, or as beautiful as these spirits, it doesn't matter if they have cleft palates and missing limbs, I will love them, I will live here until I die. The Buddha smiles from his cowl of jasmine and marigold, his eyes half closed. As is the custom, I light more incense, a candle, and bow again. The room is small, the air close and cloying, filled with the sweetness of joss sticks and flowers and candle wax. I wipe trickles of sweat away from my nose, my neck.

What are their names? I do not know.

How do you say "What is your name?" in Burmese? I will learn that soon, maybe this afternoon, or tomorrow.

My knees and elbows touch the children; the children put their hard little hands into my hands. One small girl climbs into my lap, pure affection, but the others tease her and she tumbles away, embarrassed. Pyramids of oranges and apples sit before the Enlightened One, along with cups of bright yellow liquid, and a gold-edged tea set, each cup full of tea. Yet the Buddha never drinks. A dozen children and two women stare at me as my eyes adjust to the dim light. Sunlight pours down in the street behind me, but I'm in another world now.

A heavy lady with tattoos on her arms and a wad of betel in her mouth squeezes into the room; somehow there is more space to accommodate her. That is the nature of life in Asia—there is always more space. She places a glass of the fluorescent yellow liquid before me and urges me to drink. I take a small sip. She smiles. The stuff is thick, sweet, and cold. Three of the older children bow again to the shrine. Then they back away, out of the house.

A few minutes later, they return with a tray of food separated into lacquered black bowls: deep-fried nuts and beans, roasted sesame seeds, pickled tea leaf. A tiny silver spoon matches each portion. The tattooed lady hands me a checkered napkin. The room becomes even darker as the entrance crowds with neighbors. An earnest boy who wears large, heavy-framed glasses—owl eyes, the kind I used to wear, too—leans into the room and asks in the most pure-water English, "Excuse me, miss, hello, are you a Buddhist?"

"Not really. But when I was a teenager I lived with a Buddhist family."

He opens his eyes very wide. "In Burma?"

"No. In Thailand."

"Oh, I see, I see." His voice carries the inflection of an era when white women in high-waisted dresses sipped the iced tea brought to them by boys like this clever one, who asks me, "Did you like to live with Buddhists?"

I reply, "I did. Very much. It was a long time ago, when I was just a little older than you."

"And Buddhism remains with you." A flawless sentence, and true.

"Yes. I loved my Thai family. And the Buddha believed in peace," I add. There is an irony, mentioning peace in Rangoon. Yet when he turns to translate I hear only sincerity in his voice.

Our listeners murmur approval, or at least interest. The tattooed lady lays a soft, shiny hand on my inner arm. *"Hla-deh,"* she says. I echo, *"Hla-deh,"* in response, trying the word out. The children laugh. I say this word to each of them, which elicits giggles, shrieks, downcast eyes from the older girls.

Keen to make conversation, but also shy, the bespectacled young man says over the children's black heads, "Please excuse my broken English. I study only one." He corrects himself immediately. "I study alone."

"But you speak English very well. Please excuse my broken Burmese."

He smiles, translates for the benefit of the neighbors. Then he excuses himself. "I am going to fetch my best friend. He would like to meet you. He is a teacher."

The boy leaves and a woman enters, beautifully dressed in a lavender blouse and a purple sarong. First she genuflects before the Buddha, lights more incense, a candle. Then she turns and bestows upon me a radiant smile. Speaks. I don't understand a word. After a moment of peering at my face, she rises and disappears into the back of the house. For this is a house, a family dwelling; only its small, open-to-the-street sitting room serves as a shrine.

She returns with a round disk of stone and a thick stick of wood. It must be *thanaka*. The people, especially the women, wear it as a kind of powder, to absorb sweat and to protect their skin from the sun. Ground into a paste, it has a faintly sweet fragrance and a texture like fine wet clay. I wonder if it has healing properties; former political prisoners on the Thai border told me about using the paste on their scabies and insect bites while they were incarcerated. Men don't wear it in an obviously cosmetic manner, as women do, but every man was once a small boy, and his mother smeared the delicate cream on his bare skin before he went outside to play.

Now the woman splashes the smooth stone disk with water. She pushes the heel of her hand against the soft wood; an ivory wedge has opened in the bark at the base of the stick. She rubs the thanaka against the stone in slow circles, adding more water every few seconds until the ground wood becomes a creamy paste. We watch her silently. It's a simple daily thing, something all the women do, but it becomes the first ritual of my arrival, a ceremony attended by children, women, the Buddha himself, glowing there. The woman mimes putting the paste on her own face, then gestures at me, at my cheeks, asking if it's all right. I smile. With soft, cool fingers, she smoothes the hair away from my face. The intimacy of the act makes my chest tighten. Food and drink are spread out before me, and a stranger touches my face. Without design or craving. Just thanaka.

She pats the wet stone then touches me again, smearing the mixture on one cheek, then the other. She makes two spiraling circles. Then sits back on her bare heels to look at her work. Touches the stone again and draws an ivory line down the center of my nose. *"Hla-deh! Hla-deh!"* The aspirated sound at the beginning of the word makes it soft, a breath, though the first syllable has a bright, rising tone.

I point at her with my chin. *"May May hla-deh!"* *May May* means "Mama." My voice elicits more laughter from the children, the women, the lady of thanaka, the boy in large glasses, who is back, I see when I turn around, with his friend and a few more neighbors. The woman with tattoos claps her hands.

This is my first day in Burma, my first two hours in Rangoon.

Hla-deh is the first lesson the people give me. It is the word for "beautiful."

CHAPTER 1

THE DINNER PARTY

. . . .

I said that I would find the place myself. I wanted to walk through the city, into Chinatown. "No, thank you. I do not want a ride, it's all right."

The pause at the other end of the phone was so long that I thought the line had gone dead.

"Are you still there?"

He asked again, "You . . . want . . . to walk?" Judging from the hesitating formality of the telephone exchanges we'd had earlier, I'd decided that my volunteer guide, San Aung, was over fifty, and a dedicated worry-wart.

"I do want to walk. Please tell me again the name of the restaurant. And how to get there."

He did. He described it all carefully. He said, "But it can get dark in the evenings. You will be all right alone? I do not want you to get lost."

How dark could it possibly get in a city? I said, "There is no possibility that I will get lost."

. . .

I set off gamely enough. The light coaxes me out of weariness and into in-
toxicating newness: the tea-shop stools, the bottle caps pressed like ancient
coins into the hardened mud of the streets; the scowling face of a boy as
he pours steaming water into a large pot, then tosses in a load of dirty
dishes. As I cross the street, a woman reaches up to a yellow-waterfall
tree—laburnum?—snaps off a lemony sprig, and tucks it like a bird into
her braided hair.

Even the dirt draws me in, the realness of dirt that lines the edges of
millions of flip-flop-clad feet, including my own, which I wash every
evening before I sleep, as I am unable to get into bed with dirty feet—a
habit ingrained a decade ago, when I lived with Pee-Moi and Paw Prasert
in northern Thailand. It comes flooding back to me in the flood of Rangoon, that early time cascading into this one.

I experienced a surge of those memories when I first moved back to
Thailand six months ago, a vivid unrolling of the past in a small Thai
town, my long-ago life with my Thai family. When I was seventeen, I went
to live and study for a year in northern Thailand. It was a Rotary Exchange
Program—a dry-sounding moniker for an experience that was utterly
transformative. I was a precocious teenager, already publishing my poems
and stories, and chafing for more contact with the big world. Living in a
strange, brilliant, difficult place gave me something specific to write about,
and the book I eventually published about my life in Denchai—*Dream of
a Thousand Lives*—became a bestseller. It also financed several more years
abroad and set me up, at twenty-five, as a bona-fide writer.

Earlier this year I returned to Thailand, but now I live in the welter
and roar of Bangkok, a city I both love and hate for its chaos. At the height
of the after-work rush, Rangoon seems much quieter than Bangkok, more
manageable, less noisy. Though noisy enough. The glorious disorder
slowly organizes itself into the busy face of evening. Where at first I
moved, dazed and jostled, in a thick crowd of bodies, now I float from one

stream of rushing humans to another. Young office men with soft faces, housewives confounded by the price of chicken, students who glimmer with intelligence. On Anawrahta Street, small-time salesmen with slicked-back hair have spread their wares—nail clippers, small electronic gizmos, hand mirrors, ballpoint pens, sunglasses, bottles of cologne, and loads of used clothes, much of it smuggled in from Thailand or Bangladesh, since Burma produces very little—on swaths of the wide sidewalk.

One of these salesmen, white-suited and handsome, like a Burmese version of an Italian gangster, is picking his nose when he meets my inquisitive eyes. He smiles at me unabashedly. Women walk home with their baskets of greens and onions, and other women stride in the opposite direction, toward the river and the boats that will ferry them across it. Four young Indian children in their pyjamas, their eyes kohled and their cheeks swirled with thanaka, play a checkers-like game on a set of broad steps. Normally I would stop to watch, but I must not be late for dinner.

Here is Chinatown, with its blue and green buildings, wooden shutters and elegant roofs, looking romantic in the gold leaf of dusk. The paint on the buildings is new, thin and lime-based, making the whitewashing both literal and figurative. The SLORC—that is, the State Law and Order Restoration Council, the group of generals who rule Burma—recently decreed it for all the buildings of Rangoon. Not so long ago, the SLORC also forcibly moved entire communities of the city's poorest people into primitive shantytowns on the periphery of the city so that foreign visitors like myself are not burdened with the sight of them.

The city is being beautified because, after decades of a socialist isolationist policy—the Burma Socialist Program Party was created by General Ne Win, who staged a coup d'état in 1962—the regime has changed its stripes. This is Visit Myanmar Year, and the government wants foreigners to visit, spend money, come back, and, most important, do business. The usual weeklong visa has been extended to a month; business visas last longer. There are Lucky Strike and Chivas Regal billboards on the streets; a few big hotels are already standing and more are under construction,

most of them built jointly by the SLORC and its favorite business partners, the Chinese. The shift to a free-market economy came abruptly, in
1989, after decades of mismanaged and increasingly non-functioning na-
tionalization schemes. The aged General Ne Win handed power over to
a group of generals under his sway—the SLORC—and within months
"the Burmese way to socialism," as it used to be called, became the
Burmese way to rampant capitalism fueled by the opium trade and the
plunder of natural resources. The beneficiaries of this extraordinary
economic shift are the generals—all of whom are ethnic Burmans and
Buddhists—and their business partners and friends, who are often Sino-
Burmese with connections to the Chinese business world and black market. There are Thai, Singaporean, German, French, American, and
Canadian companies in Burma as well, operating factories, mines,
pipelines in direct association with the generals, but their presence is minuscule compared with that of the Chinese. In less than a decade, most of
Mandalay's shops, hotels, restaurants, and prime real estate have been sold
to Sino-Burmese and Chinese people, who are able to buy the identity papers of dead Burmans for a few hundred dollars. The same shift of own-
ership is happening in Rangoon as impoverished Burmese people are
forced to sell their properties. When I left the guesthouse, I asked Myo
Thant, the clerk, the best way to get to Chinatown. He laughed and said,
"You're in Chinatown already." I shook my head, misunderstanding. "The
whole city," he said. "It is becoming Chinese town."

But I'm in the heart of old Chinatown now. And I am lost. Darkness falls
quickly, as it does in the tropics, and falls hard, as it does in Rangoon, because none of the lights on these streets are working. I take a moment to
get my bearings and consult my map, which happens to have several errors
on it—that is, if I'm reading it correctly. Soon I am rushing around in the
dark, flustered and big-eyed and without composure, approaching and re-

treating from the wrong pools of light and people, my glasses slipping down my nose.

But I do find my dinner party, finally, when San Aung sees a woman stumbling by on the broken pavement and calls out, "Miss Karen," accent on the second syllable, Ka-rén, like the ethnic group that has been at war with the Burmese military for half a century. I approach the table, smiling and sweating in equal measure as I greet everyone, a dozen or so dinner guests gathered together by San Aung, who is not in his fifties at all but is a good-looking man of perhaps thirty-five with high cheekbones in a long Indian face. With his gorgeous head of gleaming hair and his immaculate clothes, he looks like a movie star. He wears a blue pin-striped shirt and a dark blue longyi; both seem to have been lifted off an ironing board five minutes ago. He shakes my hand three times, then lets go and turns to introduce me to the others, giving me condensed biographies as we make our way around the table of mostly Burmese writers. But a lawyer is also here, and a history professor who works at the Japanese embassy (the pay is much better, the university is a shambles), a burly ship's captain who loves Gorky (he announces this immediately, as an intellectual credential) a woman who collects Burmese folktales, and a Swedish journalist, Anita. Even though she's sitting down, I can tell that she is very tall.

Plates of food are already arriving, heaps of greens and noodles and two whole fishes. And a pile of twisted, glistening stuff: very possibly a platter of silver worms. The ship's captain and a very rotund poet make a place for me between them and, once I'm seated, the introductory quiet closes up with voices again, like steady waves after a lull. Streams of Burmese rush around me, and English strides out into the air, directed to Anita, to me, and to a man I'd assumed was part of the local contingent but who is, in fact, Johnny, a Filipino photographer employed by *Time* magazine.

Everyone talks about books and writers, passing the names back and forth like gem dealers handling sapphires and rubies, marveling at the riches. Though at the mention of Tolstoy and *Anna Karenina,* San Aung pushes out his bottom lip in contemptuous-Frenchman style and huffs, "But it was too much, all those characters. I couldn't keep them straight. There were too many of them at the beginning and too many at the end." He laughs. "I did not read the middle, but I'm sure it was the same problem."

The ship's captain, clearly a great admirer of the old Russian writers, is scandalized. "But that is how Tolstoy . . ." He looks at me, open-mouthed, searching for the word on my white face. Apparently, he finds it. "That is how Tolstoy re-creates the world. He fills his books with real human beings. Yes, there are many of them; Russia is a big country! And all different kinds of people live in his work, not just one class or another class."

Is he really a ship's captain? He talks like a professor. I tell him, "Listening to you makes me want to be a writer."

He replies in a tone close to reverence, "You already are a writer. How fortunate!"

"But writing is hard work. And lonely. There may be a lot of characters in a story or a book, but the writer is always alone with them." I look around the table. "And there's never enough money."

My fellow writers at the table nod their agreement. But I know that none of them are spoiled as I am spoiled: by early success, by government grants and, most abundantly, by freedom. Yet still I complain. In Burma! It's disgusting.

Lately I've found my enthusiasm for my calling on the wane, partly because I know I'm stuck with it. Most of my life will be spent in a room in front of a computer, tapping out the visions in my head, reworking hand-written scrawls. This notion once filled me with delight. Now it just makes me want to get out of the room and meet someone for a drink—preferably someone who looks like San Aung.

However, the captain is right. Tolstoy has been dead for one hundred years, yet *Anna Karenina* is alive and beloved in Rangoon. It is extraordi-

nary that something so still, so lifeless—black type on the cheap paper of
Penguin's classic pocketbook—can contain a living world. A Burmese man
can step into a time machine and go to nineteenth-century Russia just by
turning one page, then another, and another, until he is entangled emotionally and intellectually in fictional lives. Strangers become his familiars.

I look around the table at the animated faces. Tall Anita is flushed, the
tip of her nose red—did she eat a chili? The folktale collector talks across
the table to the lawyer, who nods and grunts every few sentences (ah, I
know it well, the Asian male grunt—so expressive, so full of feeling!) to
show her that he's listening. He also stares, as I do, at the woman's plump
mauve mouth. I wonder if she is married. Or if he is. Possibly they are
married to each other.

Good travel is like good reading: you go inside a new world and cannot resist it. This will implicate me, I think, chopsticking a load of delicious
oily noodles into my mouth. I love eating with strangers. Nothing but sex
brings people together so quickly; dining is usually more friendly and lasts
longer. People are still chatting, but the steamed fish has displaced the miracle of Tolstoy. Under a gloss of sweet sauce and dark skin is delicious
white flesh, fat flakes of it without too many bones.

The poet spoons a tangle of worms onto my plate. "Excuse me," he
says, his voice reminiscent of Tom Waits's, a rough engine idling the vocal
cords. "This is the custom. You have not tasted this yet. Delicious. We
make sure you eat. I still do this for my daughter." He means placing the
finest morsels of food on her plate, feeding her. When he smiles, his narrow eyes sink into folds of heavy eyelid. He has great bulldog jowls, too, a
wide, lumpy nose, and a few dribbles of a previous meal staining his shirt.
He smells like a tea shop during the early-morning rush: earthy and smoky
and surprisingly sweet, as though he had an Indian pastry in his breast
pocket. He has not stopped smoking his cheroot since I arrived. Many
Burmese people are beautiful. If not truly endowed with good looks, they
have the straight-backed, slender grace that passes as beauty. Therefore it
is refreshing, even reassuring, to meet this man.

"I'm very sorry, but can you tell me your name again?"

"I am Tin Moe," he answers.

And now I recognize him. Sayagyi—the great teacher—Tin Moe, the famous, beloved poet laureate of Burma, imprisoned for five years because of his writings and his support of the National League for Democracy, the political party headed by Aung San Suu Kyi. He was on a list of imprisoned Burmese writers that PEN published a couple of years ago. Ma Thida, a young woman writer, was on the same list. Tin Moe was released; Ma Thida is still in prison.

"It's so good to meet you, U Tin Moe. I'm honored to be sitting with people who love books so much. And with such a famous poet! I didn't expect to be so lucky on my first trip to Burma."

"Oh, thank you, thank you. It is our pleasure." He motions toward my plate with his chin. "Your eels will be cold, Miss Karen. Please eat them."

"These are eels?"

The captain, who has been listening to every word, interjects, "Babies."

"Really?" Poor things! They are salty, faintly crablike, and sublime.

My fellow diners have started talking about writers again: Havel, Kundera, Faulkner—have I read them, and do I like Gabriel García Márquez, and why, and who else have I read, who is my favorite writer? Someone makes the joke that Márquez, in *One Hundred Years of Solitude,* was competing with Tolstoy for the greatest number of characters, to which San Aung responds sharply, "That's another novel I could not read. Life is too short." Then he asks my opinion about several Swedish authors. I have to admit that I've never read them.

The hunger for books is greater than the hunger for food, though there is no doubt that the conversation is enhanced by the meal. When the waiter brings new dishes, of prawns, a broccoli-like green stir-fried with garlic and ginger, and spicy eggplant, new discussions arise with the fragrant steam. We eat and talk, turning to each other as we swallow, laughing often, over many comments and turns in the conversation, our voices growing louder and louder, until Sayagyi Tin Moe says, "It's very good, to talk about all these books, these writers." His eyes shine. "But this talk makes me think of all the books that Burmese people cannot read." He heaves a sigh and picks up his cheroot again. He scrabbles in his breast pockets for a lighter. "So many of our own books are banned now. Many names cannot be printed. Her name. No one is allowed to publish her name."

The table has fallen silent and we attend him, respectfully, knowing who the unnamed woman is. His time in prison had as much to do with his unequivocal support of Aung San Suu Kyi as it did with his writing.

"Did you know"—he turns to me—"that each new book a writer produces here must be copied out four times and given to four different censors? For a Burmese writer, that is a great expense. Then each censor puts lines through any offending passages. After that, the manuscript has to be rewritten without those passages. This is not the way any normal writer likes to write. It's the way the censors like to write. One of my friends, a popular novelist, not a political writer, had to write her last book five times. It almost drove her crazy. But she had to do it. She wants to write her books. She doesn't want to go to jail and get tuberculosis."

"Like Ma Thida," I say in a low tone.

"Do you know her?"

"I know of her. One of the reasons I've come here is to find out more about her. I do some work for a group in Canada that has made Ma Thida an honorary member, and we're lobbying the Burmese government for her release."

"Amnesty International?"

"No. PEN Canada. It's an international organization. I'm a member of the Canadian chapter."

"Ah, yes," someone says. "They support U Win Tin also." U Win Tin was detained at the same time that Suu Kyi began her house arrest. His sentence was recently extended because he had made an attempt to inform the U.N. about the appalling conditions of Burmese prisons.*

"Ma Thida and I worked together," says the old poet. "She is like a daughter to me. She's a dear woman, and a fine writer."

"Do you know much about her situation?"

"The tuberculosis is under control. But she also has some—I don't know, some female problems. I'm not sure. She suffers with that, but she is doing a lot of meditation. For many hours a day, meditating. That is how she survives in the prison."

"Vipassana meditation," the folktale collector clarifies. "That is how Buddhism helps many political prisoners." She lowers her voice. "While the Lady was under house arrest, she used to sit vipassana every day, for some hours. Do you ever meditate?"

"I try. But I'm not very good at it."

She laughs. "That's normal. We need to practice every day or it remains difficult. Sometimes I go into retreat at a monastery near Mandalay, and by the end of two weeks I start to feel calm!"

Sayagyi Tin Moe snorts. "By the end of twenty years, you would be extremely calm."

"No," says the woman reflectively. "I think I would be insane."

"Insane in Insein," intones San Aung in a jokey voice. Insein is the name of the prison where many political prisoners are held, including Ma Thida.

Sayagyi Tin Moe says, "If you are a writer in this country, going to Insein is an occupational hazard. I am not allowed to publish anymore, not even magazine articles. My old poems are in the school books, but my books are banned." He looks across the table and says something to the

*U Win Tin was Burma's longest-serving prisoner of conscience. After being in prison for nineteen years, he was finally released in September of 2008, at the age of seventy-nine.

folktale collector, who breathes a few words—a consolation or a whispered condemnation, I don't know. It's not the moment to ask for a translation. Everyone at our table is silent, as though in a show of respect for all the banned words and writers, which throws the noise of the street and the voices of the other diners into sharp relief—the ongoing clatter of plates and cutlery, the hum of gaslights and music playing nearby.

Suddenly the poet lifts up his hands like an orchestra conductor. "Keep talking! Talk, talk." He raises his voice. "It is a good thing to do. We can still talk!" Then he has such an energetic coughing fit that he has to put down his cheroot. After recovering, he raises the dark green cigar and addresses it, "My good friend." Then, to me, "It is like a companion. The tea shop, the cheroot, and the writing. They go together."

"It's like that in Canada, too," I say. "And Greece. Writers love to smoke and drink."

"An international brotherhood," remarks the lawyer.

"And sisterhood," adds the folktale collector, with her mauve smile.

Sayagyi Tin Moe turns his big head toward me and asks, "Will you write a book about our country?"

Memorably, I answer, "Uh . . . I'm not sure. I'm . . ." How to dodge the question with some grace? "Right now I am still reading books about your country. I have so much to learn."

Which is absolutely true. The purpose of my visit, ostensibly, is to collect enough material to publish a few articles about political prisoners here. Because I've been living in Bangkok for the past few months, it seemed a logical step in my work for PEN Canada to come to Burma and try to make contact with former political prisoners and the friends and families of current political prisoners. Ma Thida is only one of more than two thousand. I've become attached to her because of the similarities between us— and the gaping differences. At twenty-nine, she is very close to my age. While I am free to write my books and live my adventurous life, Ma Thida is in solitary confinement, ticking the days off her twenty-year sentence. Her crime? Writing short stories that are critical of the military regime.

Both of us are young women writers. Is that where the similarity ends? The single great accident of human existence is geography: where we are born in this bordered, divided, largely unjust world. My life would have been different if I had been born elsewhere. This is an obvious enough notion, but when I was a child I used to think of it as a kind of magic. At the age of eight, when our Filipino neighbors moved in next door, I had an epiphany: "I" would not exist if I had been born in another country, to other parents. "I" was contingent upon so many things that "I" had no control over. It was a dizzying concept, and I have never ceased to feel its power. If I had been born in a country like Burma, who would I be? What would I look like?

In the depth of a Canadian winter, Ma Thida's photograph had haunted me. Framed by black hair, the attractive round face wore a small, impish smile. She regarded me with a calm gaze. It was hard to believe that she was in prison even as I thought of her; that she was suffering from tuberculosis as I prepared to return to Asia, packing up my apartment— a place I had lived in for less than six months—putting all the necessities for a year or two of travel into a small suitcase and a backpack. The least I could do was try to find out more about her, and write a couple of articles about the situation in Burma. Then, after another month or so in Thailand, I would return to my little island home in Greece and stay put, just writing and gardening, for a good long while. The past couple of years have been a whirlwind of book tours and research trips across three different continents. Though weary of traveling, I felt that this journey to Burma was crucial. And would be short: a few weeks at the most.

That was the modest, reasonable plan of a few days ago, before the plane touched down in Rangoon. Now my mind has been tossed upside down by these people. Yesterday my cab driver said of the ruling generals, "They have guns, but no brains." He grimly bared his teeth. "But guns kill us." And the merchant I chatted with at a tea shop: when I quietly asked him about the Lady—a discreet way of referring to Aung San Suu Kyi—he was so taken aback that he said, "No, I am sorry. I am afraid to talk about that." Then he stood up and left me sitting there, ashamed that I had not anticipated his fear, that I do not have the mechanism of fear myself. At least, not the fear of speaking.

Plates of fruit arrive. The end of the evening has come, but the lawyer asks me about Noam Chomsky, which in turn leads to a discussion about the failures of democracy, and how those failures are preferable to the bloodier failures of dictatorship. As the tables around us empty, we're talking about art. Anita describes the beauty of the Musée d'Orsay (her long hands in the air like white sculpture), and Sayagyi Tin Moe invites us to a gallery opening. San Aung says he knows a group of painters and asks if I would like to meet them. The fruit is finished and we are drowsy—the old poet has nodded off, twice, snoring so loudly that he wakes himself up again— but my companions are still hungry for more information, more news, more evidence of the ongoing life of the world, and how their own country, how they themselves, are connected to that world—the realm of freely circulating ideas and books and newspapers and technologies. Freely circulating people, in fact—Anita and Johnny and myself bring our worlds with us. In an isolated place like Burma, this kind of meeting is also communion that vivifies, renews, the way color comes as a mind-sparking pleasure after weeks in a monochromatic hospital ward.

The boys who clean and stack the night tables are swishing rags over the wood and the cracked Formica and sluicing the dirty water down the gutters. Our party cannot stretch the evening any further; we need to sleep. No, no, the folktale collector says, shaking her head theatrically and pressing my hand, you must not walk back to your guesthouse. San Aung will see you home—he has a car.

Goodbye, goodbye. We turn to one another with a curious mixture of formality and friendliness, not quite bowing but almost, smiling too, laughter igniting without reason, just the punchiness of being so tired, so pleased with the company. *"Now-mak dwei-may,"* I say, which brings another laugh, the colloquialism comical in the mouth of someone who cannot speak the language. "See you later."

The poet shakes my hand and whispers in his gravelly voice, "Very quickly you will learn Burmese. That will help you."

"Help me what?"

"Write the book."

CHAPTER 2

BURMESE LESSONS

. . . .

During the Days, I walk among the Buddhas of Pagan. Sometimes the coat of whitewash is gone, revealing the Holy One's countenance
as deep red, the same color as the bricks people still bake near the river's
edge. These statues are eight hundred, nine hundred, almost a thousand
years old, naked of the gold and gems that once made them so famous.

Twice in the fresh dark of morning, I have hired a horse-cart driver to
take me to the farther sites. I can die now, for I have sat atop one of the
great temples of Pagan and watched the sun rise as its own true self, a great
globe of fire. My head burned with the vision, which doubled on my retina
when I blinked. My young driver, Min Ley, sat on the stone rampart without speaking, his back to glory. He watched me for the sunrise and its dé-
nouement. After the dark plain caught red and gold fire, the mist burned
away to reveal the land's bounty: more than two thousand white-and-gold-
tipped stupas, crumbling pagodas, sister and brother temples, lines of toddy
palms, the immense gray Irrawaddy River, wide as a small lake.

Can I remember the word for "beautiful"? Humans meet a landscape
like this and all our words become second-rate. The beauty is mythical,

mesmerizing; from elsewhere, I thought, then corrected myself. The plain of temples was just there. It is I who come from elsewhere, which is why the driver stared at me with such patient interest. His was not a sexual gaze, which would have made me nervous out there at dawn in the middle of a vast ruined kingdom, in my bare feet, my shoes far below at the temple entrance. He watched me as though observing a strange animal.

I stared at the plain of fire with equal fascination, and more longing. After the familiarity of my makeshift room in Bangkok, I have become once again an absolute foreigner in another country, my notebook filling with words spelled in crude phonetics, my mind reeling, my body craving stability. Why do I keep doing this to myself—leaving, beginning with nothing, gathering other people's stories? I want to go home now: the small stone house in Greece, a view of the sea between olive trees. So why have I come to a nation ruled by a superstitious and brutal bevy of generals, with their menacing billboards and their malnourished chain gangs of intellectuals and students?

Barely two weeks in, and Burma is changing me. I know that what I see here, what I choose to write about, could be transformative. But how? Why? What has drawn me in so quickly? Several mornings in a row now, I have woken to the absolute conviction that I have to stay in Burma longer, as long as possible. A month, two, three. How long can I stay? And I must write about Burma, and the political situation here, just as the old poet suggested.

There, at the top of the temple, I thought how ephemeral the human being is, how light. I saw myself from high above: a speck of blood and bone in that extraordinary landscape. Yet still so loaded down by thoughts and desires. The Buddha knew what he was talking about when he declared that desire was the root of all suffering. When I returned to Thailand last year, I started meditating again, sporadically, even in the throb and clamor of Bangkok. Just being in Southeast Asia was enough to make me sit down and shut up, become unself-conscious, even for a breath.

Many times in my life I have wished to be a fish, or a tree, or an otter. Swimming in the Greek Aegean, hiking in the Rockies, watching seals near Protection Island: if only I could slide through the membrane, like a magician or a subatomic particle, and become something other, there would be peace. In Pagan, sitting at the crown of a world that no longer exists, I reached the bottom of such wishes: a lichen-red stone would be enough. Turn me into the temple flagstone under the driver's foot and let me give in, with igneous equanimity, to the ravages of time and sunlight.

Dawn pulled itself out of the earth and across the burning sky, drawing the mythical human past of Pagan with it. I recalled the stories from the tattered little book San Aung gave me before I left Rangoon, tales about the lavish courts of King Anawrahta—grand battles on the plains, fates decided by dreams and numbers, alchemic preparations, the lives of the princes and princesses in their riverside palaces. I could almost hear voices.

I *did* hear voices. High-pitched, lilting. Far below, just beyond the horse and cart, two children appeared, and a smattering of black-on-white goats. Their wooden slippers clackety-clacked as they stepped up the stone pediment at the base of the temple. Then the clatter intensified. I tried to lean over the rampart to see what they were doing—tap-dancing?—but Min Ley waved me away from the low edge. He pointed toward the narrow stairwell that would lead us back to the ground.

By the time we got down the many steep stairs that turn inside the temple like the swirl of a shell, the children were half an acre away, the goats salt-and-peppered around them. The plain beyond was no longer reddish, or rose, but turning back to sage yellow. We climbed into the horse cart to move on to another site. It was already getting hot.

During the Mon rule of lower Burma, Pagan was called Tattadesa, "the parched land." First kings and queens then pious noblemen and women built lavish temples here in their dedication to Theravada Buddhism, hoping to make merit for their next lives. The golden age lasted from 1044 to

1287, when King Narathihapate fled from the Mongol invaders who destroyed the splendor that was the kingdom. Successive generations of raiders and thieves came, and sun and wind. But the strength of stone and brick is surprising. And the people who have lived here for centuries— they call themselves the slaves of the temples—have protected the holy sites.

The crumbling hands of the statues are like the faces, eerily alive. See them in a certain light and you freeze, waiting for the fingers to curl or straighten. *The beginning and the ending / The final moment / My hands.* The hot dust and the sawing cicadas remind me, at every turn, of Greece. My mind grapples for foreign words that will fit the landscape, and, because I don't have Burmese, I hear the Greek poet Seferis over and over. I have spent hours reading his poems, in Greek and English, on the shores of an island not far from his birthplace: *These stones I have carried as long as I was able / These stones I have loved as long as I was able.*

At various sites, I find dozens of young women helping with the restoration work, each with fifteen bricks balanced on her head. With little regard for the demands of archeology and architecture, the generals are fixing things—laying slabs of concrete over temple pediments, crudely whitewashing Buddhas, rebuilding walls without much thought for appropriate materials or methods. Their earlier fixing of the ancient city involved forcing entire villages to move away from the holy sites.

The soldiers arrived in 1990. They destroyed the temple keepers' thatched and wooden houses, razed their little shops, and carted everything away like so much garbage. The villagers were forced to resettle in a few dusty treeless settlements on the plain, too far away from the river to easily carry water home. When people refused to leave their homes, the soldiers beat them; other troublemakers were chased down with helicopters and arrested.

All that was done for me, and other tourists like me. The military government wanted these ancient sites to be authentically empty and tidy for our appraising eyes. Near one of the "new" villages, I come upon a few children hauling water from a dubious-looking water hole. They struggle up the incline from the hole with buckets hanging off the ends of thin poles.

"Hello," I say to them. "How are you?" Several of them put down their buckets to take a break, and rattle off a half-dozen questions. I don't understand.

"Have you eaten rice yet?" a girl asks, and giggles. A boy bows theatrically and says, "Big sister, how are you?" I bow in return and say, "Very fine." A paroxysm of laughter shakes the ragtag lot of them. It's the only time one of the girls tips water from her buckets.

The spillage makes her stop laughing. Her thin face becomes thinner as she carefully lowers her load to the ground. I lean over, raise my eyebrows at her—May I?—and pick up one of the buckets. Then gasp, grimace, and rub my shoulder. The other kids laugh harder. I'm hamming it up for their benefit, but it's true. How can these small children carry two large buckets filled to the brim without spilling? Uphill? The girls and boys are so young—eight, ten, twelve. The thin-faced girl squints at me suspiciously, without a smile. Does she think I'm making fun of her? I carefully set the bucket down.

She steps forward, hooks it back onto its carrying pole, ducks under the smooth length of wood, and lifts. The tendons in her neck cinch tight. The other kids also pick up their loads; she is their leader. She bites her lower lip and walks away, quickly, lightly, catching the rhythm of the swaying buckets. The other children follow. In a moment, I am alone again, beside the brown water hole, and absurdly lonely.

We come and go, the tourists and the intrepid travelers (who differ mostly in luggage), the well-wishers and the do-gooders. I have come and I will go, taking away stories and photographs of these places. The people who live here remain. They drive their cattle and fill their water buckets; they sell rice and fall in love. They write, they push through the labyrinth of silence, they wait. Which reminds me of Aung San Suu Kyi, whom I interviewed last week. She was gracious, but also as taut as a bowstring, as pointed as an arrow. "We are not waiting," she said wearily, in answer to one of my awkward questions. "We are working."

I know they work hard, the hounded politicals, the people who believe in the inevitability of change. I have never met such dedicated, generous men and women. But the children work hard, too. While the labor of the politicals is often hidden, clandestine by necessity, the labor of eight- and ten-year-olds is ubiquitous. True, I have traveled narrowly here, only to the larger centers, on a steady journey toward individuals whose names have been entrusted to me by journalists and activists in Thailand and Britain: people who are willing to talk about dissident politics and their experiences in Burmese prisons. Sometimes these people are hard to find; sometimes they cannot meet me.

But the children meet me everywhere and share big secrets with the foreign woman: the vocabulary of their daily lives. It is the child laborers who are my most dedicated Burmese teachers.

Every day, no matter where I've been—here, Pegu, Mandalay, various townships in Rangoon—I sit in a tea shop at a low wooden table and watch children weighed down with trays of dirty teacups and bowls, children who teach me words and laugh at my mistakes. They serve, wash dishes, load and unload crates, mix the great, steaming vats of tea. For the most part it is good work, with a place to sleep at night and fairly clean air to breathe and enough food.

It is one thing to search out members of the National League for Democracy, to listen to the writers and artists talk about their lives, their prison sentences, their forms of escape, their failure to escape. But the children move through the streets, across the fields and lanes, visible and oddly invisible in their enslavement. Who wants to interview them? Their degradation is taken for granted; it is part of the new Burma called Myanmar, a country filling up with railways, roads, highways, hotels, pipelines. Eleven-year-olds have helped build them all. Many child laborers are on their own, sent to work in the cities and towns. Either they are orphans or their parents are too poor to keep them at home.

Without words, the children speak of the generals, communicating in a language filled with silences and omissions, as though their vocabulary were written with an eraser. What they do not have dictates who they are and who they can become. The lucky ones have attended school for three or four years; the unlucky ones have not, and never will. Though I use the words "lucky" and "unlucky," none of this happened by accident.

This morning at a roadside shop, I watch the smallest boy in the tea-making retinue. He perches on a low stool, scrubbing away at his pile of dishes. As he grows, he will understand more than he does now about why he has so few options, why he cannot read, why he is trapped this way and who has trapped him. He is one of the blessed ones, too—he's not hauling cement or working on a highway or a railway crew. Every morning, before I finish my tea, he teaches me a few words in his language.

Cup. Table. Sweet. Lizard. Child.

His name is Hla Win. He is nine years old. One morning, as I'm leaving, he calls out to me with the spontaneity of a songbird, *"Chit-deh!"*

Another Burmese lesson.

"I love you."

CHAPTER 3

THE CONDOM LESSON

. . . .

Whence comes my lust for vocabulary? I've had it since grade-three spelling tests, which the teacher called vocabulary drills. I loved them; I had to hide my enthusiasm from my fellow students. Once I started learning other languages, in my late teens, I became insufferable, a collector of dictionaries, a pest to anyone who would tell me the names of things. Part of the understanding Min Ley and I have involves vocabulary. When I point to something from the cart, he gives me the name in Burmese. Temple, water, horse, bell, tree, goat. I do not remember any of these words for long.

I ask, he says, I repeat, and repeat, and ask again, until I get the sound right. Then we cover more terrain, and the dust gathering on the backs of my hands and the clank-jangle of the harness and the slap of leather on the mare's bony withers combine to shake the word from my mind. I point at the same things over and over. He says the words. It took me a full day to realize that, as often as not, he gives a different word for what I believe is the same object.

Perhaps he is not saying *tree* repeatedly; he is telling me the different names of the trees. Not *temple* but its name. The names of the goats? I don't really care. I'm in it for the music. For hearing this world of brand-new things.

We travel by horse cart to his house. *Ein,* for "house." Yesterday I bought Min Ley a bowl of curry for lunch, and this morning, when he picked me up, he announced that today his wife is cooking lunch for me.

The house is simple, wood and thatch and windows without glass. I never go inside. Min Ley's wife, San San, is in the kitchen, which is outside, in a structure like a hut without walls, so that as I sit at the rough-hewn table I also watch Min Ley take the harness off the mare, drop the cart shafts, and lead her to a bucket of water under a tamarind tree. San San smiles at me from her stool behind a charcoal burner. She scoops yellow curry out of a large pot into a bowl. I smile back at her, then our heads turn at the same time, toward the high whine of "May May! May May!"

A toddler, about three years old, stands in the doorway of the house, naked but for a loose green T-shirt. The child's large-eyed, delicate beauty suggests a girl, but his nakedness asserts boy and, as though to prove it, a colorless stream of urine stretches out toward me in a falling arc. His mother squawks, we both laugh, and an older sibling, another boy of about eight, scoops the little one up in his arms and disappears into the house.

They reappear a few minutes later, the toddler looking pleased with himself, wearing baggy, threadbare underpants. He smiles at me, then presses his head against his brother's hip. The older boy tousles the young one's hair and looks past me imperiously, to his mother. My eyes are on the older boy, fascinated; he emanates pure jealous animosity—toward me. When I smile at him, he leans down and whispers something into his little brother's ear.

Two girls come out of the house as well. Their mother motions toward me with her chin—greet the guest—and they smile, link hands. Why are they not at school? Do they have a day off? Or is the family too poor to send them all to school? I know how to ask, "How old are you?" One is ten, the other six.

Four children. In a small house. "How old are you?" I ask San San. Generally, this is not a rude question in Southeast Asia but a practical one, as many intimate questions are.

"Twenty-six. And how old are you?" she asks. She ladles rice and curry onto one plate after another.

"Twenty-seven."

"Do you have children?"

Wishing I knew "Not yet," I can only say, "No, I don't." Having children is the furthest thing from my mind, though I am attracted to them, and they to me, usually, as if the living ones know how to call out to their unborn playmates. I even like the grumpy kids, the screamers and growlers, this older boy here, so covetous of his mother's attention. He sits at the bench, his head and shoulders just above the high table, waiting for his food, occasionally throwing a black glare into my eyes. Yes, it's unfair that you have to share her with so many siblings. Now there's a stranger at the table, too. Poor kid.

Min Ley, who has rejoined us, points to the little boy pee-er and waves his hand. "Here, you can take this one. To Canada. And school, far away."

San San laughs, bends down, kisses the boy's red cheek, to make sure he knows it's a joke, but he has picked up on his older brother's distrust and pouts at me.

Min Ley sits down and announces, "Twenty kyat. You can have him for twenty kyat." He is the only one who laughs. San San smiles politely, but she doesn't think it's funny, either.

I only know how to say "I don't want to" or "I don't allow it," which I hope will work in this context: *"Ma ya boo."* And I say, "He likes it here. With mother."

San San sits beside the bigger boy with her own plate of food, now that the guest and her children and husband have been served. Her body, warm and right there, is enough to settle her sons and let them return, reassured, to their food.

We eat without talking. San San is the only one without a sizable chunk of meat. Now that the boys know they're not going to be sold, they eat steadily with their hands, no utensils. My first day in Rangoon, I had the wonderful shock of seeing people eat without utensils everywhere—in the biryani shops, on the pagoda steps, under a tree in Mahabandoola Park. San Aung, my guide-of-all-things in the capital, explained that it makes the food taste better, and he gave me a brief lesson on how to avoid messing the fingers past the first knuckle.

I've been practicing my technique to prepare myself for times like this, when it is awkward to ask for a spoon. I've learned how to roll a dollop of rice and neatly squeeze or scoop up a mouthful of curry to accompany it. I still make a bigger mess than any of these children, with the possible exception of the three-year-old, but no one comments on my sloppiness.

In between rice and curry, the children slurp soup from the communal bowl in the middle of the table. The soup, a broth with root vegetables of some kind, is barely warm, almost as clear as water, and absolutely delicious. The curry is also good, though less oily than I am used to. They are not rich enough to use a lot of oil.

People in Rangoon talk often about how difficult it is to earn the money for basic necessities, to get the extra job to pay for extra costs, such as a parent's operation or the expensive journey to visit a relative in prison. I wonder how often the horse-cart driver and his wife and children eat meat. If a Burmese doctor makes sixty dollars (U.S.) a month and still has to take on other jobs to survive, especially if he has a family to provide for, how much does a cart driver make?

Oh, if only I could have a real conversation.

I can draw. After we finish lunch, I get out my notebook and draw pictures for the girls. A horse. A cat. A pig. These sketches give them a delight that is out of proportion to my meager artistic skills. When I hand the masterpieces over, the sisters squeal with pleasure and start arguing over the pages. Then a baby in the small house behind us starts to cry. San San goes inside to get their fifth child.

Min Ley shakes his head and says, "So many children." He raises his hands into the air and waggles his finger. "Difficult. We don't have money."

When he starts to smoke, I pop the question of the day, rudely, without thinking. "Do you know condoms?"

"Condo?"

"I don't know how to say it in Burmese." I've heard of a foreign NGO that uses a boat—the love boat—to distribute condoms up and down the Irrawaddy River. Hasn't the boat come to Pagan?

"Condo," repeats Min Ley. "I don't know this."

"Condom." What next? I gesture to the left with both hands open, as if to point to exhibit A, "Condom." And then, swinging both hands to the right, I announce the result of using the condom in Burmese: *"Kalay-reh muh shee boo."* You don't have children. I don't know how to say "use."

Then I remember the Lonely Planet phrase book in my knapsack. I flip through the pages until I find the section on health.

How much does it cost?

I have chest pain.

I vomit often.

My throat hurts.

Is it serious?

There is no word for *condom* in the glossary, either. What if a worthy traveler found herself in Burma and needed some handy protection? Why do the Lonely Planet writers take their title so literally? In my experience, the planet is not lonely at all.

How about *penis*?

I flip through a few more pages while Min Ley looks on with a slight frown. He takes a long drag on his cheroot.

Ta-da! Just as San San comes out of the house with a fat baby perched on her hip bone, I pronounce my new word—*penis*—well enough to be understood. *"Ingaza!"*

San San laughs and looks around. "Where?"

Min Ley sits up, waving cheroot smoke away with his hand. He leans over my arm, blinks at my pointing finger. Then blinks at me.

How about *plastic bag*? I've learned that word already, numerous times, but where is it now? Lost.

Here it is!

"Condom. Plastic bag. Penis. You don't have children."

They both stare at me. Min Ley smiles cautiously. He looks at his wife and says, "She can speak Burmese."

San San looks confused.

I have to try to explain. I grab my notebook and begin, slowly, to draw a penis. San San and Min Ley both stand over the table and watch. To clarify, I add a little spray of semen, hoping they don't think it's pee. I say, "Children."

San San laughs and announces, "Yes, yes." The baby smiles, too.

On the facing page, I draw a condom.

On the next page—the sketching gets dodgy here, I have to admit—I pull the one onto the other, just so, with the little reservoir tip in place and everything. This time the little spurt is contained inside the condom. "See? You don't have children."

Min Ley's brow furrows deeper. He tilts his head to the side and squints. "Ahhhh. I know. I know this. Condo. Good." He explains to San San, who frowns at me as she listens. She nods, taps a finger on the drawing, suddenly all business. She asks Min Ley a long question. To which he responds with a single grunt.

Exasperated, she says to me, "We don't have condo."

"You don't have it in Pagan."

Min Ley shakes his head. "No, not in Pagan, not in Burma."

"In Rangoon they have condoms." Street vendors sell them. The brand is called Apaw.

"Really?"

"Yes. Rangoon has them. Apaw."

"I don't know apaw," San San says. "But we want condo."

Min Ley explains, "We don't have this. Many children, no condo."

I wonder if this can be true. If I went to a pharmacy here, would I be able to buy condoms and give them to Min Ley the horse-cart driver who has five children and does not want any more? Would he even try to use them?

He answers this question by picking up the pen. He places his elbows on either side of my notebook. Then he writes in Burmese: "Here, my house. My address." He points at the condomed penis and continues, "Send me, from Rangoon. Very good."

San San smiles at me and hands the baby to her husband. "Thank you," she says. "Thank you." Then she turns away and fills a kettle with water, lights the gas burner. "Would you like some tea?"

CHAPTER 4

"IS IT REALLY POSSIBLE

TO BE HUNGRY IN THE TROPICS?"

. . . .

There is only one other person staying at the wooden hotel above the wide river. We've run into each other a couple of times now, going in, going out, passing the terrace on the second floor. She is an artist from Spain, a brunette who wears graceful cotton shifts. She has pale brown eyes and high cheekbones. On the evening before her departure, we dine together.

"I'm an idealist, like you. I grew up in Spain. I remember what it was like, during Franco's time. My parents were always telling me not to get involved in the politics, it was too dangerous. So I appreciate the situation here. And I think it's terrible that the people are so badly off."

"I don't think 'badly off' describes it properly. Most people are poverty-stricken. And oppressed. Hungry for many things."

Her tortoiseshell eyes search my face. "Do you think they are? Is it really possible to be hungry in the tropics? There is so much fruit every-where."

I swallow a sip of my bottled water.

She continues, "A doctor I met in the North said that he has never seen the infant mortality rate so high. I agree—that is really awful. But, in a way, it's a natural form of birth control."

I wonder if this woman has ever had a baby, and watched her baby die of diarrhea or dysentery or malaria. Those are the common killers of small children and babies born in Burma, ailments often complicated by severe malnutrition. Three in five Burmese children are malnourished.

I finish my water. The food has come, but my appetite has left me.

"And the people are always smiling!"

"The Burmese are very hospitable. That's why they smile at us."

"There seemed to be a lot of people with bad eye diseases in the North, and even they laughed a lot."

What can I say?

"I'm an idealist, but if democracy came all at once the country would disintegrate! It can't come too quickly."

"The people of Burma already voted in a democratic government. There were elections in 1990. The NLD, Aung San Suu Kyi's party, won by a huge majority, but the military refused to hand over power." She must know these details from her guidebook.

"Voting for freedom is one thing, living with it is another. A rapid transition could destabilize everything."

"The situation in Burma is hardly stable. The currency is a farce, corruption is rife, the military makes deals with drug lords, and most people can't afford to live on what they make because inflation is so high. Even the electricity doesn't work. People die after operations because the hospitals cannot afford proper sterilization equipment."

She looks at me condescendingly. "Journalists exaggerate the situation."

"I haven't been talking to journalists. I've been talking to Burmese people. Students, doctors, artists, women in the market."

"Hmm," she says, chewing a mouthful of chicken breast. "It's not bad," she adds approvingly. After another bite and swallow, she asks with alarming intensity, "What are *you* trying to do for the Burmese people?"

"Nothing."

"But you said you would not come here only as a tourist. So what are you doing here, then?"

This is a good question. I consider it. "Talking. And listening."

"Aren't you trying to accomplish the freedom of these people?"

I laugh out loud; her statement is so lofty. We sit at this table in Burma, talking about the Burmese, while the waiters stand at the dining-room doors like sleepy sentinels. They might understand everything we're saying. Or nothing, which is worse. "I don't pretend anything like that," I say. "It's too presumptuous. Only they can accomplish their own freedom. I am . . . hanging around. I will write about what I see here. That's all I can do, unfortunately. It's not much."

"Don't you think you will contaminate your writing if you become political? Art in the service of politics can only be propaganda." She smiles at me. Bitchily.

"But I probably won't write much about politics. I will write about people." This is a cowardly feint on my part; we both know it. But I'm tired of the conversation. Why are artists in so many disciplines afraid of being political? If an artist creates a work that defies oppression and violence, or offers an alternative view of history—like Ma Thida's short stories—is that propaganda?

I'm about to tell her that I disagree with her when suddenly she starts to speak again, with her earlier intensity. "You know, I have tried to talk and smile as much as possible. To let them know that foreigners are not threatening. It's absolute hell up in the North, where there are no other tourists. I wanted to go up there to prove I could, though it's very isolated. It's hard work, trying to get to places they won't let you get to, and the locals mob you, and there are no other white people. But I kept calm the whole time, never lost my temper, always just smiled as much as possible."

One of the dining-room attendants switches on the television. The news is starting. Out of respect for the diners, he mutes the volume. But the Spanish artist and I are relieved by the interruption. We turn to watch the images of a fine mango crop, box after box of the small, sweet ovals lined up and glowing. It is impossible to be hungry in the land of a million mangoes. Then come the obligatory scenes of a smiling military leader inspecting a new factory. Followed by a battalion of soldiers marching on a road through the jungle, belts heavy with ammunition.

The Spanish woman turns away from the television and talks more about the difficulties of being a tourist. White-shirted waiters come, take away our plates. After the table is cleared, we stand up. The artist smiles with her teeth. She shakes my hand and says, "Perhaps we will meet again someday in Madrid."

Perhaps. I wish her a safe journey home.

CHAPTER 5

THE EXPERT INSOMNIAC

. . . .

I've made a list of names, and added to it almost every day since my arrival; these are the ones I want to talk to, the ones who will have something to tell me. These are the ones I met, briefly, the week of my arrival, and wish to meet again. My initial intention to find out about Ma Thida and a few other political prisoners has complicated. Or perhaps it has simplified. I am willing to listen to those who want to talk, who want to describe life under the SLORC, the ruling military regime of Burma. I need to know more about this country, and it seems that learning how people live under a dictatorship is key to catching at least a glimpse of the truth—something beyond the beautiful images that are so readily available to the foreign eye.

A magazine editor happened to be at the opening of a new art gallery that Sayagyi Tin Moe invited me to attend. This editor gave me his card and asked me to call him upon my return from Pagan. I'm back in Rangoon; I called him today. But the woman who answered the phone said he was unavailable. She hung up while I was still asking when I might call back. An hour later, I called again; she answered, heard my voice, and put down the phone.

So I called the gallery owner, who quickly explained that the editor has been detained. By the MI, the military intelligence, the SLORC's extensive spy, interrogation, and torture network. Everyone I've spoken to mentions the MI. Its web stretches across the country, through every organization in every city and town. The civil service, universities, colleges, high schools, hospitals, marketplaces, taxi stands, the photocopying shops: they all have their watchers and their informers. The generals who make up the SLORC are the leaders, and people speak of them angrily and scornfully. But when they say "MI" their voices are hushed and fearful. The MI operatives are on the ground, doing the nasty work, knocking at the door in the middle of the night, taking people away to the interrogation centers, picking people up off the street in broad daylight. It happened to the editor just a couple of days after I left Rangoon. He's been sent to prison for an article that he published in his magazine last month. The gallery owner told me this. Then he also hung up in my ear.

I cross the editor's name off my list. One dark line. I move the pen back and forth until his name is indecipherable. As I'm doing this, I become aware of a crying baby, somewhere down the road. A howler. The sound seems so close. Maybe it's not down the road but in the next house? The black scrawl becomes solid, as impenetrable as the ink the government censors use to blot out offensive passages in periodicals. What is wrong with the baby? A pre-verbal wail is the human siren. *Do something, help me, do something, help me, do something.*

I put down my notebook and pick up the editor's card again. He has become a political prisoner. Why am I surprised? I know what happens here. I tear up the card and mix it in with the other paper in the garbage in the communal toilet.

Perhaps Pagan was too beautiful; it made me forget where I am.

.   .   .

There are two realities for the new foreigner. Two worlds, both legitimate, both real: the seen and, kaleidoscoping deeply, endlessly, the unseen. Unspoken, unexplained. The unseen world does not yield easily. Facts swirl and shift rather than settle. Repeatedly, a new layer of knowledge displaces the older, simple pattern.

I need years to learn. What I've had is two weeks in the Golden Land, as Burma is sometimes called, and many conversations about the country in Bangkok, sometimes with Burmese exiles but more often with other foreigners—Free Burma activists, NGO workers, journalists. Until recently, I've been living with a couple of journalists. Their house was an open center for international members of the Fourth Estate—American, Canadian, English, Irish, Australian, Kiwi. All these nationalities passed through, to do work in the studio, voice-overs and film editing for the BBC, CNN, NBC, CBC, ABN (Asia Business News, out of Singapore).

The journalists were the ones who most strongly suggested that I visit Burma. They supplied me with names and addresses here, people to visit. They also told me to be careful of my list of contacts; if it seemed potentially dangerous to anyone to keep the names, it was better to get rid of them. Scribble them out. Throw them away. I am grateful to the journos.

But now I'm thinking traitorous thoughts about their dinner parties. I've always had these thoughts. Now that I'm in another country, I can write them down. The dinner parties involved crates of red wine, loads of Carlsberg beer, joints so powerful I literally toppled over after smoking them, fried chicken and cashews, Italian pasta, and—always as the true main course—energetic, loud, smoky political conversations.

So. What is there to complain about?

During every intense, hand-waving, half-drunken rant or dissertation about Cambodia, Vietnam, Burma, and Thailand, I remained on the far edge of the dialogue. When I did speak, attention invariably strayed, or the topic changed. I was always reaching for the detail or the individual or the subjective truth contained in the particular moment. That's how poets talk, and women; among hard-nosed journalists of either sex, my approach was embarrassing. They knew everything. They spoke in broad strokes, with assurance and conviction. Even when they didn't really know what they were talking about, it sounded as if they did.

And I was younger than any of them. Why does everyone think youth is so wonderful? Most people won't take a woman seriously if she's under thirty. If she's under thirty *and* beautiful, too many men want to fuck her and too many women are jealous of her. And still none of them take her seriously. I look forward to being over forty, wrinkled and tough. At least, I hope that toughness will come with the other two.

At the dinner parties, the talkers dazzled me with their encyclopedic knowledge of Burma and "the region," their many stories, their wealth of experience. I gratefully accepted their advice; they are experts. But something disturbed me more and more as the months went on: though the talk was often about those with brown faces, and though we were eating and drinking and living in a land of brown faces, there was rarely a brown face among us. I started to wander into the kitchen to chat with the maid, who was my link, in that house, to the Thailand I lived in years ago, as a teenager.

During the day, she sometimes took me to the nearest street market, or to the temple hidden on the other side of it. She spoke Thai with me all the time, until the language reasserted itself in my mind and my mouth. I felt uncomfortable that she was the maid and washed my clothes and brought me fruit in the morning and cleaned up after me. Of course there are maids here, servants, people to wash our dirty clothes, by hand, brown people to send to the market, who shop and cook for us, the white people. Social hierarchy is the way of things in Asia, and many Thais and Burmese have servants of various orders. But it gets stickier when you mix color into that hierarchy, especially when the only brown person in the house for days on end is the one who cleans the toilets.

Oh, hierarchies! I noticed, too, that most Western experts think of and treat the Thais differently than they do the Burmese dissidents, who are the subjects of white concern and deference and genuine admiration. The

Burmese political struggle is inspiring and exciting. The dissidents are heroic. Not like the Thai maids (who need to be told everything twice or three times and still don't understand—why don't they learn better English?). Not like the Thais in general (who are considered unintellectual and shallow and spoiled).

I should know that the Westerner is allowed to make such distinctions between one Asian race and another. The Westerner knows. We are entitled to knowledge, among other things. That is what makes us experts. Everything becomes territory to us, everything becomes ours. Is the tendency to colonize genetic? Even the political struggle of a small country can become our colony.

Thus, I become suspicious of myself. What am I doing here? Really? Why do I *need* to know more about Burma?

I get off the bed and stand at the window. The street below is empty and dark. The baby stopped crying awhile ago.

Sleep, then, if you can. Make use of the silence. I lie down, my mind whirling through countries and words and conflicting allegiances.

Just before I drop off—two in the morning? three?—I hear the breath-stilling clarity of trishaw bells. The ring seems to come from below my window. Who is out there so late at night? Is he leaving home or arriving?

CHAPTER 6

"EXACTLY WHAT

WE WANT TO TELL YOU"

. . . .

Today San Aung will introduce me to some Burmese artists, so that I can see their work for myself and ask them about living and working under the SLORC regime. In the car, he asks how I slept. I remember the trishaw bell, so late at night, ringing in the dark street. "That was the last thing I heard."

"In Burmese, there is no trishaw," he says. "We call it *si-caa*. From 'sidecar.' Like the sidecar on an English motorcycle. Another word for your vocabulary." San Aung is pleased with my word obsession; he thinks it's a reasonable objective to try to learn his language in a few weeks' time. I scribble "si-car" in my notebook.

In the beginning, all language is innocent—*tree, cup, flower, love*—but San Aung wants me to learn serious words. He has taught me *death* and *freedom. Democracy, cruel, trust, don't trust.* I learn quickly, but as I fill my notebook with phonetic spellings I lament the loss of my innocence. Why can't I just have sweet chats with the tea-shop boys? Or repeat the number of siblings I have? Or ask, "Can I take your photograph?"

No. I am infected with the desire to grasp meanings, which makes it difficult to keep things simple. And any language makes a home for those who speak it. Even a few shreds, a few building-block phrases, provide shelter. San Aung is at home in English. Unlike his parents' generation, he didn't have the opportunity to take language classes in school; General Ne Win had forbidden the teaching of English as too colonialist. Years later, after Ne Win's daughter was denied entrance to a British university because of her poor language skills, the general put English back in the curriculum. But that was too late for San Aung. He learned the language from his mother and various tutors.

I watch him from the corner of my eye. In a country of gracious hosts, I find myself attended to by a prickly, impatient man. He is a friend of a friend in London, and has been explaining things that I wouldn't notice otherwise, taking me to meet people I would not be able to find myself. He has the same alternately madcap and black humor I noticed among Burmese exiles in Thailand, but sometimes there is a caustic, unnerving edge to his jokes. In a Southeast Asian context, this stinging humor is unfamiliar to me. More than once he has said of himself, "I am not very Burmese," meaning that he does not much subscribe to *ana-deh,* that essential trait, not directly translatable into English, which is a mixture of decorum, grace, and exquisite tact. He is more direct and more openly critical—of just about everything—than any other Burmese person I have met so far. "I sometimes say out loud what others think in private," he tells me.

Hanging on the walls are a dozen works by the senior painter's students. I use "senior" to denote well known, respected—I cannot tell the man's age. He might be fifty and not so healthy; he might be seventy-five and excellently preserved. The deep hollows of his cheeks make the upper half of his bald skull seem abnormally large; only after looking again do I realize that he is missing most of his molars. Like the stick limbs of a scarecrow, his pale, hairless wrists and lower legs poke out of his brown sleeves and brown longyi. His rheumy eyes examine me briefly through thick glasses. Then he turns to talk to San Aung. As he speaks, intelligent energy beams out of him like electricity. I take an involuntary step away, as though he were giving off sparks. His head seems to shine harder the more he talks.

As if reading my mind, he turns back to me, puts his hand to his naked skull, and says, "I went away to a monastery last year, during the rains. Just two months. But I continue to shave my head."

When we shake hands, he does not smile. "Please, feel free to look at the pictures. That is why they're here." He invites San Aung to sit down with him at a low table. Three young men are already sitting. The senior painter explains, "They are my students. They have made these pictures." They stare at me; only the one who wears a baseball cap smiles. Not one of them says a word. Perhaps they don't know any English. Or maybe they're just deferring to their elders. Even when San Aung begins to exchange rapid-fire Burmese with the old painter, the young men remain silent.

I walk around the low-ceilinged room, looking at the mostly abstract canvases. Unlike the representational art I've seen in Rangoon's large, expensive galleries, there are no exotic Burmese scenes for tourists, no berobed monks, no women carrying water pots on their heads. If there is lushness here, or some common Burmese example of culture—as in the painting of the mythical stone lions that guard the overgrown entrance to a temple—it has a menacing quality to it. The lions are dangerous; the vines on the temple walls resemble snakes. For ten minutes I stand before a series of small watercolors. Each picture shows the same brick wall from a different angle, a different position. There are three paintings of the same closed door. The images remind me of Sayagyi Tin Moe describing how many Burmese artists and writers struggle with self-censorship. The outer system of repression calcifies into internal paralysis. The wide-open circle of the mind shrinks, turns into a shackle, a handcuff, the mouth shut tight, unwilling to speak.

. . .

When I've finished viewing the paintings on display, I thank the artists. No one indulges in any encouraging chitchat. Their teacher looks away from me and bends forward to wave the fan around his bare shins; the mosquitoes are out already. The young men just slap at them, then apologize to the older artist, who gives me a cadaverous smile. "I don't kill them. Because I have spent a lot of my time in monasteries. As a monk. So I try not to kill anything. Even things that bother me." He holds my gaze for a moment.

San Aung clears his throat. "Why don't you ask some of your questions now?"

I shoot him a glance of irritation. He makes it sound as if I am the interrogator. Which I am, but I don't like to present myself that way. It's not as if the crowd is overly friendly, or interested in talking to me. The atmosphere in the courtyard is heavy, like the weather. The sky is purple-gray and low; the scent of unfallen rain comes to us from the garden.

I begin, "What do you, as artists, think of Burma's new free-market economy?"

The senior artist replies, "It is our own Free Nazism." No one else says a word.

A dust-laden ceiling fan turns and turns above us. Two of the men relight their cheroots. San Aung flicks his cigarette butt out the open door. I see amusement in the line of his mouth.

"Do you have paintings that relate directly to the political situation?"

Their teacher—their Saya—immediately replies, "No."

But most of the paintings here relate to the political situation. Clearly they don't want to talk to me about that. So I talk to them, trying to explain my interest. Painters transform essence into the visible. They render mind and emotion into actual color and form. I know how much can be expressed with a finely wrought image in words, but visual artists get closer: they create an exact image with materials. The metaphor is the work of art.

Only poetry can claim a similar directness. But language is always an interpretation, a translation, while a painting is a visceral, physical experience, both in the making and in the viewing. What a power, to be able to get so close to the mind's vision, to enhance and deepen the real.

The artists nod as I talk, but say very little. Does any of this translate? I'm still not sure how much English the younger ones speak. They glance repeatedly at their revered Saya, who unconsciously sucks in his lower cheeks from time to time, making his cheekbones stand out even more.

I know the ban on speech comes from him. Will he give them a signal, to release us into conversation? San Aung does nothing to help. Among these men I hear only my own voice, and the slow stuttering of the fan. For the past two weeks in Rangoon and Mandalay, I've talked and I've listened for hours to people's conversations—sometimes in English, sometimes in French, sometimes in Burmese hurriedly translated by the best English speaker. I thought San Aung's presence here would be a reassurance that the artists could talk safely with me. I was wrong.

"Why are artists so dangerous?"

Silence.

I look at the man in the baseball cap. How old is he? Twenty-five? Twenty-seven? He has an impressive series of inky, rough tattoos on his forearms, letters I don't recognize; I don't think they're from the Burmese alphabet. Like San Aung, he smiles occasionally, though not at me. He seems to be amused. I repeat my question. "Why do you think artists are so dangerous?"

He makes a noncommittal, sideways shrug. Still, Saya has the last word. "Silence is better than talking. There are many meanings behind silence." This sounds like a line from that kung-fu show I watched as a kid, but he is not an actor.

We sit in uncontested dumbness. Our rattan chairs creak occasionally; the fan clicks. As the invisible sun begins to set, muted orange light fills the air. Heat lightning flashes above the city.

I look from one face to another. "Would any of you like to say any-thing?"

Saya replies, dryly, "They haven't got enough inspiration to talk." This comment makes the others smile.

Amazing. Every one of them understands English and no one will talk to me.

"Well," I say, too loudly, then reach into the bag at my feet. It's like knocking a glass to the concrete floor. They look in my direction. I rummage around in my bag of notes and papers and books. Their faces are immediately expectant, curious. What is she going to take out of there? A rabbit? A pair of American blue jeans? I bring out a book, one of my own, because the political books I brought with me about Burma and South Africa have been given away. That is my one regret: I didn't bring enough books. People have been so grateful to have them—small publications put together by Burmese dissident groups and NGOs, two of Bertil Lintner's books about Burma, Nelson Mandela's autobiography, a couple of recent newspapers—that I should have brought a suitcase full of books and magazines. I hand my slender volume to Saya; it's a collection of po-etry.

The book is an opening. We begin to talk about poets. I tell them about meeting Sayagyi Tin Moe at the dinner party, then again at the new art gallery. The gallery owner kindly seated us on the only two chairs in the room and we had a long conversation. For close to an hour, the old poet made me laugh with his stories. He talked about his youth, his education in a monastery school, his love for teaching and for his students. His self-deprecating humor was irresistible. "I know I am very ugly, I am an ogre, but that is part of my charm," he says. "Ugly men are the best poets. Look at Shakespeare! Or Pablo Neruda. And I am sure there are many more international examples. I am the Burmese example!"

Then, for another hour, he had me close to tears, talking about his time in prison. His prison stories were not about himself. Instead, he de-scribed the struggles of his fellow inmates, their health problems: rheumatism, from sleeping on cold concrete; scabies, the itching-skin parasite; amoebic dysentery, a feared and common killer; TB and hepatitis, from the lack of sanitation. Everyone suffered from the constant lack of food and clean water for drinking and bathing. He talked about how much his family suffered during his absence. "The authorities make it difficult for the family, not allowing visits, sending the prisoner far away and so on. That is why prison is so harmful. It is not just one man or one woman who goes to jail. It is a whole family."

He was kept for some time in a dog kennel, without a latrine pail, exposed to the elements. I told him that what those idiots did to him made me sad but also furious. He patted my hand consolingly. "Yes, some anger is good. But that emotion is not so useful. It is better to be . . ." He couldn't remember the English word; we had to find the gallery owner, who gave us a translation. "Ah, yes, crafty. It is better to be crafty!"

Sayagyi Tin Moe was warm, fearless, and fat with happiness, despite those lean years of incarceration. Because he spoke so candidly of his political involvement, I thought (naïvely) that other artists would be like him. By talking about the great poet, I try to tell the painters that they can trust me; Sayagyi Tin Moe did.

The conversation does put us on a different footing. Saya is pleased when I give him the definition of the word *crafty,* and its synonym, *sneaky.* "I am an expert at the sneaky," he says. We talk about the craftiness of creating an image and imbuing it with meanings beyond the obvious. Burmese artists in every discipline have become consummate practitioners of the art of metaphor, setting images alight while simultaneously finding ways to hide them from the Censorship Board. Saya jumps up and flips through a bunch of canvases leaning against the wall. He knows what he's looking for, and when he finds it he pulls it up and raises it in front of his body, then slowly turns around. Gray-blue and green-blue ghosts swirl and howl out of the depths of cobalt mixed with black. It's called *The Sea,* and evokes stormy waters clearly enough, but it's also a chilling portrayal of suffering. Though more abstract, it recalls Munch's *The Scream.*

Saya smiles down at the nightmarish image with obvious pride. "This made it past the censors, into an exhibition abroad."

The baseball-cap painter asks me, "How do you make a living?"

"Some money comes from my books, some from teaching. And grants."

Saya leans his painting, face out, against the pile and sits down again. "We have heard of grants from a Dutch painter. The government gives artists money to do their art—is this really true?"

"Yes, it's true." Blessings and a long life to the Canada Council!

"You can do anything you want?" As Saya opens his bony hands wide, his mouth opens, too, and this time it is his long, thin face that reminds me of *The Scream*. The young painters talk excitedly among themselves. It is a bizarre reversal for them, to hear of governments that actively support artists and make their lives easier.

"We're not allowed to do *anything*," I explain. "You need to fill in a lot of forms, and have a project. And you describe the project you want to do."

"And then the government lets you do it," one of the young painters says.

"And gives you money," adds another.

In this instant, all my past complaints about the odious task of applying for grants become pathetic. "You have to explain what the project is, and then a jury, a group of other artists, chooses which projects to support. Sometimes you don't get the grant because there's not enough money for all the artists."

Saya nods and leans back in the rattan chair. "There is not enough money. This is the normal problem for the artist. Do you also write for magazines?"

The question leads to talk of censorship. When the censors don't like something in one of the popular journals, they paint over each copy of the offending line or article with silver or black ink. Saya picks up a magazine and shows me what he means. Above an article about a drug runner in South America, the popular Burmese proverb "No one escapes from his own crimes" has been silvered out. He holds the page up to the light and points out the words.

One of the young men explains, "On the bus, you know who is trying to read the censored articles because they hold the pages up to the windows. But if the ink is black this trick doesn't work."

San Aung explains the context of the article. "It's about a South American criminal, but it will remind readers of a famous Burmese one, Khun Sa, the Shan drug lord. He made a deal with the SLORC and is now a free man. He lives in a big house here in Rangoon. The U.S. wants to arrest him for heroin trafficking, but the generals take care of him. He has a swimming pool."*

The baseball-cap painter says, "Stupid to paint over the proverb. We all know it very well. They're not hiding anything from us."

One of the other young men adds, "The generals know it, too. They can't escape their crimes, either. They feel guilty."

Saya relights his cheroot. Before inhaling, he says, "They are very crude. But more afraid of us than we are of them."

"That is what gives us hope." This comment comes from the third young man, who has not made a sound until now.

Saya explains how difficult it is to receive permission for public shows. The Censorship Board has to review the paintings, and the censors can take as long as they want before making a decision. Sometimes paintings go missing. "Two years ago, I was lucky," he says. "A gallery in Bangkok asked me to join a group show of artists. And it took many months of vis-

---

*The Shan leader and druglord Khun Sa died in Rangoon on October 26, 2007, of complications from diabetes and high blood pressure. He had lived in seclusion and relative luxury in the Burmese capital for over a decade. Though he had been at war with the Burmese military regime for much of his life, the generals gave him amnesty in 1996 and refused the U.S.'s request to extradite him on heroin trafficking charges (for which he had been indicted by the U.S. District Court in New York in 1989). In return for the protection of the generals, Khun Sa disbanded his powerful Mong Tai (Shan) Army.

iting people at the Censorship Board, but finally I could send the paintings. And I was permitted to go to Bangkok."

"Did you go?"

"I went."

I wait. I incline my head, lean forward a little. "And?"

"And I showed the paintings there." He looks at San Aung and asks something in Burmese.

"Ya-deh," replies San Aung. This important little word, which the foreigner learns quickly, means "All right" or "Go ahead."

"And a journalist interviewed me about my work. I asked him to be careful. I told him some things that I did not want to go in the newspaper. I told him to be careful. For me. Because my government would be watching." He falls silent.

San Aung finishes. "The journalist published several articles, in Bangkok and Hong Kong, and he used Saya's name. He interviewed other Burmese people, too, and used their real names. People were afraid of what would happen to them, because they had been critical of the government. No one wants to go to prison. Sometimes it's hard for foreigners to understand how dangerous it is for the people here."

Now their reticence makes sense. "But I would not use anyone's real names. I'm not even sure that I'll write about meeting you." I look around the circle of unimpressed faces. "I could pretend you were all potters."

Saya shakes his head. "Potters?"

"They work with clay." I knead the air. "And make pots."

"Political potters," one of the young men says, nodding.

In an attempt at non-threatening conversation, I motion toward the garden and remark, "Look how strange the light is." Before anyone can respond, the electricity in the studio shorts out. We laugh. San Aung quips, "Yes, in Burma the light is strange." Electricity shortages are a routine part of life here.

Outside, the air seems washed with orange; the clouds are clamped over the city like a rusty lid. The baseball-cap painter makes his own pun.

"It's the new light of Myanmar." *The New Light of Myanmar* is the name of the state newspaper.

"No, no," his colleague rejoins. "This is the old dark of Myanmar."

Saya says, "Let's go into the garden." When he stands, San Aung and I follow suit, and the three young painters spring into action, picking up the chairs and rearranging them on the rough gravel in the courtyard. They won't allow me to lift my own chair.

When we are sitting again, the young painters return, spontaneously, to the subject of censorship. One of them says, "When I was twelve or thirteen, I sketched some soldiers during the big Army Day celebration. There was something funny about the picture. I made the generals who were watching the march look like pigs. My father used to talk about the fat generals all the time, but when he saw my sketch he was angry. He asked, Did you take it to school? Do your teachers know about this? He made me tear it up. And he hates the government! But he was afraid of his son's getting into trouble."

The baseball-cap painter adds, "Now we are adults, but our father is the Censorship Board. The board always says no and don't, just like a father. That's all they do. It' so boring."

"Why do you think they want to control you?" I ask. "What are they so afraid of?"

Saya speaks while waving away the mosquitoes around his ankles. "Oh, that is simple. They are afraid of us because we can see."

If the artist is a historian of the personal, the images he creates are artifacts—evidence of lives lived, lives broken. Subjectivity doesn't detract from the reliability of personal history; it adds to it, makes it irrefutable truth. This happened to me, to my family, my people. Here is the record I have made.

The third young man, who has been so quiet, speaks carefully. "They are even afraid of colors. The Censorship Board does not like red in our paintings. Or black. We try not to use red and black, but it's hard." He shakes his head. "They don't like anything with strength or strong emphasis. If the pictures are not monks or elephants, if they are abstract, they accuse us of criticizing the government. Whether or not we are allowed to hang the paintings depends on their interpretation."

"Everything depends on their interpretation!" Saya exclaims, his tone betraying exasperation for the first time. And then irony: "Some of the generals are great artists."

"Some of the greatest in the world!" agrees the baseball-cap painter.

"So they know what they are talking about," Saya finishes.

The orange light has faded into deep rose. We talk until we're sitting in the dark. But we can still see one another. We listen to the frogs. Crickets ring in a second chorus. I listen to the growing choir of creatures singing around us. How free they are, frogs and insects and the final birds of the day. When a clap of thunder crashes above us, we jump in our seats, shaken from our separate reveries.

Saya says, "You hear that big sound? That is exactly what we want to tell you. That is how we would like to speak. But we cannot."

CHAPTER 7

HORROR WITH LAUGHING

. . . .

~~On our way~~ back to the guesthouse, I tell San Aung about the editor who is now in jail.

"Yes, I heard about it while you were away. He is well known. Every month, after the publication of each issue, he would say, 'Maybe they'll come and get me now.' So they went and got him. It's no surprise."

"Are you afraid sometimes?"

"Of what?"

"Of going to jail?"

He grunts. I'm not sure if this means yes or no or if he's just showing his disdain for the question. "I like to think the military intelligence network isn't interested in me anymore. I don't do much."

"But you do enough. Don't you?"

He thumps the big, bare-looking steering wheel. "This is enough. Driving around with you, an external destructive element." This is a joke, a reference to one of the SLORC's ubiquitous red-and-white propaganda billboards: *Crush all internal and external destructive elements as the common enemy.*

"What did you used to do?"

"You asked me that already."

"I'm just curious."

"Don't you have a saying in English about curiosity? And dead cats?"

"Curiosity kills the cat."

Another grunt, and a lurching lane change. There is not so much traffic on the streets in this part of town, but somehow we're stuck in a little posse of cars with ailing mufflers racing down the wide thoroughfare. "I used to work with underground agents. Find places for them to stay, food to eat. I'm retired now. But I should not tell you anything about it. If the MI agents pick you up and torture you, please don't mention my name." He laughs.

I say, "Ha-ha."

"It wasn't such a great job. The pay was bad." It's hard to tell if he's joking or not. "You know when you go back to your guesthouse and write things down?"

"Yes?"

"Things that you see, the talks we have, about what happens here? You know?"

"Yes?"

"For you it's notes on paper. For me it's my life."

Silence. But not really: the close roar of traffic, to which I add, "I'm trying to understand that." He takes a sharp corner onto Mahabandoola Street and I sway toward him in the narrow car.

"Sorry." He's referring to the turn, though he doesn't sound apologetic.

I try, and fail, to hold my tongue. "Do you think it will always be your life?"

"Yes, I think so."

"Even when democracy comes to Burma?"

He clears his throat of phlegm and spits out the window. "In '88, we thought the change would come immediately. The military would step down and a caretaker government would rule, then we would have free elections. You would not believe what it was like—the protests, the streets filled with people. So many people!" Now he flings his hand out the window, toward the past, when the entire nation was convulsed with indignation and propelled into action. "Then the soldiers killed thousands. And many others left. But we still had plans. There was Aung San Suu Kyi. We thought, All right, two years, five at the most—there were still many people in the movement. But now we don't know. She is not really free, even though the house arrest is over for now. She can't travel. They will let her speak for a while, but they will make her be quiet again. And what if she had power, right now? The military will not disappear.

"Right now, not many things work in my country. The university system has been destroyed by all the shutdowns. If you get sick and have to go to the hospital, you need to bring your own bandages, your own plastic bags, your own blankets. And if you get a blood transfusion you might get malaria or HIV. Or hepatitis. A friend of mine got two at once: hepatitis and malaria, from an operation on his leg. And he had already paid for the blood that infected him! There is no money for schools and hospitals because the generals keep it for themselves. I understand why the intelligent people are leaving."

"Do you think you'll ever leave? There are many exiles in Thailand and India."

"I know someone who was on the border for a long time, but then he got sick and had to go into the U.N. refugee camp. Now he lives in Norway. What could I do for Burma in Norway? I would be very busy learning to speak the Norway language, like my friend. I know the exiles on the borders are working hard, but here we are also working, fighting. Quietly.

"That drives some people crazy—to fight and to be quiet at the same time. And nothing's getting better. People in outer Rangoon still get malaria during the rainy season. Right here, in the city, malaria kills people! I spent my youth doing politics—going to meetings, copying and distributing strike manuals, waiting, translating documents, copying U.N. reports out in the middle of the night. Then we finally did it, we had our people's revolution. And it failed. Some of my friends died. My two cousins went to prison. My uncle went to the border. I did not leave. Now my mother is sick and I can't go anywhere. Thirty-six and I am an old man, taking care of an old woman. I haven't traveled the world. I haven't been free."

"You have every right to be bitter."

San Aung laughs. He has the habit of laughing before offering up a particularly scathing observation. "Yes, I am bitter. Many of us are. We are angry, we are sick of this shit. But most people will not talk about that, especially with foreigners. Why would they tell you? Regret is not a very Buddhist emotion. How can my Saya show his unhappiness to you, his guest? It would be inhospitable. Bitterness is un-Burmese. Saya is a great artist whose work will only be recognized in twenty or fifty years, long after he's dead. Maybe. Or maybe not. The Burmese people of the future will not be interested in his paintings. They will be more interested in . . . computers. And these things called mobile phones. The Japanese people who come here on tours can't believe we don't have them."

"It was sad today, how the painters were afraid to talk to me."

"It's not just because they are afraid of stupid journalists. It's because sometimes they don't know how to talk about their own experiences, even in Burmese. It's hard for people to talk about what they don't have. It's hard to imagine.

"But we will smile for the foreigners. We are happy to talk about all the old writers over dinner—Gorky and Lu Xun, people no one in the West reads anymore because there are new writers now, writers we don't know. The country was closed to the outside world for over thirty years, and now that it's open what do we get? Art exhibitions and new translations of literature? New schools, medical journals, hospitals? No. We get high-rise hotels and the sex trade, like Thailand. That's what the government is giving us. Tourism and HIV." His voice changes suddenly, just as serious but no longer angry. "You will write a book about Burma. Just as Sayagyi Tin Moe said."

"I wonder. I don't know."

He acts as though he hasn't heard me. "You will write about something that the tourists never see. That is why you have come here. That is why I met you. To help you."

He stares straight ahead as we barrel down Mahabandoola Street, as if he has made up his mind. I wait for a speech, a list of reasons why I should write a book about Burma. But he says, "I've read too many English and German books. I've often thought, reading Kafka, that I could not possibly experience anything more un-Burmese. His world is so Western, so cold. His people are cut off from each other. Yet he describes exactly how our government works, and how funny it is. Horror with laughing. That's very Burmese.

"Two years ago someone brought me a copy, in French, of Fernando Pessoa. Though my French is not good, I think he is another absurdist. He has many names, no? He knew that there are several men in one man. That is like Burmese people, too. The activists used to have two or three names, even four, to confuse the MI. Maybe the next time you come you could bring some Pessoa in English?"

"I will try. It might not be so easy to find his poetry in Bangkok."

"When do you go back?"

"In a week."

He smiles at me and murmurs, "A lot can happen in a week." He comes to an abrupt stop half a block away from my guesthouse. "Maybe it's better if I let you out here today."

"Sure," I say, hiding my bafflement. "Whatever works for you."

He gives me a serious, penetrating look. "I will try to call you in a few days. But I don't know if I'll be able to see you before you leave. I have a lot of work to do. I may have to go out of town on business."

"That's fine. If you can call, great. If not, I'll see you when I come back. Thank you, San Aung, for all your help."

Confused by the sudden farewell, I hop out of the car and watch him drive away.

CHAPTER 8

WHO COMES

TO THE LADY'S HOUSE?

. . . .

Dark-Bellied clouds hang above Rangoon. The heat carries the threat of rain but none of its coolness. I am one among hundreds of people who don't care if they're caught in a downpour. We stand and crouch and sit along the curbs and on the little patch of earth outside the gates of 54 University Avenue. Old people wearing straw hats are here, and young men with stylish eyeglass frames. Men who must be hard laborers—judging from the size and shape of their hands, their threadbare clothes—crouch and smoke cheroots. Girls with thanaka on their cheeks are pressed close to one another, and dozens of burgundy-robed monks stand on the periphery of the growing crowd. A hawkish Indian man with thick eyebrows stares at my pen as I make notes; I resist covering the paper with my hand.

Like so many others, this man sits cross-legged on an empty rice sack. Though it has rained heavily in the past two days, I didn't think to bring anything so practical. The woman next to me offered up a square of newsprint, making the joke that it was a government newspaper and "fit to sit on." The good-humored neighborliness of the crowd includes the odd jab at the SLORC. People know there are military intelligence officers circulating, snapping photographs, watching, waiting for the Lady like the rest of us. Some people I've interviewed have refrained from using even that moniker, simply referring to Aung San Suu Kyi as "her." But it's hard to imagine this lively throng whispering the Lady's name. If they feel fear, they do not show it. It seems that just waiting for the famous opposition figure gives them courage. Twisting around, I scan hundreds of faces, perhaps more than a thousand.

Not only here, but everywhere I've been in Burma, faces turn to my face as I cross the street or sit in a tea shop or walk into a market. The eyes look at me so directly; their aliveness is shocking. In most Western cities, strangers avoid eye contact. Our glances are usually fleeting—it's impolite to look too long. If you smile at a stranger or talk to a child you don't know, many people will disapprove. Some will fear that you are mentally deranged.

People in the crowd smile at me; they smile at one another. More remarkable than the smiles are the stories the mouths can tell. I've heard some of them simply by going to tea shops and little biryani joints and sitting around for hours at a time. People don't always want to talk, but sometimes they do. If we have time and enough common language to move past the preliminaries, I try to scratch below the surface.

How easily the gold flakes off the Golden Land. People want to tell the stories that are forced under the surface of daily life. Everyone knows these stories, yet they are treated as secrets. The father dead in prison, or at a work camp in the North. The husband, son, sister, brother in prison. The fear of prison and the fear of hunger: these are the twinned specters in my impromptu interviews with strangers. One afternoon, when the lunch rush was over, a tea-shop boss came to my table and sat down for a chat. "You ask me what Burmese people think about the government," he said. "Now I have time to find an answer. You know what? A lot of them don't think about the government. They think about eating. They think about their children, eating."

Some ex–political prisoners are so weakened by malnutrition, torture, and disease that their physical bodies, to say nothing of their minds, are never the same again. One such man told me that food didn't seem to make a difference. He still felt as if he was on prison rations.

Familial separation is another common fear. Burmese family ties are strong. The potent glue of the family holds an individual's world together, further secures that world in the firmament. Yet many families here are broken, not by divorce but by imprisonment and exile.

Aung San Suu Kyi also lives this experience, separated as she has been for years from her husband* and children, who remain in Britain, where she lived before returning to Burma in 1988. The SLORC has mostly denied them the right to come and visit her. Most of her first continuous six years of house arrest were passed in profound isolation; even letters didn't reach her. This family tragedy—the mother lost to her children, the husband separated from his beloved wife—is the most well known of thousands of similar stories that make up recent Burmese history.

Suu Kyi's famous, revered father, General Aung San, was the architect of Burmese independence from the British and later, during the Second World War, from the Japanese. He was a brilliant young statesman whose early assassination left Burma vulnerable to the military he'd helped create. His name has become the prefix for her own, to remind the ruling junta that people still remember her father as a heroic freedom fighter, and that she is following his path.

But people are not here just because of who her father was. She has be-

---

*Dr. Michael Aris was a professor in Asian studies at Oxford, and one of the leading Western authorities on Tibetan, Bhutanese, and Himalayan cultures. A dedicated and outspoken supporter of his wife's political work in Burma, he edited an important book of essays by and about her, *Freedom from Fear*. When he became seriously ill with prostate cancer in 1997, he wished to spend his last days with Suu Kyi in Rangoon, but the junta repeatedly turned down his application for a travel visa. The U.N., Western governments, and many prominent world figures petitioned the regime to grant him permission to see Aung San Suu Kyi before he died. The generals refused their requests. Suu Kyi refused to leave Burma for fear of not being allowed to return. Michael died in London on March 27, 1999.

come a politician and a leader in her own right; years of house arrest have
not been enough to erase her from people's minds. The generals continue
to publish slanderous, mocking articles about her in the state-run press,
but the burgeoning crowd around me proves that government hate cam-
paigns haven't succeeded. She is joined to her people not only by the will
to change a corrupt political system but by a common experience of loss
and sacrifice.

Here they are, the people: expectant, patient, ordinary, remarkable.
Their military leaders have failed them badly and with increasing violence
over a period of fifty years. Behind closed doors, many would say that
Burma is governed by murderers and liars. When the National League
for Democracy, with Aung San Suu Kyi at its head, took over eighty percent of the country's votes in the 1990 federal election, the generals had already placed Suu Kyi under house arrest, "for her own protection." Instead
of taking her rightful position as the leader of the country, she remained
locked up in her childhood house on University Avenue, the old colonial-
era building behind the blue gate.

When she won the Nobel Peace Prize in 1991, her young sons, Alexan-
der and Kim, accepted the award on her behalf. She was released from
house arrest in 1995, and very soon after started to give weekend talks.
When I asked San Aung about them, he told me, "Go to one. See for yourself. You'll like it. Everyone likes it. Except for the army, of course. I don't
think they'll let her speak publicly much longer. That's why you should go.
It will be different from the interview you had. More interesting."

"But it *was* interesting to meet her." I interviewed her during my first
week in Burma, because Ma Thida, the young woman writer in prison,
had worked with her on her election campaign in 1989. I also thought that
Suu Kyi would have some insights into the prison experience, having spent
so long in solitary confinement. But she refused to compare herself to the
prisoners in prison, and she knew no more about Ma Thida's situation
than anyone else did. But, like Sayagyi Tin Moe, she cautioned me against
trying to interview her family; they could be under surveillance by the MI.

"I think I interviewed her too early in my stay. I didn't ask her the right questions, and I was nervous. Despite that, she was very gracious. But I didn't know how to talk to her. She's in this immense public position—national heroine, international Nobel laureate—but she's one of the most private people I've ever met. That much was obvious just from her posture—she's like a wall. A beautiful wall. I was afraid to ask her anything too personal, anything unexpected. I didn't want to offend her or invade that privacy. So I asked boring questions. Or awkward, overly complicated ones. And I didn't dare ask if I could take a portrait of her."

"You know, every Western intellectual who drops into Rangoon tries to get an interview with her."

"Exactly. I was just another Western intellectual. She must get sick of us."

He laughed. "You should have asked her about that, to see what she would say."

"Oh, I know what she would say. She'd say of course not, she appreciates the support of the international community. Boring answer. Correct."

"Karen, she cannot be outrageous and incorrect! She's a politician. But I know what you mean. Other foreigners say the same thing—she's charming but stiff. Not a typical Burmese woman. And she's not, is she? She has spent most of her life abroad, and a lot of that in Britain. I don't mind the stiffness. But I wish she would agitate, like Gandhi. Tell people to go out and march on the streets again. He's one of her heroes, but marching in the streets is not her style."

The crowd is now so big that it spills out across the pavement and up onto the other side of the road. Cars drive carefully through the masses of people, the drivers blaring their horns—"to show support," says the woman beside me. Another festive sound is the metallic clink-clink-clinking of vendors knocking cups against their metal water coolers. Sun, not rain, suddenly pours through the heavy clouds, and the water sellers begin to do a brisk business.

When a young couple rises together to change position, hoping to squeeze into the welcome shade of the tall trees lining the street, they carry their shoes in their hands and place their bare feet gingerly on the ground in front of sitting people. They smile and talk to strangers as they go. An old woman holds the shoulder of a young man as she lowers herself down. Young girls hold each other's hands.

Here and now, outside the pale blue gates of 54 University Avenue, the familiarity is such that we might be attending an enormous family reunion. The Lady will speak, as she does every Saturday and Sunday, at 4 P.M. We're packed in tightly, faces and hands, feet and folded knees. People fan themselves with newspapers and pieces of cardboard. Sometime after three o'clock, a young man appears and tests the microphone. The crowd goes silent with expectation as his voice rings out into the avenue, but he goes away again and the people return to chatting.

A few minutes later, two groups of supporters come through the gate. A row of young women in traditional cotton jackets sit facing the crowd in a half circle, the first band of a human shield. The second band consists of white-shirted men who file out of the compound and face us with earnest expressions. The talkative people grow silent. Two men step up onto the unseen platform behind the gate, leaving a space between them. A wave of sound rises up and crests into the shockingly articulate syllables of her name: "Aung San Suu Kyi! Aung San Suu Kyi! Aung San Suu Kyi!" Despite the heat, goosebumps rise on my skin.

I've never heard, in Burma or in any free country, how quickly a thousand voices can join together. People shout this rallying cry at the tops of their lungs. I hear and I feel the words vibrating through my head, against the roof of my closed mouth. The force of it is almost frightening.

Suddenly she is up there, between the two men, in front of the microphone. Even after the photographs in newspapers and books, even after meeting her in person, it's surprising to see how beautiful she is, how upright, and how small. A string of white jasmine flowers hangs from the knot of hair at the back of her neck. She dips her head for a moment, waiting for the chant of her name to ebb. Then she greets the people, smiling, and begins to speak.

It doesn't matter that I don't understand. I hear something in her voice that I did not feel with her at all in person. Ease. Her public Burmese persona is not the woman I met in the front sitting room of the house in the compound. The authority and intelligence are the same: sharp, undeniable. But the small woman who stands on a table and smiles at the crowd as she speaks, and pauses to let them digest her words, and pauses again to look up from her notes and meet the eyes of her supporters—this woman is the myth incarnate, the beautiful, warmhearted heroine, the daughter of the hero father. She speaks without earnestness or anger. She is attractive, almost sensual in appearance. It's a complete transformation from the rigid-backed person I met during my first week in Rangoon. Though she stands behind her gate—both fulfilling and pushing against the SLORC dictate that she must not speak outside of her own home and compound— she brings herself close to her audience. What astonishes me most is how funny she is.

And how the crowd laughs! She makes her witty remarks and her jokes and laughs with them, throwing her head back and opening her mouth wide. That's the essence of the alteration: she is open. She unlocks her heart for a thousand people. They unlock their hearts for her. Their faces shine as they listen, their eyes follow her, reverent and focused. I must be the only shifter and fidgeter in the crowd. Unlike everyone else, I am unable to ignore my pins-and-needles legs and numb feet.

When she begins to speak with the crisp, hard consonants of British English, the private, cool woman returns. She speaks English politely, giving the few foreigners in the crowd a brief summary of her talk, which will "concern the struggle in South Africa to end the rule of apartheid." She explains that she has recently read and been inspired by Nelson Mandela's autobiography. But we are not her real audience. Rightly, she doesn't waste much time with us. She opens her mouth again and becomes Burmese once more by speaking it.

A moment later, she must offer another joke or a play on words, for a big swell of laughter washes over the people around me. An answering smile animates Aung San Suu Kyi's face. With one hand, she grapples with her notes and the unwieldy microphone. The other hand she stretches out toward her listeners. At first I think the gesture is meant to quiet them, as a teacher hushes an unruly classroom. But she is reaching for them.

It makes me think of the words San Aung taught me the other day. *Let pwa-deh,* a verb: to open the hand, to give. To be generous.

CHAPTER 9

DO-AYEY

.   .   .   .

I hear a knock at my guesthouse door. "Telephone!" Myo Thant crisply announces. He waits for my acknowledgment, then thumps back down the stairs.

I suspect that San Aung is calling to tell me that he *does* have time for a last visit. But when I pick up the phone a woman's voice surprises me. It's Anita, the Swedish journalist I met my first night here. I ran into her at a coffee shop recently and we had a long chat. She's been doing work in Burma and on the border for years.

Her words tumble out breathlessly. "Yes, it's me. I remembered the guesthouse you were staying in—that's how I found you. I've been wondering how you are. No, no, everything's fine. Could you meet me for a drink at the Strand around seven? It would be lovely to see you again."

I go back up to my room, close the door. How odd. Anita is on a tight schedule. She cannot be calling me just to have a drink.

.   .   .

She needed a partner, a fellow watcher. For the past four nights, we've gone out together to small student protests, which have been held in or near busy downtown pagodas. We try to keep an eye on each other, especially when the soldiers come. The rallies begin with a group of twenty to forty students; some of them hold up pictures of the Lady's famous and beloved father, Aung San. He is particularly beloved by politically minded young people because he was one of the country's first student activists, a fervent protester turned revolutionary against the British colonialists.

A young woman who had a small photograph of him pinned to her shirt told me why she and her classmates were protesting. Three months ago, after a minor argument between a small group of students and a tea-shop owner, police arrived on the scene, arrested the students, and beat them up in a nearby police station. Apparently, the tea shop was owned by an MI agent. The students were eventually released, but several had been seriously injured, and all were angry about the unjust treatment. When Rangoon University administrators refused to support them in their demands for a public inquiry into the affair, the students began to organize these small demonstrations.

As the young woman gave me this background, drawing maps of Rangoon University's campus and listing the names of the main participants— she had a photographic memory and was an excellent sketcher—I was struck by how familiar the story sounded. It was almost a play-by-play repeat of the incident that launched the 1988 democracy uprisings, when a student was killed by the police after an argument at a tea shop. This time, too, police brutality has ignited a firestorm of indignation. The university students are like a collective human barometer that reveals how frustrated and angry the entire population is. Often they arrive at the protest site empty-handed and begin yelling political slogans that attract sympathetic passersby. Small but supportive crowds gather quickly and join in with the chanting students. The most rousing slogan now was also the rallying cry of marchers in 1988: *"Do-ayey, do-ayey!"* Our business, our concern!

I felt a mixture of awe and anxiety the first time I saw one of these shouting knots of protesters. After so many hushed conversations and so many descriptions of the 1988 marches and how violently the army quelled them, I was amazed to watch these brave young people claim public space yet again, volleying chants back and forth, clapping their hands whenever someone yelled new words of protest above the din.

One young man recited their collective goals: "We want justice for the students. We want the SLORC to stop shutting down the university every few months." He looked around at his friends' faces, and I did, too, moved by the pure vulnerable youth of them.

New indignation entered the young man's voice: "We want a new government. We want democracy. Our government has nothing good to offer us. And our teachers are cooperating with the government because they are afraid. Instead of accepting these conditions, it is better for us to risk our lives!" With that pronouncement he started yelling again, punching the warm night air with his fist.

The student-led revolt of 1988 spawned a strike that spread across the country. I doubt the students will be able to manage that again. Along with the crippling university closures, increased SLORC surveillance on campuses all over Burma has kept student bodies from organizing and mobilizing. Even these guerrilla protests—or hit-and-run rallies, as Anita calls them—are a feat of organization, arranged without the benefit of cell phones or email. Inevitably, after about half an hour or so, the army and the riot police arrive in their big trucks, and people scramble into side streets, away from the uniforms and the guns. Some of the students are caught, but their comrades move on to another pre-selected site. In the past three days, hundreds of soldiers and riot police have spent hours running around Rangoon, trying to catch up to these bands of ingenious young activists.

The soldiers have set up a large barricade of wood and barbed wire blocking the way to Aung San Suu Kyi's house; she is no longer allowed to give her weekend talks, and the young people holding the rallies say that before long she will be put under house arrest again. There's a visible army presence in Rangoon, hundreds of machine-gun-toting men in berets and boots. Some of the students being held in detention have been badly beaten. A writer whom I had arranged to visit two days ago sent a message to the guesthouse canceling our appointment. Her note said, "Now is not a good time to talk."

Yesterday afternoon, Anita and I arrived too late to witness a student march down Insein Road. We were stopped at a barricade after riot police had broken up the march and detained dozens of students, whom we saw confined in big blue cagelike trucks. A girl stuck her hand through the bars and waved at us. As surreptitiously as possible, standing behind Anita, I shot a few photos. But a commander saw me and ran across the road, yelling. A soldier let him through the barbed-wire barricade; he rushed at me and grabbed my camera. There ensued a frightening yet horribly comic scene as he struggled to remove the film, screaming the entire time. When he managed to get the roll out, he pulled at it until all the black film lay twisted on the ground. Then he thrust the camera into my chest. "Thank you," I said in Burmese, pissed off about losing my pictures but grateful that he hadn't smashed the Nikon. The day before, a Japanese photographer had had both his still and video cameras confiscated. Then he was deported.

He was one of several foreign journalists who have arrived in Rangoon to cover this latest outbreak of unrest. The young activists have told us that a much larger, more significant rally is planned for tonight at Hledan Junction, a historic spot near the Rangoon Institute of Technology, where political marches have taken place for decades.

I've spent the afternoon trying to rest in preparation for the evening, but I can't sleep. I'm wound up tight with adrenaline and the excitement of so many unexpected events. I'm also plagued by a feeling of uselessness. Why am I not a journalist, like Anita, who has been filing reports for the past several days? She has been here for the past month because she's researching a book, but she also writes for a couple of major newspapers. I should be doing the same thing right now, telling the world what I've seen.

I sit up on the prickly bedcover and listen to the sounds of the midday street, si-car bells and honking horns and the cries of fruit sellers. It sounds so . . . normal. As if nothing untoward were happening outside. This doubleness makes me feel unbalanced. That is how life is every day for Burmese people, even those with uncommon privileges. Here is the surface—the sun shining down, the man on his bicycle, the nun with a deformed face selling candles, as usual, at the corner. There are the schoolboys in their green shorts and white shirts playing on the curb. But another reality also exists, hidden though in full view, known by all but secret. That is the nature of life in any politically oppressed country: reality itself has a personality disorder. I know this intellectually, but for the first time I feel it in my gut.

After scribbling these notes, I flip back through my book, rereading. Then I find a felt marker—bought this morning, for this purpose—and start blacking out particular names and meeting places, erasing the list of people I've met with here. Unexpected things are happening these days, and several people have asked me to be careful with their names. Anita has told me about activists and journalists who have had everything confiscated by the MI agents—computers, notes, address books—and she has learned to keep all her contacts on a single piece of paper that can be disposed of quickly.

It's amazing how easy it is to become paranoid. Suddenly the inquisitive taxi drivers who want to know my name and my friend's name and "What are you doing at the pagoda?" could be informers. And they could be. A network of informers and spies really does exist throughout the country; it is no longer something I read about in a book.

Two days ago, I interviewed a Shan man whose father had been executed by the regime in the 1970s. The Shan people are one of many ethnic groups who have demanded land and language autonomy from the central government. They've been locked in conflict with successive regimes for half a century. The man I spoke with lost not only his father; he lost the land and the way of life that had belonged to his extended family for generations. The government stole their ancestral property, impoverishing thousands of people in the process. He asked me not to record our conversation on tape, because "I trust only myself. People do things we do not believe that they will do. You have to be careful, Karen. Especially when the generals are upset."

I am cautious enough, I think. I hope. I'll be leaving the country in a few days anyway, and the MI agents must be very busy tracking down student activists and organizers.

However: Myo Thant said that a Burmese man he has never seen before came by the guesthouse yesterday, asking for me. Anita also had an unknown visitor, but she, too, was away from her hotel when he came by. He waited for her in the lobby for a full hour, then went away without leaving his name. Neither of us has found out who our mystery callers were.

CHAPTER 10

HLEDAN JUNCTION,

DECEMBER 6

· · · ·

When we arrive, Hledan Junction is already crammed with people, most of them under twenty-five. We are on the street—in the middle of the large intersection, in fact, where Insein merges with Pyay Road and University Avenue. In the thick of this mass of people, it seems like we're inside a vast circular stadium, with apartment blocks surrounding us instead of rising seats. Several thousand more faces look out on the protesters from the windows and balconies of these apartments. Many people call out slogans of their own, to encourage the students. Some throw down packets of food. We watch a man carry out a box of water bottles, which he hoists into the arms of one of the students, then he hurries back inside his building.

This gathering is nothing like the small rallies of the past few days. Those felt like taunts, gadfly stings at the authorities. Anita and I estimate that there are between two and three thousand people here. Row upon row of faces shine under the chalky streetlight. We walk through, burrowing into layers, sometimes pausing to talk to other foreign journalists and observers.

When we get to the core group of several hundred at the center of the crowd, we stand and listen to the speeches. Young men and women yell through bullhorns, their voices sometimes strong, sometimes hoarse— they've been speaking for hours. They gesticulate as they make their speeches, outraged by the events of the past few days. They invoke names from the last generation of young activists: Min Ko Naing, who has been in prison since 1989, and Moe Thee Zun, who left Burma to become a revolutionary on the Thai-Burma border. Between speakers there are often a few moments of group chants, and the most popular one is in English: "We want demo-cracy! We want demo-cracy!" In 1988, the people yelled the exact same words.

Suddenly I hear someone behind me start to cry. I slide through the crowd until I reach the source. A young woman is pleading with her parents. They want her to leave the rally. Her hair swings over her shoulders when she whips her head from side to side, spreading her arms to indicate her friends—the hundreds of people, thousands, her comrades. How can they take her away? She wears a white blouse and a green longyi—the uniform of the high-school student.

The mother does the talking, moving her hands to and fro, weaving the reasons that her child should come home. I can tell she's winning the girl over. The older woman glances nervously, beseechingly, at the onlookers. Hers is the tear-stained face; she is the one who was crying before, and now she begins to cry again, shamelessly.

Who knows what their story is? A son might be dead, or he might be a guerrilla soldier on the Thai border. Maybe they never lost a child and cannot bear the possibility of losing this one, a pretty girl who walks slowly into her mother's arms.

A few young women come forward and hug their friend, but it's too late to argue. The mother has clamped her arm around the white-bloused shoulders, and the father walks behind the two women, a hand clasped on either elbow.

Not long after the girl's departure, a murmur runs through the crowd, building quickly, transforming from sound into attention. Everyone turns toward the massive lights far down Pyay and Insein Roads and University Avenue. The trucks have arrived. Or maybe they've been there for a long time already, and the lights were off. I wonder if the girl's parents, on their way to find their daughter, passed the five fire trucks—I can see them now—and the six trucks loaded up with soldiers, and the empty cage trucks ready for the students they intend to arrest.

The regime announces its presence with high beams. The lights shine blindingly down each thoroughfare, informing the large crowd that it will not be so easy to get away. The faces around me, and presumably my own face, appear raw, exposed. To run would draw attention. Better to slink. As the trucks roll down the streets, more than half of this huge crowd does precisely that, dispersing into small lanes. People who live in the surrounding houses and blocks of flats have already gone back inside, their willingness to support the students having evaporated. The metal grilles that seal many apartment buildings for the night are pulled down with a resounding clank.

Several hundred protesters form into a thick ring, at the center of which stand perhaps eighty young men and women, some holding aloft portraits of Aung San and pictures of the golden fighting peacock, the symbol of student protest. The young women form the nucleus of this group; the young men stand around them in a protective, if futile, gesture. How bravely, foolishly, and profoundly dedicated they are to their cause! They knew the soldiers would come. They know they could be arrested, imprisoned. They know they could be tortured. Yet here they are.

The fire trucks begin their approach.

Anita and I lost each other when I went to watch the family drama with the young girl. I stand by myself at the far edge of the main group of students, in front of a block of flats. Faces behind me peer out from the closed grille. The students at the center of the gathering have finished yelling their political slogans. They light candles and pass the small flames through the circle. They remove their shoes or slippers and kneel down on the pavement, facing one direction. When they begin to intone Buddhist sutras, I realize that they've turned toward the Shwedagon Pagoda, Burma's most revered place of worship. As their voices rise in a mournful, steady chant, the hairs on my arms and neck stand on end. Here and in Thailand, in temples and meditation halls, I have listened to hours of similar prayers uttered by monks and by laypeople, repeating together the ancient words that call for loving-kindness, for compassion, for equanimity.

The water shocks me. A wide white arc of it shoots through the air, then another, and another. I feel only cold, heavy gusts, but the water cannons knock over some of the kneeling students; others swing at the air as they try to keep upright. The posters and portraits of General Aung San shoot up and fall back on people's heads. The drenching is meant to humiliate them before the final assault. More liquid salvoes come before the trucks pull aside to make room for the riot police and the soldiers. When I look around at the crowd, I find it mostly gone: the demonstrators in the outer ring have melted into the dark side streets beyond the lights.

Sitting in a ragged circle, the students murmur quietly. The soldiers make a tremendous racket when they jump out of the trucks that have carried them here. The riot police stand aside while the soldiers push and pull the protesters off the ground and drag their limp bodies to the army trucks. I am so mesmerized by what's taking place in front of me that I don't realize how alone I've become. The remainder of the crowd has gathered across the intersection. I stand in the glare of the lights. As soldiers lift the last of the girls into the trucks, I walk slowly along the face of the apartment buildings, touching the rough plaster walls with my fingers. The intersection is filled with trucks and troops, yet I hear only the thud of blood rushing in my ears. An epiphany of adrenaline pours through me: I have witnessed how oppressed people fight back and forge a new history with their own bodies. The hunger for justice shrinks the self; at first it makes the word *sacrifice* possible, then necessary. In the moment when people hurl their lives at dictatorships, they hardly care if their lives return to them.

I reach the intersection where the last group of demonstrators and observers huddle together. A row of riot police stand across the road. The students of the inner circle are in the trucks now. I glance at the person next to me and am relieved to see the familiar face of a young man I spoke with earlier in the evening. He asks, "Are you all right?"

"I'm fine."

I look around, trying to find Anita. Usually her blond head sticks up in a crowd. The young man catches my elbow as I am knocked off balance. People are running, pushing past us. "What happened?" I ask, but he doesn't need to answer. I turn to see the riot police charging us, their batons raised in the air. Shields and guns, helmets and boots, the black sticks. We run. Everyone is running and shouting. Flip-flops slap the pavement, and behind them comes the pounding of boots. I feel little fear, only the clear-headed desire in the midst of noise and bodies to get away, to be safe. Several open apartment blocks are the only places that offer immediate refuge—the side streets are too far up the block.

I follow the white-shirted young man and two younger men who have joined him, boys really—neither of them can be over sixteen. Knees and elbows pumping, we climb up one floor, two, three, four floors—no effort at all, I might be flying—into a dark hallway. A woman has opened her door, she ushers us into the apartment. "Shh," she whispers, "the children are asleep." The room is lit only by bands of streetlight. She closes and locks the door, then we all freeze, because we hear the boots hammering up the stairwells. The riot police yell to one another. It's depressing how easily their voices cut through the concrete walls. They begin to pound on people's doors.

The woman holds her hand out in front of her, telling us without a word to keep still. For the first time, I feel real fear. Why have we come here? What am I doing? What if the police break in and discover us and this woman gets into trouble? What about her children?

They've reached the third-floor landing. Their voices are so clear that they could be right outside the door. The woman murmurs, "Come quickly," and we follow her down a narrow corridor into a small room. I'm shocked: she has brought us to her children. She pulls boxes and blankets out from under each of their cots and whispers to the Burmese students. The white-shirted one translates: "If the police come in, you and he"—he points at the smaller boy—"will hide under there, and we will hide under the other one. But don't do it unless they come to her door. She doesn't want the children to wake up."

I'm in awe of the slumbering forms. It's too dark to know if they are boys or girls or one of each. How have they slept through the noise? One bare arm sticks out from beneath a blanket; softly bent fingers hook the night air.

We listen to the shouts of men and their thumping feet. From outside comes the crash of breaking glass—storefronts, windshields, streetlights—and people yelling.

The footsteps never come to the woman's apartment; no fist pounds on her door.

The younger boys have begun to breathe more slowly. The mother brings us a tray laden with glasses of water. We thank her and gulp it all down. She and the young man whisper together, then he turns to me. "She thinks the police have gone. I will go on the balcony to see what's happening."

We follow him as far as the dark sitting room. When he reenters the apartment, he tells us there's nothing to see; too many streetlights have been broken. Farther up the road, people still shout into the dark, and more glass shatters. We wonder if the police themselves are doing the damage, trying to frighten people.

Our hostess brings some blankets. We lie down on the floor.

Is the night long, or short? I nod off once or twice, but mostly I'm awake, listening to the breathing of the young people beside me. At one point, I drop into a disturbed sleep and wake up so disoriented that I think

I am dreaming. Then I see the boys' sleeping faces beside me, and feel a deep pang of sadness.

Young people always look younger when they are sleeping; the child returns with the slack mouth, the guileless forehead. Before they dropped off, the two boys told me their ages: fifteen and sixteen. Each told his parents that he was staying over at the other's house. By now their lies have probably been discovered and their parents are sick with worry. But the woman told us we couldn't think about leaving the apartment. She said it will be safe only in the morning, after residents in the building start going to work and school.

Soon enough, dawn light appears and grows in the room, revealing what we couldn't see last night: the color of the kitchen table, the family photographs on the wall above the little sofa, the English and Burmese titles on the bookshelf. Though dazed with sleeplessness and stiff from lying on the concrete floor, I realize that I must have slept more than I thought, because I missed the woman's husband coming in. Once we're all awake, he brings us a tray of tea as though he regularly entertains young strangers at 6:45 A.M. He couldn't get home last night because of barricades and rumors of a curfew; he stayed at the home of a colleague.

He has a long, low-toned discussion with the young men. The sadness I felt in the night emanates from all of us. The older man nods a lot and kneads his big-knuckled hands. We've finished our tea. The young man and I thank our generous hosts. There is so much emotion in the room that the boys tear up when they say their thank-you.

They will leave together. The young man gives me his address, carefully written out on a small scrap of paper. "I will meet you again someday," he confidently predicts, though I know better. The three of them give me surprisingly lighthearted smiles and walk out the door.

Twenty minutes later, I follow them down the stairs and step into the morning sun. It is a normal day. People cross the intersection. Smoke-belching buses hurtle over the spot where the protesters kneeled, reciting Buddhist sutras. Walking away from Hledan Junction, I pass a woman whose plastic baskets are packed with green leafy stuff and mangoes. She has just been to market. As though nothing happened here last night. As though no one was taken away.

I step off the curb too lightly. My body floats across the road, as insubstantial as a ghost.

CHAPTER 11

"THE SKULL IS MADE

OF SUCH THIN BONE"

· · · ·

~~Anita is missing.~~ I called her hotel repeatedly through the morning and afternoon. Now it's past five, but she's still not there. Since the protests started a week ago, we've telephoned or met each other every day, to compare notes and to check in and make sure all is well. My gut tells me that all is not well, but I resist the obvious conclusion. I don't want to believe that she has been picked up by military intelligence agents. The generals are not very good at public relations, but I don't believe they're unwise enough to hurt a white woman journalist.

On the other hand, why wouldn't they? Like me, Anita is here on a tourist visa, but she is writing articles for major European newspapers and collecting material for a book about Burma's dictatorial politics. It's foolish to assume that our white skin can protect us, yet we assume precisely that. At least I do. There is a measure of arrogance (how much?) mixed into this assumption. Even if I don't act arrogantly, I benefit from the racism that is part of this world, the discrimination that adds a layer of value to this white-skinned body.

Yet today I feel like a ghost, invisible, erased because the acts of brave protest I witnessed have also been erased. Ghosts are white, aren't they? Does it matter that I saw what I saw? I have no newspaper to write for, no report to make to anyone who cares. The students who did not run were hauled away in trucks. What is happening to them?

I go downstairs and call Anita's hotel again. Then I ring another journalist, who is also worried about her, but he has news only about last night. The riot police roughed up dozens of onlookers who didn't get away fast enough (though they didn't touch any white foreigners). They also beat up some people who sheltered the fleeing protesters in apartment buildings. More than a thousand students have been arrested in the past three days. Some of them have been released, though organizers and leaders are still being detained; they will probably receive long prison sentences. Word has it, too, that a man who handed out water bottles to the demonstrators has been sentenced to several years in prison.

In two hours, another rally will begin downtown. Students told me about it last night. Part of me doesn't want to go. I just want to lie in bed and read John Ruskin. I want to hide. But the day after tomorrow I leave the country—I've already overstayed my visa by several days. Who knows when people will protest this way again? I feel I must go, to watch, to witness the protesters' courage. It's the least I can do.

I'm afraid of touching one of the monks accidentally. People are crushed together on this side of the street; half a dozen monks and I are among them. With news of the crackdown at Hledan Junction, the bystanders are not so brave; none of us mingle with the student protesters in the middle of the road. The monks stand in a tidy row beside me. I keep getting elbowed and jostled ever closer to them. Owing to monastic vows of abstinence, Buddhist monks are not allowed to touch women.

Around us and across the road, people angrily shout the rallying cry, *"Do-ayey, do-ayey!"* When cars pass, the celebratory sound of honking horns and pop music crescendoes and fades, replaced by people's voices.

The monks don't join in the yelling, though sometimes they politely smile into the crowd. After a particularly loud volley of chants, I find myself locked in a stare with the tallest monk, who is at the end of the row. One by one, each monk bends forward past the shoulder of his fellow to smile at me. I smile back. We nod. It is a formal, wordless acknowledgment, but the solemnity ends when the monk nearest me, a youth not yet twenty, starts laughing merrily. I begin laughing, too. The tall man at the end of the row asks me in Burmese, "Do you understand?"

The language? Burmese politics? Their laughter? Karma?

"Yes," I lie. "I understand."

The monks laugh again, concluding our exchange. We turn our attention back to the demonstration. A new group of students have entered the fray. The energy in their voices gusts toward us like a strong wind.

But it will not be like yesterday, when the military let the young people occupy the street for hours before closing in. Another salient difference: there is no foreign-journalist presence here that I've been able to see, unlike last night, when there were a dozen or more of us running around, taking pictures, watching, shooting videos. Some of the students told me that several embassies sent cars out last night, too, and posted observers at different points around the intersection. I'm not sure where the white people are tonight, but the military has less reason to show restraint, because the soldiers won't be on film.

They'll come soon enough, following the pattern of the earlier rallies. News of the recent arrests and beatings has spread through Rangoon, which makes this group of young men and women doubly admirable. Undaunted, they keep shouting, *"Do-ayey, do-ayey!"* Our business, our concern! Our cause!

Sure enough, not ten minutes later, big army trucks turn the corner and stop a short distance down the street. The student protesters fall silent. Everyone hears the metallic clamor of armed men jumping onto the pavement. It's the most formidable international language: automated rifles rattling and clattering against buttons and cartridge belts. Heavy boots batter the pavement. How strange that I recognize these noises.

Then I pick out another familiar sound, closer, more immediate: the thwack of flip-flops slapping the road. The feet above the rubber soles are so bare. Shins and calves and knees appear as men hoist up their longyis in order to run faster. I turn my head again. Across the street, beyond the stream of frightened people, the soldiers stand in a line, holding their weapons across their chests.

The juxtaposition is riveting. This is the finale of a small street protest in a half-forgotten country, but it's also the face of war in the late twentieth century: the heavily armed, overdressed enforcer preparing to run after shoeless people wrapped in cotton. I can sense the attraction, the hunger to fulfill the machine's purpose. Raise the gun and fire. The release like orgasm, but against life. How difficult it must be for the commanders not to give the order to open fire, how challenging for the soldiers not to shoot. Because that is the heart of the gun, the only reason it was made: to shoot and kill human beings.

A few brave souls cry out, "Don't run, don't run away!" It sounds both absurd and heartbreaking. I, too, am startled into movement, but I let people pass me at a fast clip. I keep turning around to watch what happens. I slow to a stop. What is wrong with me? Is it the stupidity of youth, or the arrogance of the white brain, believing it is safe inside its still-colonial skull?

The soldiers form two rows.

Carrying a wooden truncheon, their commanding officer marches down the pavement, offering a sort of pre-charge introduction. I watch him come on. Here he is, there is his face, a man in his late forties or early fifties, trim, close-lipped. Like most of the commanders, like the one who took my film the other day, he wears a wide-brimmed, turned-up-on-one-side safari hat, Crocodile Dundee style.

As he walks past, he brandishes the truncheon at my head, motioning a swift whack with the stick, but he is four or five paces away and there is no real danger, no reason to flinch, and I do not. I just keep looking at him, knowing that he, too, has a history, and a family, probably children, and tenderness coiled inside him. Farther down the road, a few demonstrators stand poised on the pavement, waiting for the soldiers to charge. The commander stops about twenty feet away from them and begins to yell, furiously, taunting them. His voice is full of hatred. The sound of it bounces from building to building in the narrow street.

My stomach churns. The jeering voice makes me afraid. Yet I remain at the side of the road. What will happen if I stay on the street when the soldiers start running? Will they crack my head open? Will I be beaten up or arrested or killed? Or will the soldiers just pound past me?

I want to find out.

A voice whispers out of the side street to my left. The language is the old-fashioned British English of a young Burmese man: "Miss, perhaps you might not remain in the road. We fear they will hurt you." There is concern, but no command: the voice proffers a useful suggestion. I look from the faintly glinting shields down the road to the speaking darkness.

No one is there. The speaker must be hidden. In the other direction, the commander stops yelling, pivots, and starts to walk back toward his soldiers. He will pass by me again in a few seconds.

I step toward the voice.

It's the group of monks whose bare arms and burgundy robes I struggled not to touch. The six young men are squeezed into the doorway of a building. Just inside the vestibule, I stop. To move backward is to leave the hiding place, to move forward is to press against a member of the holy Sangha.

How stupid I've been, exposing their secret nook to the commander. He must have watched me step into the path and disappear. The monks murmur amongst themselves. Then the one who called out, their spokesperson, asks me, "Would you like to watch the SLORC?"

Would you like to watch a movie?

Would you like to watch the sunset?

Would you like to watch the soldiers beating people up?

It's a reasonable question, assuming, in the discreetly polite Burmese manner, that perhaps I do not want to see such a thing. The question also assumes that if I say, "Yes," I am willing to be a witness. Implicit in the act is some kind of responsibility—though who knows what kind, how much.

"Yes," I say.

"Then let's go," responds the tallest monk. We quickly step out of the doorway. Three monks walk in front, three walk behind. We glide through the dark. The houses and shops are closed, without lights, not even candles. We pass a line of huts, a healthy cluster of trees, then move through a walled compound of small buildings. I am disoriented, and getting nervous. Far from the street where the soldiers and the remaining protesters were, how will we "watch the SLORC"?

We enter a two-story wooden building, take off and pick up our flip-flops, then ascend a narrow, steep staircase. At the top, we step into a large, empty room. Streetlight shines in the row of glassless windows along one wall, our destination. I crouch down beside the kneeling monks and look out.

What I see baffles me. The street of the protest is below us. The soldiers are far down in one direction, at the intersection with another street.

The commander's voice gives a one-word cry. The soldiers begin to run. At first I can hear only the clatter and pounding, then they surge into our field of vision. The rare streetlight gives the scene the hyperrealness of theater, as does the first line of riot police, holding up their shields like warriors. The second line are soldiers. The men gallop over the place where I stood and disappear from view. The military commander strides behind his men. As he passes by beneath us, he adjusts his safari hat.

At that moment, someone—a protester who broke away early from the knot of students? a sympathetic observer? a pedestrian?—runs across the path of the commander. The two of them are about fifty feet apart. The commander shouts; the man slows to a hesitant jog. He looks ahead, glances back. He must be measuring the distance to the safety of the side streets against the relative proximity of the man in the safari hat. The commander strides on, speaking all the while. I hold my breath, willing the man to run. *Runrunrun!* As though to push him into action, I grip the windowsill harder, forcing energy through the wood and the air, down into the legs of the man below us.

When he steps toward his escape—a path into the darkness similar to the one that led me here—the commander shouts at him not to go. And the man stops. The tension goes out of him. He begins to shrink, to cover himself.

I know what's going to happen. The monks also know. We sit transfixed at the window, unable to look away and unable to act.

We hear the thwack of wood on his head.

From farther along the street, where the soldiers have charged the students, we hear the shatter of glass. Below me, the armed man clubs the unarmed man on the head. Some of the monks look away. The intimacy of the violence is shocking. The two men are so close to us.

When frantic hands with widespread fingers shield the skull, the back of the neck, the commander clubs the narrow back. The sound of the wood hitting the man's back is like that of an ax when the blade misses the chopping block and sinks—*thunk*—into hard earth. When the man pivots to save his back, the commander shoves the truncheon under the elbows to bash in his face. The officer changes tactics suddenly and aims for the man's belly.

We watch the man sink heavily onto his knees and sway. The commander hits his head again, and once more the man raises his hands to shield himself. When he twists his body away, I see a ragged diamond between his shoulder blades. At first I don't understand what it is. Then I do. The blood must be coming from a split on the back of his head.

I am afraid for the thin bone of his skull.

San Aung told me about the 1988 protests, how soldiers cracked people's heads right open. "They did not hit to hurt, you see. That was the problem. They hit to kill you."

When the commander shouts, I jump six inches off the floor. His bellowing reverberates against the buildings. He abruptly stops the beating and begins screaming. Then he stops screaming and kicks the man once in the upper thigh. He pivots on his heel and stalks off toward the battalion farther down the road.

The man pulls himself off the ground and slowly stands. His longyi has unknotted. As he rises, it drops down his hips and thighs. He grabs at the material of the longyi and, missing it, almost falls down. A second time, more slowly, he pulls the longyi up, reknots it, and begins to walk.

The monks whisper among themselves. One of them rises and leaves, thumping back down the wooden staircase. "Has he gone to see if the man is all right?" I ask.

The spokesman-translator doesn't answer my question. Instead, he observes in a doubtful voice, "That man is very lucky."

I can't reply. My fingers won't release the windowsill. I say to my hands, "Let go of the sill." It hurts when they uncurl. I grit my teeth to stop them from chattering.

The monk turns to me like a teacher whose lesson is finished. He says, "When you return to your hotel, be careful. Take a different road. My friend will show you how to go. Please come and visit us sometime." Then he tells me where his monastery is. He tells me his abbot's name. We crouch out of the room. I hear the soldiers returning now, boots thumping steadily on the asphalt.

At the bottom of the stairs, in a darkness so complete that I have to squint, the monk produces—from where I will never know—a box of crackers. "Please take these crackers with you, for the journey back to your hotel." As though that trip were several hours by train rather than half an hour by foot.

"But it's really not that far, thank you. Please, I am very grateful, but you need this food." They are monks; their food comes to them as daily alms. "You are a guest," he insists. "Please, you also need this food."

Need is not the point. They are offering the antidote to what I've seen in the street, a gift of civilization that I can understand and ingest without fear: English water biscuits. This is a talisman against harm. I must not refuse.

Holding my right elbow with my left hand in the traditional way, I lower and open my right palm to accept food from a monk. I thought monks were forbidden to give objects directly to a woman, but perhaps because of what we've seen this rule has been set aside. I thank the monk in Burmese. The other monks smile and nod; we whisper thank you to each other repeatedly.

The youngest monk leads me through the same walled compound, that maze of buildings. We walk quickly through the narrow streets and into another compound, where he opens a gate and points to a passage-way of shops. At the end of it is a thoroughfare that I recognize. I'm surprised again. We're at the edge of Chinatown.

I thank the monk and walk alone into the street, which is empty save for a few sleeping si-car drivers and, farther on, two young men sitting on the curb. One of them is strumming a guitar, which seems bizarre to me, discordant, though late-night lazy playing is common in Rangoon. My teeth have begun to chatter again. A large rat scampers slowly along the gutter toward me. It pauses to inspect some refuse, and begins to eat. I stop, too, and stare at the rat for a long time, seeing it, not seeing it at all, clutching the box of crackers to my chest.

CHAPTER 12

THE ICE CRUSHER

. . . .

I wake to a steady pounding. The sound causes my empty stomach to roil. I dread looking out the window, but up I get—how heavy the body is—and pull open the thick green curtains. Sunlight pours in. I squint down into the road.

It's the ice crusher. I've seen him before. Bent over with a crowbar in his hands, he beats a massive block of ice. Soon the block is no longer solid. With the wedge of the bar, he pries open one fault line after another. White and bluish chunks drop onto the pavement. With loose-limbed precision, he smashes each of them with a heavy mallet. As he shovels fragments into rusted barrels, I waken fully to the morning clamor. Bicycle bells ring on the main street, car horns beep and blare.

The ice crusher slides another block of ice off the back of the truck and begins his task anew. Watching him, I think how easily he could smash in a man's skull. My hands are stiff from gripping the window ledge last night. I gaze up the street. Down the street. The limbs of the trees remind me of guns; the broom propped over an old woman's shoulder has the shape of a gun. A si-car driver, riding past with a piece of old cardboard, is carrying a shield.

That man, in the sunglasses and the white shirt, sitting on a motorcycle—who is he? The peaceful world outside is as real as the bass thump of the woman downstairs in the kitchen pounding chilies. But a corrosive power is alive around us. It permeates the buildings, the markets, gnaws through the floors and walls, menacing everyone. I won't be able to look at a Burmese street again, or a Burmese face, without being aware of it.

I glance around the familiar drabness of my room and feel a jolt of surprise. I'd forgotten about the box of biscuits. There it is, on the night table. Alms, given back. If I eat these buscuits, will my head and my heart remain intact? Will I know how to proceed?

As I tear open the box, the phone rings downstairs. I hear it clearly. And I know that it's for me.

Anita was arrested the day before yesterday. And interrogated all night. She was deported yesterday morning, sent out on a plane to Thailand. One of her friends in Bangkok called the journalist colleague who has been trying to find her. That was him on the phone, speaking in a monotone. He said she is all right but badly shaken. He didn't have any details, and didn't want to talk for very long. The last thing he said was "I don't think I need to spell it out for you, do I?"

"No. I'll buy a ticket this afternoon."

"I've already got mine—4 P.M. flight. Take care."

He hung up before I had a chance to say goodbye, but I held the phone for a full thirty seconds more, and pretended the conversation was still going on. Myo Thant eyed me furtively as he swept the lobby. He often sweeps while guests are talking on the phone.

Anita, arrested. Interrogated. I repeat the words, but they do not work. It's hard to sit her tall, comely Swedish body in a chair and allow Burmese men to bark questions at her. I have a generic Hollywood interrogation scene in my head that rolls quickly into torture and sexual intimidation. Yet the journalist who called said nothing about such treatment. It is my democratic, guaranteed-human-rights country that readily supplies the images of dehumanization. I try to turn off the screen in my brain, but it's not as easy as I would like it to be.

I will buy a ticket, leave tomorrow. Though part of me wants to stay. I want to see what happens next. But, more than that, I want my being here to be useful. Oh my God, I have hero delusions! I want my very presence to make some difference. How very white of me.

My visa expired almost a week ago, but I will claim ignorance at customs, a confusion over the dates. I could stay on awhile and make up a story about losing then finding my passport. It would not be prudent to remain here in Rangoon. But what if I went north and lay low in tourist fashion, taking photographs of the monuments? Or I could travel to famous Inle Lake and do a boat tour.

Unfortunately, the thought of partaking in regular travelers' delights is repugnant. I am too tired, too sad. When I got here, I was a tourist, and I enjoyed being one, reveling in the beauty and strangeness of this new world, confident, too, that I was not merely a tourist because I was aware of the dire political situation. I was prepared to do my bit by writing an article about Ma Thida.

That seems a long time ago now.

I think about San Aung, but I don't call his house. It's possible the line is bugged, and a call would disturb his poor old mother. I think about the monks last night, who led me to the center of the maze, showed me what was there, then led me out again.

I wonder what I've been doing with my life. I wonder why I'm not doing more.

CHAPTER 13

TOUCH STONE

. . . .

Myo Thant, man of many talents, sits proudly behind the wheel of his boss's black car. He beams at me in the rearview mirror. Usually the boss gets someone else to escort departing guests to the airport, but today Myo Thant is the lucky chauffeur. While driving, he polishes the steering wheel with a soft cloth.

The polishing becomes flamboyantly aggressive when we roll into an unexpected pod of bicycles. The young clerk meets my eyes in the mirror and apologizes. "Please do not worry. We have much time."

I do not worry. For different reasons, we both want the drive to take as long as possible. He karate-chops a flat hand at the bicycles and mutters under his breath, but the displeasure is just evidence of how much he enjoys his motorized stature. We roll slowly past the worn cotton longyis and wiry calves of the cyclists, who carry all manner of stuff in baskets and on their handlebars and backs. Through the mill of wheels and laboring bodies, I see a crippled man using his crutch as a broom, knocking white flowers off the step of his cheroot-selling shack. A group of pink-robed young nuns pass under the flower-spilling tree. I feel the same ache

I felt this morning, and ignored. I would like to visit a temple before I leave.

After the bicycles, on the tree-lined boulevard that will take us to Mingaladon Airport, billboards blur by, advertising foreign cigarettes and liquor, and blaring the usual propaganda in English and Burmese, that people must oppose external elements and foreign stooges. No wonder I want to visit a temple.

But there is no time. We have reached the ocher-colored houses on the outskirts of the city. A cow walks down a muddy road, following a little boy.

There is no pagoda in sight. It is a simple balm, to touch one's head to the earth. Good soil, hard dirt, solid rock: another sort of holy trinity. Several river stones from the wide Irrawaddy weigh down my bag. I rarely buy Buddha icons, or any other religious paraphernalia, but I covet rocks with an odd fervor, and carry them around with me.

Many images of the Buddha show him touching the ground with his right hand. The traditional story has it that, upon achieving Nirvana, he touched the earth so that it could act as a witness to his enlightenment. But why would he need a witness? And why would it be the earth? The Buddha's hand touching the ground is a gesture to the earth, honoring animist religions that Buddhism displaced.

The earth is already enlightened. It is itself, purely, in this moment, solid and ever-changing. Lower the vulnerable forehead to any stone floor and the third eye sees that even the dust is sacred.

Soon I will be high above the Buddhas and the dust, in a plane passing over green trapezoids and yellow rectangles, crops squared off and parceled out in an orderliness that deceives, suggesting that the wild grass and the weather have no agenda of their own. Flying south to Bangkok, I will look down at the wide rivers and the glimmering tributaries dropped into the mud of the Irrawaddy Delta like a handful of silver chains. The silver thickens and pours blue into the Gulf of Martaban, the Bay of Bengal.

I'll have no problem getting on that plane. An immature part of me wishes that an MI agent would stop me. I would weasel my way out of difficulty with my voluminous wit and charm. Stupid. I don't actually want anything bad to happen to me. I just want it almost to happen, so that I'll have the story.

But my departure is uneventful. Leaving is my consummate and cursed talent.

CHAPTER 14

THE CITY OF FILTHY ANGELS

· · · ·

The sound of birds.

A raucous argument among birds wakes me. The voices fly through the screens, dive up, down, crash against leaves. The birds—jackdaws? parrots?—roost in two tall trees that grow near this concrete block. New place, new sounds. Rangoon is gone.

I am dislocated, like a bone, and in pain.

In the middle of the night, a lizard woke me. How does it manage to live in the roaring city? *"Too-kay! Too-kay!"* The sound seemed to be inside the room, at the foot of the mattress, but that was just a clever reptilian trick with echoes. The tukae, a big gecko. It must have been outside, clinging to the balcony wall.

The light was so bright I winced and swore aloud at the streetlights. Then squinted and rose clumsily from the mattress on the floor. But it wasn't lights: it was the full moon gaping through the window.

Afterward, I lay in bed, frowning at the glow on the walls. I kept thinking of the question. On the plane from Burma, a curious man asked, But where do you actually live?

Presently, in a small rented apartment on a *soi* off Phaholyothin Road. A friend of a friend owns the place, empty but for this mattress and a fridge. And a working phone line, thank God.

But I won't be here for long. I want to go to the Burmese embassy and get a visa to return as soon as possible. And find out the bus schedule to Mae Sot, a border town where many Burmese exiles live. I need to get in touch with Anita, too, though I suspect that she has already left for Sweden.

But first, breathe. Breathe. When I came back to Thailand over a year ago, I went to visit an old Thai monk. His unsolicited advice was identical to that of the monks I met in Mandalay: "You just need to sit. And breathe."

How do they know?

And why do they give such harsh counsel? Monks are used to tremendous rigor. They probably forget their old lives. Breathing in and out is supposed to be enough to keep the mind from running around like an ax murderer. Some small measure of calmness would be good, though enlightenment is out of the question; I can't sit still long enough to apply nail polish.

And, right now, I'm hungry. I roll off the mattress and prepare to meet the city.

To leave Rangoon and land in Bangkok is to leap from the nineteenth century into the future of the entire planet. Think *Blade Runner* without Harrison Ford.

The rush of the morning hordes flays me awake. Millions of people are on their way to work and school. Those who commute from one side of the city to the other have been traveling for two hours. I walk in the direction of Pratunam with a bathing suit in my bag. If I can stand the smog, I'll get there an hour before the bus does.

In Thai, Bangkok begins with the syllables *Glung-tape,* but the full name is several lines long. A small part of that extravagance translates into "city of angels." If angels still reside here, they must be filthy, asthmatic, and covered in mange, like the torn-eared dogs that plod across my path. I've been outside for less than forty-five minutes, but a thick layer of grime coats my arms and face.

What are you? I ask the place as I walk through it, dazed by the car and bus exhaust, shaking from too much caffeine in the blood or from the press of bodies in the street, or both. What are you? The angels refuse to answer me. The beggar outside the neighborhood shrine waves away the flies that feed on the raw stump of his amputated leg. The journalists I used to live with told me that the beggars wound themselves, so I shouldn't give them money. But after standing over his stump for a whole minute I pull out a few baht and drop them into his cup. I feel obliged, because I've been watching a squirmy cluster of maggots have their breakfast. I ask him, "Shouldn't you take those off?," meaning the maggots, but he just puts his hands together in prayer position against his head, thanking me for the money or wishing for more.

Receptionists and office workers in high heels walk past (making me self-conscious about my clunky shoes), along with salary men, factory employees, pizza deliverers (at ten in the morning), and dozens of teenage girls (wearing the same navy-blue-skirt-and-white-blouse uniform I hated when I was seventeen). The crowd spreads over the broken sidewalks, hurrying toward the new Asia. The Mercedes and Saabs inch by slowly, trapped in the traffic like the cheaper cars and buses.

City of filthy angels and garbage, metropolis of smog and children. The gleaming tops of the pagodas disappear among the skyscrapers, Siam's new temples, the usual gilded and gleaming centers of commerce. They are flanked by an architectural cancer of shopping malls that has destroyed most of the city's old buildings.

What makes so much noise? Revving cars, the traffic cop whistles, two-stroke engine motorcycles, three-wheeled whining tuk-tuks, much human- and machine-generated clamor around building sites (which are ubiquitous), sledgehammers falling, rising, falling beneath the slow pirouettes of cranes, and here in front of me: a man tapping together finger cymbals to entice people to his fruit cart.

Only money makes this much noise.

The stinking, lung-burning serenity of the traffic impresses me. Few drivers honk; no one screams. Buddhist patience informed by habit civilizes the mayhem: people listen to music, talk on their cell phones, and do crossword puzzles. Unwilling to walk any farther, I stop at a corner and enter into negotiations with a motorcycle taxi driver. After a deal is struck, I follow his lead and hop on the back of his huge bike. He hugs the gas tank and enters the gridlock, weaving between vehicles. Perched behind, higher up, I try not to grip the young man's hips too hard with my thighs. This is not so easy, because my first loyalty is to my kneecaps, which must remain attached to my legs as we speed past jagged fenders and side mirrors.

To keep themselves safe from harm, the motorcycle drivers wear strong amulets. Strong helmets are not as popular, though they sometimes use plastic caps, like the one I've got on my head, held on with an unraveling, sweat-stained chinstrap. These young entrepreneurs know that hundreds of people die on Bangkok streets every year, sometimes bleeding to death on the pavement because the traffic is so thick that ambulances can't get through. The police occasionally have to fly in helicopters to crane-lift wrecked cars—to get the traffic moving again, not to save the accident victims. Self-appointed squads fight over who gets to clean up the bodies.

The traffic makes me miss Rangoon. Away from that beleaguered city for less than twenty-four hours, I am already nostalgic. Less development—read grinding poverty—means fewer cars, less noise, not so much pollution, thousands more trees. I know the generals have kept it that way, inadvertently, through mismanagement, corruption, and lousy public relations. As we cut through the diesel-y nooks and crannies of Bangkok traffic, I mentally compose a letter.

> *Dear Generals:*
>
> *Look at what you're missing. Computer chips as abundant as grains of rice. Art galleries thick with rich white buyers. Crates of real Johnnie Walker Black Label. Never mind your little mountains of opium and the brisk trade in methamphetamines. If you really want to make money, drop the nasty isolationist neuroses and liberate your citizens! Their freedom will free up your markets. The world will come begging for everything you've got.*
>
> *P.S. What I really mean is, don't sell the works to China. There are many other suitors salivating in the wings.*

Thailand has responded enthusiastically to the multinational come-ons. The West promises prosperity for all, or at least for a showy few, forever and ever, or until the market crashes. Thailand, black eyes shining, laps up the dream of a rich future and smiles its famous smile. Unlike every other little country in the region, old Siam was never colonized. The Thai people never struggled vociferously for independence from foreign rulers. Instead, Thai kings and their envoys managed to make alliances and deals with various Western countries, preserving old Siam's freedom while learning the art of compliance. The most obvious recent example of this gift for accommodation took place during the Vietnam War, when the country became a major site of R and R for American soldiers. Their presence helped create the blueprint for sex, tourist, and service industries that have brought Thailand some financial prosperity and a lot of painful problems.

My motorcycle driver deposits me a couple of blocks away from the Regent Hotel, so I squeeze through the Pratunam Market district, where shops are stuffed with gorgeous bolts of fabric and stalls almost disappear amid piles of clothes and gadgets. I love the anonymous intimacy of market streets. People push behind me, beside me, until they get past; and I push past other people coming in the opposite direction. Strangers rub against each other matter-of-factly. Your body is also a thousand bodies, two thousand, more, all of us platelets of blood bumping together then giving way as we slip through the artery, rushing onward to do our little blood-tasks in the giant pulsing organism of Bangkok.

I cross a large intersection and begin a perilous walk beside a sprawling construction site, tripping over broken chunks of cement, blowing dust out of my face. The workers' heads are wrapped in cloth and sometimes hidden under wide-brimmed straw hats. Bandannas cover their mouths, though the cloth will not protect them from the stronger poisons of the trade or the smog in the air. I pause in my walk to look up at a mountain of bricks, upon which sits a young man, cross-legged, eating dust and diesel with his rice. He pulls the bandanna up from around his neck, wipes his mouth, and smiles down upon me, beneficent. I wave back.

Construction workers' shifts here are twelve hours long. Why smile?

When the day crew finishes, the night crew begins, hammering and hauling and welding—usually without protective glasses—under floodlights. The building sites are hardly different from the ones in Burma, though there is a merciful absence of child laborers. At this site, and at the dozen others my motorcycle driver sped me past, the dark hands of men and women carry buckets of rock and dirt, moving out the debris of the old city as they build the new one.

What is this building-in-progress? No billboard shows the shining computer-generated structure that will rise from the rubble. There is only a vast block of the rubble itself, and people carrying it around. The great boxcar-shaped loads of bricks seem like a beginning. Of what? More established civilization is just a few meters away, across the road.

On the other side, I buy some pineapple from a squat middle-aged man with inflamed acne and layers of acne scars. He bears an uncanny resemblance to the thorny fruit he sells. Using his machete, he hacks a yellow pineapple into chunks and gives me a quarter of it. I take the fruit, hand him the money, and ask, "What are they building over there?"

"Condo," he says, the second *o* lifting, stretched out in a rising tone. The word makes me think of the dearth of prophylactics in Pagan.

"How long have the people been working here?"

"Several months. They took down the other buildings."

"The workers are from the North, right? Esaan?"

The pineapple man looks offended. "No! I am from Esaan. We don't want that kind of work anymore. All of them"—he waves a dismissive hand toward the construction site—"they are *kohn baa-maa*." Burmese people.

I see the scene before me anew. Burmese migrant workers. Unable to speak Thai. If they have work permits, they're still vulnerable to the unscrupulousness of their employers. I eat my fruit as I watch the men and women hoisting, scurrying, carrying. No wonder there are no earthmovers. Burmese laborers are cheaper than machines.

On the next block, I find myself walking up the gentle slope to the entrance of the Regent Hotel. As casually as I can, I step between the tall white pillars. Thai doormen in pith helmets nod at me solicitously.

Now I'm no longer part of the throng. I am a white woman. I try to look the part as I walk among the carp and turtle pools, realizing that scruffy khakis and a T-shirt are not the best costume for an illicit visit to a fancy hotel. But here I can be a mess because of my white woman–ness. I could be staying here, slumming it among the natives. I ascend the wide staircase and smile into the Thai employees' eyes. Their deference is horrible; I don't deserve it. I'm an impostor.

I've brought my bathing suit because I want to go swimming in the hotel pool. The proper way to return to Bangkok is with a ritual bathing in turquoise-tinted chlorine.

In the change room, I scrub my face with a linen hand towel. Gray water swirls around the sink. Whatever I blow out of my nose is the color of the roads I've recently crossed. I get into my bathing suit and walk out

to the shimmering aquamarine rectangle. Water belongs to peace and freedom and that Mediterranean island where you can swim six months of
the year. I dive into the pool and put the last harrowing weeks in Burma
out of my mind. I think of the Aegean, and remember Seferis:

> . . . *the road left us miraculously by the sea*
> *The eternal sea to cleanse us of our sins . . .*

CHAPTER 15

THE ACTIVIST AND THE ENEMY

. . . .

"The thing is, you were indiscreet."

How to answer this accusation? I often am indiscreet, by nature and by choice, but I think she's wrong about this incident. Unfortunately, I'm not good at arguing, especially with older women. I so badly want them to like me that I perform the metaphorical equivalent of whining, rolling over, and pawing the air: a submissive bitch. Later, on my own, I abhor my groveling and spend hours defending myself.

She continues gravely, "What you did—or, rather, didn't do—put other people, Burmese people, in danger. You should have switched guest-houses."

I am still silent, puzzled by the sanctimonious tone I've never heard her use before. Where is the Marla I knew before I left for Burma, the tough-talking American activist and journalist, the storyteller who gives impassioned speeches about the Burmese cause? She has two distinct ora-torial traits: she punctuates her main points with staccato gestures of her long, thin hands and, when finished with a story, she throws her heavy dark hair over her shoulder with the finality of someone closing a door. I like her very much.

Or, rather, I think I like her. I have liked her in the past. She tutored me before my trip to Burma and introduced me to Burmese people, both here and inside the country. But something fishy is going on.

"I don't understand why you wouldn't have changed places after the first protest. You and most other foreigners were probably being watched from the moment you appeared at the demonstrations."

Despite the glacial air-conditioning in the coffee shop, Marla's chest and neck have flushed red. "It's like you weren't taking the danger seriously. I've stopped phoning into the country, because phone lines are tapped. We have to be careful. We don't go into the country to endanger Burmese people."

"Marla, there were protests every day for over a week. I would have called more attention to myself by repeatedly changing hotels. Besides, not everyone changed hotels. One reporter who worked for a major American newsmagazine stayed at the Strand from beginning to end. I chatted with him the night of the Hledan Junction showdown, and he said he was going back to the hotel to file his story over the phone."

"But he was staying at a big hotel. No one person would have to take responsibility for his behavior—calling out on a line that was probably bugged. No one person could get in terrible trouble because he was staying there."

"Well, I can't afford to stay at the Strand."

"That's not the point. I told you that if the situation got tense it was best to switch guesthouses."

Frankly, I was just too tired to switch guesthouses, but I don't want to admit this to her, so I cast about for some ammunition. "Anita didn't switch guesthouses." I hear the petulance in my voice.

Marla spits her rejoinder. "She did, actually, earlier that week." She and Anita are friends.

"But she didn't change hotels once those intense days began. There just wasn't time. We were running around all day long."

"And look what happened to her."

"Do you mean that the arrest and interrogation were her own fault? Because she stayed in the same hotel for a few days? If the military intelligence agents in Rangoon decide to pick up a tall blond foreign woman who's been meeting with Burmese people, obviously they will find a way to do it, no matter where she's staying."

Her eyes narrow. "Do you know what else they do?" Her voice cuts loud and sharp through the coffee shop. Several Thai patrons look up. "Do you have any idea?"

I don't reply. Marla's fury doesn't make sense. Is she angry that she wasn't in Rangoon when the protests took place? After years of filming in Burma and on the Thai-Burma border, she missed recording some of the most significant political events of the past decade.

"Well, do you? I'll tell you. The MI agents also intimidate and extort guesthouse owners when the 'wrong' sorts of foreigners are staying there. That's what they did to the owners of the guesthouse where you stayed. Personal friends of mine! Who knows how much money they lost."

I am shocked. "How do you know this?"

"I was told."

"Who told you?"

"A contact. I think you already know more than you should."

That comment hits its mark. I don't reply.

"If you had changed guesthouses like I'd told you to, they would have been safe."

"But . . . if I'd been staying elsewhere those guesthouse owners might have been harassed. The MI harasses whoever it wants to. The way you've explained this makes it sound as if I'm the enemy."

She crosses her arms. "I didn't say you were the enemy. I just said you were indiscreet." She fixes me with a hard blue stare. "Not everything, not every experience, is for the artist's palette. You are not allowed to use every-thing."

My mouth dries up; there's no debating juice left. She wins. I am not allowed to use everything. What does that mean? She knew that I went to Burma to gather material—at least for a few articles.

In order to part, we have to speak to each other. Which means that I need to get my voice past the rock in my throat. How do I respond to Marla the avenger?

I bow my head and mumble, "I don't intend to use everything. I won't." I stop myself from adding the obsequious phrase "I promise," but it's burning my mouth like acid.

After a week of self-loathing, I give up and begin to feel less guilty. I make a few phone calls to people in Bangkok and Chiang Mai, lightly fishing, trying to find out who in the NGO-activist community recently stayed at the guesthouse. No one. Who could have given Marla that information? She didn't just call the guesthouse owner. By her own account, she hasn't taken the risk of phoning Rangoon.

Not knowing why I'm asking about who's been in Burma, someone gives me the number of a young American woman who will be going. Next week. She has spent a year working in a Karen refugee camp and plans to visit the relatives of some of the people she worked with, to deliver photographs and a small sum of money. Which gives me an idea. I ask her if she'll take two hundred U.S. dollars to the guesthouse. It's a significant sum of money for me and a large one for a Burmese family. Hopefully, it will cover the money they lost through the MI extortion.*

But I'm still smarting from Marla's reprimand. I call Charlie, a Kiwi

---

*In 2001, on a return trip to Burma, I found out directly from the guesthouse owner that he hadn't been extorted by the MI after my stay. He kept some of the money I'd sent and do-nated the rest to a charity.

filmmaker who lives in Chiang Mai. Charlie is famous in Burmese circles for her films about the revolutionary student-led army, the SLORC's campaign against ethnic people, the tragedy of the child soldiers who work on both sides of the civil war. We met at a party in Bangkok and laughed a lot. I asked if I could call her with questions about border life. She's been everywhere, met the ethnic leaders, lived in the camps.

Though I'm embarrassed to ring her just because my ego is smarting, she responds with a clear-water accent and a raucous cry: "Welcome to the snake pit!" Her voice through the phone makes me see her: the striking sun-lined face and the sharp blue eyes, thick blond hair pulled back in a ponytail, the slash of lipstick on a mouth that is often open. She is a force.

"We whiteys are very territorial. You'd better get used to it. It's a touchy thing, because we know the Burmese struggle isn't our own, but for those of us who've been part of it for a long time it feels like it is. So people are very protective. But sometimes we take political events too personally. Hazard of the job. The thing to remember is that we are all on the same side, you know? We can't let the SLORC make us into enemies. That would give them too much satisfaction."

I want to crow self-righteously that that is exactly what I said to Marla, but I continue doodling on my notepad.

"Listen, to take the sting out you should come to the Christmas party. A bunch of the guys'll be in from Mae Sot and Mae Sarieng—they'll be people from the camps. You'll get to meet everybody—ABSDF, DPNS, NCGUB, some NGOs. We'll sing and get drunk and feel like utter shit the next day. It'll be lovely."

CHAPTER 16

THE STRING BREAKS

.   .   .   .

I surrender. I give up on the Chiang Mai Christmas party.

After an hour of wandering around in a dark, dog-infested maze, I can't find the damn house. Twice I've gone back down the hill to Huay Kaeo Road and started out again—up, right, past a row of shops, two lefts. But the directions don't work. They only bring me closer to the temple and monastery at the top of the hill, with the lights of the inhabited houses winking derisively below me.

Under a lone streetlight, I pick up broken chunks of brick—ammunition against the nastier stray dogs—and start back down the hill. A street over, a pack of mutts begins to yip, "Thai-Thai-Thai-Thai-land!" and howl "has-a-very-hiiiiiiiiiiiiiiiigh-incidence-of-rabieeeeeeees!" People tell me that it is because of Buddhism that there are so many stray dogs in Thailand: no one wants to kill an innocent animal. The dogs, however, eschew the Buddhist precepts. Tonight several of them have growled and raised their hackles at me. I wish I had a big stick.

The numbers on the gates make beyond-quantum leaps—32/121, then

47/223, followed by 64/3. It's like obscure wartime code: 54/125. None of these puzzling numbers are the same as the one on the piece of paper below the chunks of brick in my pocket.

Forget it. I'll return to my hotel and have a few screwdrivers in the lounge, where a heavily made-up Thai lady sings to loud synthesized music, crooning for the benefit of Thai and foreign men who lovingly nurse glasses of whiskey. I'll make some notes on Culture.

All at once, the dogs cease their menacing chorus.

And I hear, distantly, the strumming of an out-of-tune guitar.

The guitar is old, its varnish worn away to raw wood. In my hand is a large glass of atrocious wine. My second, or third. Which I am drinking quickly, surrounded by perhaps one hundred other fast drinkers, mostly Burmese men, some Burmese women, and a handful of white people, the majority of whom I've never met, though Marla is here, and back to normal.

When I first walked through the gate an hour ago, she greeted me warmly, led me to a table laden with alcohol and scoured of food, and introduced me to a dozen people: "Here's the Canadian writer I've been telling you about." Not a word about my vampire palette.

Smiling, drunken faces turned to me. One man made a small bow. "Oh, a writer," he said. "What a pleasure to meet you." Then his comrades elbowed him out of the way and started interviewing me about my work. People asked about my time in Burma, the recent protests, my favorite writers, and my goal.

"My goal?"

The one who asked the question clarified, "Is your goal to write a book about our country?"

"Well. Yes. Yes, it is."

"Then we will help you in any way we can. I promise, we will.

But please, not tonight. Tonight is a rare occasion. We are having a party!"

At that, we laughed and crushed our plastic glasses together.

"The A string on this guitar," the strummer announces to his swilling, milling audience, "has broken twelve times." A dozen people stand around, waiting for him to fix the problem, tune up, and play. I recognize their desire from other places, other countries: the collective tension of those who want to sing.

I have my suspicions about the guitar. It called me here with its dreamy burr but has not yet produced any real music. Soon after I arrived, the A string broke. Someone jumped on a motorcycle and rumbled off to find another one, which has been presented to the dapper man who's holding the instrument in his arms.

I stand in the small crowd, trying to sort out the names I've heard in the past hour. The names of individuals are a challenge; the names of political parties and organizations are easier because they're in English. I get out my notebook and scribble them down:

ABSDF: All Burma Students' Democratic Front
DPNS: Democratic Party for a New Society
NCGUB: National Coalition Government of the Union of Burma
NLD-LA: National League for Democracy—Liberated Area
DAB: Democratic Alliance of Burma

That's just a few. The friendly young men of these and other organizations have placed their cards in my hands. The more I drink, the more difficult the names get. Back at the booze table, I think about prudently switching to soda water but fill my glass with liquid the color of oxblood; the nose is armpit and putrid cherry. Why stop now?

. . .

There is something inherently pathetic about writing in a notebook at a party. But the scuffed book is my protection, my loyal companion. I talk with some of the partygoers, jotting facts as I learn them. The Democratic Party for a New Society was formed by students in Burma during the nationwide protests against the SLORC in 1988. While the DPNS is important, it's not as big as the All Burma Students Democratic Front, which split into two groups a couple of years ago, though both groups use the same name. The ABSDF, both sections, is the most militant group of former university students. After the SLORC violently crushed the '88 demonstrations, these brave young men and women left Burma to become revolutionaries. Both the DPNS and the ABSDF are closely allied with, and were trained in the jungle by, the Karen, the Karenni, and other ethnic armies that have been fighting different incarnations of the Burmese central government for fifty years. Some of these ethnic groups, and the student organizations, have military camps in the jungle up and down the border.

Though I have to do more research to establish the accuracy of the following claim, my observations suggest that the men of the ABSDF, both factions, are the best-looking. The most beautiful man here—aquiline features, an elegant mustache, a gracefully erect bearing—has just introduced himself, unsurprisingly, as a member of the ABSDF. Through one of those little genetic twists that connect strangers half a world away, he bears a striking resemblance to a Mexican composer I once knew; they could be brothers.

When he sees me glance at his cane, he answers my unasked question. "I was injured during the Manerplaw offensive. Now"—he smiles, thereby exponentially increasing his handsomeness—"I am a retired guerrilla." He offers a practiced laugh; this is what he says to all the curious white people.

The 1995 fall of Manerplaw was a decisive, disastrous loss for the revolutionary and ethnic forces fighting against the SLORC. The fortress-like headquarters of the Karen National Union, which were also the headquarters of the ABSDF, were attacked and destroyed by the Burmese military. "A mine exploded," the retired guerrilla continues. "But I did not die. Obviously." He takes a contemplative drag of his cheroot. We listen to more dissonant twanging. The guitar player has finally pulled the new string up over the frets and threaded it through the tuning peg.

When I tell the ex-guerrilla my name, he nods. "Yes, I know. It's like the ethnic group. You are the writer. I am happy to meet you. I hope we will talk later, but now, I'm sorry, I will sit down for a few minutes." Leaning heavily on his cane, he calls out to some friends, joins them at a table, cups his hands around a candle.

The warm glow reminds me how chilled I am. I stuff my stiff hands into pockets full of political name cards and brick dust. I'll wait five more minutes. If there's still no music, I'm going into the house.

A man behind me says to the guitarist, "We are getting old, waiting for you." The guitarist responds by putting down the guitar and lighting a cheroot. He mutters something in Burmese.

Looking over my shoulder, I ask, "What did he say?"

"He said I'm getting old anyway, whether I wait for him or not." The man takes a step forward to stand beside me. He turns himself in my direction. Full lips offer me a wet, sexual smile.

I ask, "Are you a member of ABSDF?"

The smile doesn't change as he steps closer and answers, "Yes, I am."

"I am not surprised."

"No? Why not?"

We've been staring at each other gamely throughout this exchange. Finally I have to look away—I never win staring contests—but I do manage a straight-faced response. "Because the members of ABSDF tend to be quite handsome."

He doesn't miss a beat. "That was part of the recruiting process."

"Really?"

He nods. "No ugly men allowed. Like Canadian writers. All very beautiful."

I try to keep a huge grin from opening my face. I fail. I cannot believe that the news of my presence has traveled so fast through such a big party. It's a disconcerting form of flattery.

"I am pleased to meet you," says the ABSDF man.

He puts out his hand and I shake it, surprised by how warm he is.

"You are very cold," he exclaims, and puts his other hot hand over mine. This is too forward a gesture for me, and for most Burmese men, at least in my limited experience. Maybe he is the revolutionary movement's number-one bad boy. I slide my hand out of his with impeccable timing.

Because the guitar player has begun to play.

Song rises up like sparks from a fire. People come carrying candles, shoulders shrugging off the cold. Many of them are not as young as I thought but well into their thirties, early forties—a group of men and women growing older near the border, as the guitarist said. What an exile they've had, these onetime university students who walked into the jungle to become revolutionaries. In the early years, dozens of them died of malaria, snakebite, battle wounds. But these ones survived.

I don't know what the words of the song mean, but I know the people sing them to go home. Music is a vehicle that traverses every terrain, carries over oceans, through air, across time. This is a song they have sung for years. The guitar is not that bad; the new A string holds. The player's fingers spider easily from one chord to another, accomplishing the slow rise and sudden drop of the melody, then the bridge when the chorus becomes something new, the place where most voices would drift off, unsure of the key change. But these singers know every word and how it rests in the music.

When the first song is finished, the guitarist noodles around until he works his way into another tune, and the voices move again. The next song is familiar, though I can't remember the American band that sings it. Sounds like the Eagles, but not quite.

The flirtatious man beside me has been singing, bass voice thick with alcohol but serious. Now he cants his head close to mine and whispers, "Do you know the song?"

" 'Dust in the Wind.' "

"This is a different song using the same music. A revolutionary song." People sing it with growing intensity. He translates the song haltingly:

> Oh brothers, our people's blood on the asphalt road
>   has not yet dried
> Don't be shocked, honor the martyrs who died
>   for democracy
> Keep fighting for our true revolution.

I watch the faces. Everyone is either singing or listening quietly.

I wonder if this means the party's over, literally on a sad note, but I underestimate the partygoers and their appetites. The guitar player lets a moment of silence settle between his last song and his next, which is, my translator explains, "a touching love song." People sing their hearts out again, but with ease and some mock crooning. After another song, someone makes an announcement in Burmese and everyone begins to walk toward the house. My translator stands directly behind me, and walks close to me as I follow the group up the terrace steps into the living room, where perhaps fifty people are crammed together on the parquet floor. When I sit down, he sits next to me. We're both cross-legged; our knees touch. When he lets his hand rest on his knee, his knuckle brushes my leg.

Candles flicker on the staircase, lighting the room. Someone turns on traditional Burmese music and a man descends the stairs. He wears a stunning Burmese dancing dress, with a tight bodice and flowing bits of material and sequins sewn along the seams and hem. After he gives a graceful bow, a young woman approaches him and lights the candles he holds in his palms. He begins with elegant, highly stylized movements.

The man sitting close to me whispers into my ear, "In the traditional dance, the woman holds small oil lamps."

"Why is a man dancing?"

"Because there are not so many women here, and they are shy. This man dances because he loves the music. As you see, he knows the steps."

Burmese mandolin sweeps beneath xylophone and drums, finger cymbals open and close. The dancer cups the candles in his hands while weaving his arms around his torso. He goes down on one knee, the other. Then, birdlike, he lifts his arms and rises again. His upper arms extend straight from the shoulder and the elbows bend downward like a marionette's. Wrists swivel toward his body then away, toward the audience. The lights flare out toward us. His body plummets again, but never once do the candles gutter, proving his expertise. He ignores the spill and splash of hot wax. The flames light his face and glow through the skin of his fingertips.

The xylophone and the drumbeats become increasingly feverish; the dancing gets faster. Everyone in the room wears a smile or a look of astonishment. The guerrilla soldiers on three days' leave and the dissidents in from Bangkok and the people in from the jungle camps: they watch this man dance himself into a woman, his body lithe and beautiful, his face beaded with sweat.

I don't know if he dances for thirteen minutes or for thirty-five. I'm lost in the close room, the faces around me, the man at my side watching the dancer and sometimes watching me. Keenly aware of his eyes, I ignore him and feel the full measure of my delight. I am happy in his presence.

After the dancer falls into a motionless pose, he raises his hands to his mouth and blows out the candles. The people laugh and clap hard, clap harder, like a herd of horses stampeding into the room. We all cheer for him. As everyone smiles at the dancer, my translator smiles at me. People begin to stand up, then flood out of the room, but we remain sitting.

The long, serious drink we're taking of each other's face is interrupted by one of his friends—I have noticed them, too, these hoverers—who bends down and whispers something into his ear. My companion turns to me and says briskly, "Excuse me," then springs up off the parquet floor and leaves the house. I get up tipsily, laughing, wondering where he's going.

He has disappeared. I stand on the raised terrace, picking through the faces. I don't know his name. Now that he's gone, my high quickly metamorphoses into morose-drunk-and-rattled.

I scan the crowd again. Among the Burmese people are white faces, too, mostly belonging to women: Angie, the activist who rents this house; Marla; Charlie the filmmaker, very fetching in a formfitting blouse and jeans, spiky heels at the bottom and a cascade of blond hair at the top. There's another woman who works with Burmese migrant workers, a feminist academic from Britain, and an activist, married to a Burmese revolutionary, who started a Burma-focused NGO years ago and continues to run it. Her name is Anna; she invited me to her office to browse through her library of Burma books. She and Charlie are the most welcoming and relaxed of the foreign women I've met in Chiang Mai and Bangkok. A few of the others here tonight, upon meeting me, radiated such grim antipathy that I shrank away, removing myself from their company. I am at the bottom of the pecking order here.

How did these women fall through the world and land on the border? How did they decide to stay? Technically, "the border" refers to military encampments in the jungle—sometimes on the Thai side, sometimes on the Burmese side—and to refugee camps and Thai frontier towns: Mae Sai, Mae Sot, Mae Sarieng, Mae Hong Son and, farther south, Ranong, Sangkhla Buri, all the places for crossing over. But the border is also a mental and emotional state.

Even when people spend most of their time in Chiang Mai or

Bangkok, they still talk about living on the border, or going there, or what was happening when they were last "on the border." Though contemporary Burma may be the yearned-for home and the heart of memory, it's not the first point of reference. The border is the invisible, shifting country they inhabit now. Most of the Burmese exiles move around a lot, partly because of work but also to avoid the Thai immigration police. None of them are here legally. Even my mystery companion talked about traveling from elsewhere to come to this party, and about going to a different place on the border after a few days of respite.

There he is. With the guitar. He takes a swallow from a plastic cup, hands it to one of his friends, then starts toward me with a purposeful though weaving stride. I quickly descend the steps of the terrace, not wanting to be Juliet. He stares at me with burning eyes. Oh, no. No!

He stops walking. He has to break his gaze in order to carefully put his fingers around the frets. He begins to play, poorly, and sing, better— he has a rich, resonant voice—but I do not want to be serenaded. At least not in front of a crowd of people who know that I am a writer: a serious person.

But he does not care about my reputation. Or his own, apparently. The two men he left ten steps behind him are grinning indulgently, as are a few other revelers nearby, who watch the scene unfold. Loudly and goofily, he sings the chorus of a pop song about a brown-eyed girl.

I am mortified. I laugh, trying to make a joke of the whole thing.

His fingers jump off the frets. He takes an unsure step backward and squints at the neck of the guitar. "Oh! Too bad. The A string has broken again!"

"How unfortunate." I laugh some more. Thank God.

"Very sad," he agrees mournfully, but tries a few more bars before giving up. He walks past me and up the steps to the terrace, where he collapses into a low-slung wicker chair. I follow and sit in the chair beside him. He puts down the guitar and pats his shirt pocket. "Too many of us smoke cheroots. It's not good."

Again he smiles that sexy smile. In response, a current of lust snaps through my belly, makes me sit up straighter, more sober than I've felt for hours.

He says, "I do not smoke cheroots." He taps his jacket pocket. "I surrender to Thai consumer society and smoke Marlboros instead." He pulls out his pack of cigarettes and proffers it.

"No, thanks. I don't smoke."

"Better." He lights up. "Come tomorrow. I will see you tomorrow, yes?"

"Well, I don't know. Where will you be?"

"Here. Just come here in the morning. For tea. Or coffee."

"You're staying here, in this house?"

"I stay here when I come to Chiang Mai. Me and some of the other men."

I wonder about Angie, the activist who rents this place. What is it like to let a group of revolutionaries regularly stay in one's home? Marla does the same thing; she has a spare room at her house in Bangkok, and Burmese dissidents and refugees often occupy it, coming or going from one place to another. I doubt that I could ever be so generous. I'd never be able to get any writing done.

I'm such a hypocrite. How often am I a part of that vagabond stream? I cannot count the times I've taken succor in other people's homes, depended on their comfortable domestic worlds. When will I pay back the debt of hospitality that I owe to the universe?

My translator asks, "Why are you smiling?"

"Because I wish I could stay in this house, too."

"Maybe you should ask Angie."

"No, I don't think that would be a good idea. I just mean her house is lovely."

"Yes, it is."

"By the way, what is your name?"

He flinches. "I told you my name already!"

"No, you didn't."

"I did. When we were listening to the music."

"Really? I don't think I heard you. I'm sorry."

He stares at me, as though reconsidering his first impression. "My name is Maung."

"And you already know my name."

"Yes, I do. Karen." He puts the accent on the second syllable. I don't correct his pronunciation.

"Will you come tomorrow for tea? Or we could have dinner."

"Maybe tea. I'll see how I feel in the morning. I am going home—to my hotel—now." When I stand up, I have to make a conscious effort not to sway.

"I will walk you to your hotel."

"No, no. That's all right. It's not far." A lie. "I'll just catch a songtow at the bottom of the hill. Not to worry."

He walks me through the dregs of the party, toward the gate. I say goodbye to people as I pass them, feeling conspicuous and awfully drunk. I'm thinking about the dogs, and rocks to throw at them, and finding a bamboo cane before I leave the compound. But it's too awkward. If I tell Maung that I want a stick for the dogs, he'll insist on coming with me— to protect me, of course—and that could lead to all sorts of inebriated lust-ful foolishness. Bad enough to have been serenaded; how much worse to take a revolutionary to bed on the first meeting!

I wave goodbye to Maung gaily, as if I were going for a picnic in the dark. I'm barely past the property line of the house when I hear the dogs barking down the road.

CHAPTER 17

THE CHAMELEON HEART

. . . .

In the morning I find Angie's house with irritating ease. The garden compound has been cleaned up already, and a small group of people are gathered on the terrace. I am curious to see Maung again. Will the attraction prove as strong in the warm, revealing light of day? Maybe last night was pure drunken revelry and the only real thing about it now is a pounding headache and dehydration.

People are chatting, eating Thai coconut sweets, and drinking tea. One of the Burmese men makes a spot for me on a bench—beside Maung. Everyone laughs about being hungover and agrees that our hostess gave a wonderful party. Maung stands and asks me what I take in my tea—all the fixings are on the table just inside the house—and brings me the warm cup. We touch fingers as he hands it to me. When his phone rings, he walks down into the garden to talk, but I can feel him watching me as I talk to Jenny, an Englishwoman who works for the Burma Border Consortium, an organization that brings food and aid to Burmese refugees and dissidents.

It's hard to be present for the conversation when I feel an invisible umbilical cord stretching between myself and a man I don't know. But I nod and try to listen to this intelligent woman talk about her work. She tells me she is married to a Burmese man who is a member of the ABSDF. Her husband is here; he's the one who pointedly made a spot for me on the bench beside Maung.

Without expecting much of an answer, I ask Jenny, "How did you decide to make a life here?"

Her reply is striking. "I decided I didn't want to be an observer anymore. I wanted to be a participant, whatever that meant. The Burmese struggle is . . . remarkable. It made me think about human solidarity. Does that sound out of date? I suppose it is. But I guess I came to the point where I didn't want to just watch the struggle. I wanted to struggle with them. And so, in a way, I do."

I do. Two small, fateful words.

Maung returns from the garden. I shift places to try to put some distance between us, but within five minutes he insinuates himself into the chair next to mine, looks me straight in the eye, and smiles, as if to say, "It's not that easy to get rid of me." As a newcomer to this society of foreigners who do Burma-centered work, and as someone who doesn't know any of the Burmese people here, I try to be quiet in conversation, and respectful. Not too talkative. "Inconspicuous" is not an adjective I can claim as my own, but it is a state I aspire to on occasions such as this.

Maung makes being inconspicuous impossible. He flatters me, he stares at me, he sticks to me. He asks three times if I want another cup of tea, and when I finally say yes he leaps up to get it. His charm is a catalyst; I can't help reacting. Whatever comes out of my mouth charms him right back. I'm not even trying! I'm trying not to, in fact, but we flirt with each other in small but obvious ways. Angie, our hostess, glares at me from time to time. I want to tell her it's not my fault—I can't help the torrential flood of pheromones and the girlish smile.

Maung's friend—Jenny's husband—teases me about the tragedy of the broken A string. "You need to hear Maung sing. The sooner, the better," he says knowingly. My face burns as hot as a stove.

A few minutes later, Maung stands up to help himself to more tea, but before he goes inside he lays his cotton jacket over the back of my chair. It takes monumental strength not to lean my body against this material that has touched his skin. Hilarious. Infuriating. He's done it on purpose, too; he's tempting me. But I will be strong.

After some more conversation, I stand up and say goodbye to everyone, thanking Angie for the party last night and for the tea this morning. She grunts an unintelligible reply and throws a look like a machete between my eyes.

Maung once again walks me to the gate of her house. Before I turn out into the street, he asks me, "Are you busy tonight?"

"Why, is there going to be another party?"

"No. We're just having a dinner." He tells me the name and location of the restaurant while I back away from him.

Dinner will involve at least a dozen people, so I'll be safe. I don't want to be safe, of course. I want to be my impetuous, passionate Greek self and act on my lustful impulses. But this is hardly the place for that kind of thing. I'm in Thailand, with Burmese political exiles, people whose lives are defined by dictatorship and revolution. The past twenty-four hours have been a respite for all those I met last night—and for me, too. I know nothing about these people, but I felt in the music, and in that magical dance and the mostly happy drunkenness, that I had entered a rare oasis of pleasure. It continued into the morning, the teacups and the chime of spoons, people talking on the terrace in the dappled shadow of a tamarind tree, a man flirting amusingly with a woman: all lovely, lovelier because unexpected, fleeting. Not unreal, but not reflective of the daily life of struggling Burmese dissidents, to say nothing of the hundreds of thousands of refugees in camps up and down the border.

I have so often chosen pleasure, taken it as the right of my body and my mind. I love Greece because the world I experience on the island feeds the passionate animal I have been. The easy dry heat, the reasonable winters, the Mediterranean, the physical body cherished through swimming in that brilliant salty blue, enlivened through eating, dancing, gardening. The Greek landscape calls forth a sensual response partly because it's covered in human fingerprints: the earth is both body and living memory.

But I am here now. How do I know what my real self is, when I owe so much of what I am to the places that have made me? Thailand was my first foreign home, the country my chameleon heart cleaved to a decade ago; I will always be comfortable here. But I've further complicated myself with Burma.

I know that I lived too much there, leaped into events that I didn't fully understand. I feel frayed at the edges. When I close my eyes, I see image after image from those last days in Rangoon—the monks who led me up the stairs, the man being beaten, the child's arm hanging out of the bed I was supposed to hide under if the soldiers came.

Could I have contained the trip? Could I have turned away from unexpected events and departed unscathed? I didn't think I had a choice, but I did have a choice.

Why must I love?

I've been served an unreasonably large portion of love for an insane world, yet the world does not serve the same portion back to me. Why would it? I don't mean romantic love, not even human love. I love the feral dogs as I love the thick dust and the filthy mess of broken streets in Mandalay, as I love walking into the market at the bottom of this hill and seeing the human faces over the pyramids of fruit and, farther back, the stalls bloody with chunks of meat and the guts of animals laid out like augury that always comes to pass: cooking, dinners, people eating together, taking in the life of the animal to feed their own lives.

I love, I love, I love. The language of the world calls me, wills me to know it. To become it, in a way. That is why I'm obsessed with new words. To speak another language is to think anew, to be born again—eyes, mouth, sky, blue, hand, heart, open, open. I still carry around my Burmese notebook, full of phonetic spellings, scribbled notes, the many words that San Aung wanted me to learn. Where is he? Lying low with friends in Mandalay? Or having tea on Mahabandoola Street?

Burmese will be my sixth language if I ever learn to speak it properly. Isn't that just another form of gluttony—wanting to take it all in, have it, know it? In one of his notebooks, van Gogh scribbled the words I live by: "The best way to know life is to love many things."

But should I live this way? To love widely is not to love deeply. I love, yes, but I am also lonely. I remember talking to an NLD member in Burma. Early in the interview, he inquired if I was married. I said no. He responded, "Always alone! You modern women. Alone, alone, alone against Rome." We laughed. Then he became thoughtful and said, "Daw Suu Kyi is also alone. Alone against the SLORC!" We did not laugh.

Sometimes my loneliness is like a well I cannot get out of, though I see the human light up there, the people coming and going. It's partly why I am interested in these amazing women who have married Burmese men and settled here. How I admire them!

There are precedents—that's the point.

Though I still think it unwise to become involved with a man who belongs to a guerrilla army, even a small one.

CHAPTER 18

THE DATE

. . . .

Should I blame my naïveté on youth? But I will be twenty-eight years old in two months. That's not so young. By my age, my mother had three children and a house to run. I need to smarten up.

I arrive at the lovely garden restaurant expecting a group of Burmese men and women dissidents, foreigners who do Burma work, maybe a smattering of journalists. But there are no large tables. I check out the diners seated among potted palms and hanging orchids—several couples, a group of four, Thai businessmen drinking a bottle of Johnnie Walker. I wonder if I'm at the right place, or if the dinner was called off; I didn't give Maung my number, so he wouldn't have been able to contact me at the hotel.

Then I realize that the one solo diner in the restaurant—in the far, candlelit corner—is him. Maung. My date. This is a date, not a motley gathering into which I can slip, one more motley among many. Self-consciously, I walk through the restaurant and sit down across from him. "I thought some other people would be here, too." I don't know whether to be amused or irritated.

That smile again. The earliest form of foreplay. How does he do that? "You look beautiful," he says.

Inwardly, I scoff, "You've got to be kidding." Out loud, I murmur, "Thank you," and stare down at the napkin I unfold over my lap. The lowered eyes, the fluttering lashes—that's Southeast Asia making me unrecognizably demure. I'm behaving like a Thai girl.

We do what a couple does on a first date. We talk about the food—excellent northern Thai cuisine, the ground-pork *laab moo* a dish for gods and luckier mortals—and we chat about the weather, the cold last night, the chill already rising at eight in the evening. He offers me his jacket, which I decline. When he smiles, I take a sip of water.

"It is surprising."

"What?"

"That we met at a Christmas party. A strange coincidence. I am Buddhist. We do not have Christmas parties."

More internal scoffing on my part. Christmas was a pretense for that souls-of-the-border gathering, not a reason. If one is an illegal alien in tough circumstances, a party in a safe haven is an occasion not to be missed.

I hold Maung's gaze for a few seconds, sounding his eyes. Fathoms deep, heavy-lidded. I look away and address the ashtray. "But a party is a party. And a religion is a religion. I have Buddhist friends in Bangkok who go to church just to make sure they have all the bases covered."

"But you were there."

No. No. No. I must resist the romanticism. Someone around here has to be skeptical.

But why? Instead, I describe in graphic detail how hard it was to find Angie's house, how the guitar music led me there. So the conviction grows around us like a bubble that fate conspired to allow us to find each other. After being used for thousands of years by millions of people, why does this trick continue to work?

"Too bad the A string broke," he says wistfully.

"Are you kidding? I'm glad it broke. You were embarrassing me."

He seems not to hear. He prods one of the newly arrived dishes with his spoon, scrutinizes one chunk of food, sets it down, lifts up another. I wonder why he's being so picky. Eventually he chooses a tasty-looking morsel of curried chicken—and floats it over the candle to place it in the middle of my rice. This congenial gesture makes me smile. *"Tzey-zu-tin-ba-deh,"* I respond in thanks. He beams at me.

I think, Now I will reach across the table and kiss him. But the risk of knocking over a glass is too great. I put some more rice into my mouth, wondering why this man affects me so dramatically. It's confusing. After tidily cleaning a chicken leg, Maung leans back to light a cigarette.

He is a chain-smoker. I do not like chain-smokers.

"Maung, it's hard to eat when someone is staring at you."

"You seem to be doing fine." When he smiles, wisps of smoke escape from the corners of his mouth, giving him momentary white Fu Manchu whiskers. He doesn't stop staring.

"Where are your bodyguards?"

"There is only one. And I don't like this word 'bodyguard.' He takes care of me. He is like a brother." With a single question, I have broken the little romantic-conviction bubble. Good!

"Does he have the night off?"

"No. He is outside somewhere."

"Outside the restaurant?" I didn't notice him out there when I came in. Was he hiding?

"Yes. I saw him a few minutes ago, through the plants. He is in the parking lot."

It takes me a moment to digest this. I chew and swallow another mouthful of spicy chicken. I sip my beer. His caretaker/bodyguard is in the parking lot. I wonder if Maung is in actual danger. If not, why does he have a bodyguard?

"So. What do you do with ABSDF?"

"A lot of organization. Decision-making process."

Vague. He can't spend a lot of time in the jungle anymore; he has some fat on him. At the party, the men and women I met who were visiting from their military camps were thin as rails. Maung has a happy layer of flesh on him, as do a couple of the other ABSDF higher-ups. Officers vs. those in the trenches, I think.

Not that he's eating much tonight. I dig my way, as delicately as possible, through three dishes. "Aren't you going to eat any more?"

He shakes his head—distracted, I suppose, by the mention of work. He smokes hungrily and peers through the lanterns and plants out to the parking lot. Disappointed to have lost his attention, I eat the last of the morning-glory vines.

He stubs out his cigarette so decisively that I think he's going to get up and leave. But he doesn't. He moves his plate out of the way and puts his hands on the white-clothed table. "I have to tell you something. Can I tell you something?"

I nod.

"The men and women who are doing revolution on the border, we are not like other people. I see Thai men with their wives and families, doing the normal things. But that is not how my life is. We left our homes behind in Burma a decade ago and we do not have homes here. I move around Thailand a lot, but I also travel to China and India for meetings with other revolutionary groups.

"We would like to be as the other people are, but we cannot be. We must try to fight for Burma. Even if we cannot continue the guerrilla war, we have to prepare for the future—when we will go back to our country and rebuild it. It will happen. We will go home."

He has explained his life to me in a few sentences. Not the normal routines of domesticity, not the unfolding of career, marriage, children. It's good to know what a person is. I hold his gaze, and ask, "Will you keep doing politics?"

"It is all I know now. I did not do politics when I was a student. There were many political students, having meetings in secret. I only studied medicine. And had a good time. I wanted to be a doctor, but I loved school, too. We had so much fun. Singing and playing the guitar and falling in love. Politics was not part of my life.

"The '88 protests changed that. I woke up. The democracy uprising was something that we were doing together, the whole country. After the crackdowns, I knew that I would join the armed revolution. We thought that other countries were going to help us—they would give us weapons maybe, or money. We were wrong. There was no one but the KNLA, and how much could the Karen army help us? They didn't have many resources for their own people, and then thousands of university students wanted to become guerrilla soldiers. We needed training and food and clothes. And weapons. At first we trained with sticks. It was crazy.

"I did what I knew how to do: I helped organize the students in the military camp, and I worked as a doctor, and ran a clinic without supplies, with little medicine. Dozens of people were getting sick with malaria and dysentery. And snakebites."

"Did anyone help you?"

"Sometimes one of the young women or men would act as a nurse, but few had training. When I went to university in Rangoon, I was like a child—we were all like children. In the jungle, we grew up. I slept four hours a night for a couple of years, because the clinic was so busy."

He looks around the restaurant. "Sometimes, in a place like this, I cannot believe I am here. I think I am still there, with my sick people, or walking miles through the trees. I remember one march, we kept going though we were very hungry. We wanted to wait until the rain stopped, to have a meal in peace. But it did not stop. We halted to eat in the rain. The rice in our hands filled with water before we could get it into our mouths." He shakes his head, tosses out an unexpectedly loud laugh, and lights another cigarette. "I miss that time, too, somehow. I miss the jungle."

He shakes his head. I want him to keep talking, so that I can keep watching him, but our coffee comes, interrupting his reverie.

After the coffee is finished, we're tired. It's like sunstroke: we've exposed too much. I've talked about my work, my unrooted existence, my little home in Greece. Strangers, we've laid out the simple lines of our lives so that the other person can try to imagine fitting, somehow, into that shape. We haven't even touched each other.

Maung pays the bill. I ask to share it, but he refuses, which makes me feel uncomfortable. Should the revolutionary forces fighting against the Burmese military regime buy my dinner? I think not. Where does he get his spending money, anyway?

I yawn. He yawns back. We grin. I tell him, "It's not because I find you boring."

With deadpan delivery he replies, "I find you boring. That is why I am so tired."

We walk along the little path beside the parking lot—no sign of the bodyguard, but I'm not going to bring him up again. "Do you want me to send you back to your hotel?"

I believe that he means it—that he would accompany me to the hotel and leave me in the lobby. Many people in Burma wanted to "send" me back to my guesthouse, or accompany me to my next appointment, or go out of their way to make sure I was safe.

But I decline his offer. "A songtow taxi will have me there in less than ten minutes. It's quick. You're staying at Angie's, right?"

"Yes." He quickly adds, "A group of us are staying there. Not just me."

I don't flag a songtow out of the traffic, and neither does Maung—not yet. He takes a deep breath, and a step closer to me. "I feel something special with you. It's hard to say in English. I hope I don't make you angry by saying that. Can I see you again?"

"Yes. I would like that. But I'm not sure when." I knew we would arrive here, at this key piece of information, but I've put it off as long as possible. "I'm leaving Chiang Mai tomorrow. To go stay with friends for a while. They have a little resort near a lake. I'm going there to write for a couple of weeks."

He looks shocked. "A lake? Where is it?"

"Three hours south of here. It's called Nam Waan, near the province I lived in when I first came to Thailand, as a teenager."

"I won't see you before you go?"

"You've just seen me!" The jokey tone of my voice sounds false. I'm not happy to be going away, either, but I'm determined not to change my plans. Too often I have changed my plans for attractive men. It's a habit I'm trying to break.

"Will you call me when you get there? I will give you my cell number."

When he puts his card in my open palm, he grasps the back of my hand with his thumb and folds our hands into a double fist. And then lets go. "Thank you for having dinner with me," he says, raising his arm in the air. For a moment I think he's making some bizarre salute, then I realize that he's flagging a passing songtow. The small canvas-covered truck grinds to a stop a few feet beyond us. I tell the driver where I want to go and hop in the back.

Maung doesn't come closer while the songtow waits to merge into the traffic. He just stands there, smiling his sleepy, delectable smile. He brushes his hair out of his eyes. I smile back, and wink, which makes him laugh. As the truck pulls away, he lights another cigarette.

CHAPTER 19

TWO FISH

. . . .

The lake is not really a lake. It's an old gravel quarry filled with cool green water, surrounded by long-needled pine trees. I swim from one side to the other in less than half an hour, and then have to go back again, of course, as my shoes and towel and the easiest path out of the little forest remain on the other shore.

I am actually a marine animal. As a child, I kept frogs and salamanders for pets and copied their swimming techniques. I used to hold my breath underwater for long periods of time—and once made it to two minutes, but fainted as I was climbing out of the pool.

Is it just a coincidence that I am a Pisces? Two fish swimming in opposite directions. In water, you are yourself—a body encased in skin, capable of swimming only so far. But you are also other—almost weightless, almost free.

Freedom was much on my mind during the three-hour bus ride from Chiang Mai, and it's much on my mind in the lake-that-is-not-a-lake, because I'm thinking of other water, in my other country, Greece. Part of me feels that I should return to the island as soon as possible, because I feel depleted, exhausted. I was planning to go back in March, two months from now. On the island, I would be able to digest my experiences and write about them. But I can't leave Asia that soon. I want to go back to Burma.

And, possibly, become involved with Maung. Possibly? All I've done for the past several days is think about him. But being here, walking through the gardens, floating in water, reminds me that I need to rest. I crave peace. While imagining a relationship with a revolutionary.

In the middle of the body of water, the coolness turns cold. My stomach seizes, flips over. It's deep here, in the center. I'm unused to swimming so hard. And there is supposed to be a ghost in the water. That's why the people of the nearby village refuse to swim here.

The ghost of the lake is a child. But he or she—the gender is not specified in the story—didn't drown. There was an accident a long time ago, when the place I'm floating above was still a rock quarry. The child died on solid ground; I don't know how. As she haunted the quarry, now she supposedly haunts the water I'm treading in.

With a big splash, I kick below the surface, glide down three feet, four, five, and open my eyes. Do skeletal hands reach out? Does a ghoulish child-face waver below me? I see nothing but pillars of sunlight. Flecks of algae float through them like shattered jade. The only dangerous thing in the lake is my mind, its complicated uncertainties and longings, which attach it so irrevocably to my body.

Pretty blond Zoë showed me the lake, and took me to swim there the first time I stayed here a few months ago. Now we sit at the bar of her restaurant. After listening to me talk for a while, she interrupts. "Karen, give me a break! Why are you talking about being in love? You haven't even slept with the guy. Can't you just have a wild affair?"

She is the smart, easy-in-her-skin American woman who runs this resort with her Thai husband. Expert dispenser of free advice, she answers her own question on my behalf. "No, they never just want to have an affair, do they? They fall in love with you after the first kiss, and after the first night they expect to marry you. Look at me! Three kids and a Thai husband because of one youthful romance!

"You never know where an affair with a Thai guy will go. I don't think the Burmese are any different. Especially someone who's doing dissident work—wives must be scarce. Do you really think he's a revolutionary? I mean, gun-toting and everything?"

I shrug. "What's the difference between a revolutionary and a dissident, anyway? He wasn't toting a gun."

"You were in Chiang Mai. It's not like he'd be able to carry around an AK-47."

"I don't think he has much to do with guns. At least not now. I think the focus is more on making diplomatic connections, building up an international lobby. He talked about trying to get the U.S. government to implement economic sanctions against the regime. And one of the NGO women said that politics on the border is also about education. Dissidents are learning computer skills, and 'democratic conflict resolution'—whatever that means."

"Sounds like an NGO. They've got their own language. The NGOs who come down here for R and R from the hill tribes all talk like that. Sawan hates it." Sawan is her jack-of-all-trades musician husband. "He says the CIDA people can make 'taking a shit' sound like a major triumph for Third World development."

I laugh. "I think Burmese dissidents have to learn to talk that language, too, to get funding for education projects. A lot of people are studying either English or computers or both. It's become part of the movement, part of resisting the isolation that is so much a part of Burmese life. It's incredible, really."

"What?"

"The whole story. How these university students walked out of Burma to wage revolution in a jungle war. They're amazing people, dedicated to this cause that has taken over their lives."

"You think that's amazing?"

"Of course it is. They've sacrificed years—their youth and sometimes their futures—trying to bring democratic change to Burma. Don't you think that's admirable?"

She stirs her gin and tonic. "I do think it's admirable. But it's ... it's also ... tragic. Sad." I can't read her expression. Dubious? Amused? Cynical? She cocks her head to one side and says, "Sooooo. What does Maung do? Do you know?"

"I don't, really. He travels a lot. His group works with other border groups. And there are several battalions. He talked about that, too. Visiting the jungle camps."

"Hmm. That sounds like he's one of the leaders. It's bizarre that he's still single." She pokes her straw at the ice cubes in her glass.

How does she know it's bizarre? Was Che Guevara married?

"Are you sure he's single?"

"Uh ... I don't think he would have been so stuck to me that first night if he were married."

She raises one sun-bleached eyebrow. "What about girlfriends?"

"I don't think so."

"But you didn't ask?"

"Well, no. I thought that if he was following me around in front of all his friends and colleagues—his comrades!—he must be single."

"You're awfully trusting, aren't you? But I suppose there can't be that many Burmese women out in the military camps. It's been, what, almost ten years since they left Burma, right? So most of the girls would be married by now. With a kid or two. Good God! Those poor women, in the fucking jungle." She shakes her head, then, a split second later, gives me a sexy pout. "Well, you were probably the prize of that Chiang Mai party, honey!" She lifts up her gin and tonic again and gives my half-empty glass a good crack.

I suddenly regret talking to Zoë about Maung. She has a surplus of the attributes I lack: skepticism, practicality, long experience. She is twelve years older than I and feels trapped by her married life, her children, her endless responsibilities. She loves her family and her (sometimes overly) charming husband, but I know that her restless, unsatisfied energy comes from longing for some of the booty in my camp: unfettered freedom of movement, adventure, self-direction. She and Sawan have built a business out of a couple of empty fields, and it's a great success: fourteen small wooden houses for guests, several extraordinary gardens full of vegetables, flowers, and stone sculptures, an excellent open-air restaurant (which is a favorite with Thais—everyone in the know, traveling to Chiang Mai or Bangkok, stops here to eat), and a large fish pond. The foreigners who stay in the little cabins work in Thailand; it's not frequented by tons of tourists. It's a gorgeous place to visit. But perhaps a dull place to live?

She doesn't say that, exactly. Yet I know that she wants me to preserve in my own life what she doesn't have enough of in her own. But I'm envious of her, too. She is fully steeped in the rich, complicated muck of marriage, attached body and soul to this land and to her husband and their lovely kids. It's no surprise that such attachment sometimes feels confining.

My own life is so open-ended. I've been vanquished by one country after another, as though I have no center, as though I belong everywhere, nowhere, touching the world but not bound to it, like wind. How many realities can a person contain, how many languages? Not as many, apparently, as I would like. That is why I need to escape to various bodies of water and pretend to be a fish.

I feel guilty for being in this peaceful place, though. Guilty for this ease and luxury. I think of the students back in Burma, dozens of them in prison, thousands of them, disillusioned by their own brave efforts at protesting the regime. I doubt that Maung—like most of those who work on the border—is able to run away from his responsibilities and wallow in questions of selfhood beside a green lake.

CHAPTER 20

VISITATIONS

.   .   .   .

I've come here to write, but I wake up in the mornings full of reluctance. The usual ache in my back and right shoulder radiates down into my hands. I turn away from my notebook and turn off my computer. I just want to swim or sit in the sun or walk around the town. How I love that sane, friendly world of temples, markets, and noodle shops, the easy banter I have with shopkeepers and children buying rice sweets outside their walled schoolyard. Doing these things, I am able to hide from my recent experiences and growing interest in Burma.

Though I hide, he finds me. In the middle of the night, when I wake up for my bout of insomnia, a man's voice whispers in my head. No, not Maung. This Burmese man has been with me since the interviews I did with ex–political prisoners in Rangoon. He is not one of those ex-politicals, not exactly. He is himself. I would have expected a woman, some familiar of Ma Thida, the young woman writer whose tragic case got me interested in Burma. But that is not what—not whom—I have received.

This man does not talk to me. I have no personal connection with him. He addresses two worlds, his own and a much larger one beyond him, countries and people he has never met. Not in a didactic way, not grandstanding—just talking. He wants to communicate with the world outside the prison. That is where he is, in a solitary-confinement cell. But the greater world ignores him.

It's horrible. And captivating, because I hear him so clearly. He talks about his own life. The history of his country is recorded in his body. That is always the first record, written as it unfolds for those who live it: flesh as memory. The official accounts, mythic or laden with propaganda or detached, come later, and do not smell of human skin or taste of tears. This man who speaks is not detached. One of the most painful things about these visitations is that I already know some of what he has suffered. I know that he will suffer more. Yet, disconcertingly, I've also heard his laughter. I've heard him sing.

I've always been suspicious of those interviews in which novelists describe how they are "taken over" by their characters, as though the writer is privy to some kind of mystical experience that eludes the rest of us. In fact, I am not at all "taken over" by this as-yet-nameless personage; he is not me. When I hear him speaking, I feel unbalanced somehow, unsure, but full of curiosity: it's the ideal mental climate for good writing. At the same time, I feel I've entered a world that I probably shouldn't have entered, in which I have no rights.

Yet here I am. A man in a prison in Burma. He is not the only one. There is a boy, too; the boy I saw once early in my stay in Rangoon, in the railway yard, at night. I stumbled down a hill, toward a fire that was, in fact, the center of a tea shop, and he was there, a worker, presumably, taking his break. A miniature man with tough hands, stained fingers on the white tea cup. A boy. But a man, knees spread wide, an unlit cheroot stub in his mouth. I could not stop looking at him. The human self was sharply present, almost commanding. Sometimes the child laborers are so tired that vacancy fills them; they look benumbed. He looked fierce. He relit his cheroot, the flame of the lighter flaring briefly in front of his face, darkening the smudges of dirt, the small scars on his cheek, his forehead. After a deep inhalation, smoke rushed straight out of his nostrils. Little dragon, sharp-faced and wire-limbed, the wildness held in but there, as fire was there inside the cheroot, capable of burning down a house, or a train station. So small, so vulnerable, yet such a power.

In my imagination, in the story, this boy does not talk. At least, I cannot yet hear his voice. He watches; mostly he is looking for something to eat. An old, crafty monk will help him, but I don't know how they are related to the prisoner yet.

Who are these people? To find out, I have to write about them. But I can't. Not yet. I'm too indignant. I spend many notebook pages ranting at the cruel generals of Burma and praising the bravery of those who fight against them. Fair enough—the generals are brutal tyrants, their opponents are courageous—but it's still a girl's journal writing, simplistic and embarrassing.

I fear I'll have to wade through a lot of that crap before I'm able to transcribe the stories of my nightly visitors. Equally daunting is that their voices and the images of deprivation that accompany them threaten me in a visceral way. They are imaginary—as illusory as the ghost in the lake—but they are literally haunting. They call to me from a dark place, a world I have glimpsed vividly but in small degree, from the safety of my white skin and my Canadian passport. I don't know if I can write my way out of that safety—beyond my noisy self—into the truth about a wounded country whose language I cannot speak.

"Are you writing?"

"I'm doing what comes before writing. This is a quiet place. I'm able to think."

"What are you thinking about?"

"My life. Burma." I pause, wondering. "You."

He pauses back. Then says, "Do not think about the first two too much. The last is more important."

"Really? What makes you so sure of that?"

"I am older than you. Wiser. You must listen to me."

"Comrade, you are dispensing propaganda."

"The revolutionary forces will do what is necessary to achieve their goals."

I laugh. "What are you actually doing? Right now?"

"Having meetings with some people from the Karen army."

"Are you still in Chiang Mai?"

"No. But we're not too far away. So tell me, the place where you are, is it beautiful?"

"It is. There is a green lake, where I swim every day, usually twice, and there are some lovely gardens." Mimicking the postcard line, I add, "I wish you were here."

To which Maung quickly replies, "I will come. Can I come to see you? Tell me how to get there."

The next two days consist of waiting. Waiting is an odious task, which I've disdained for almost as long as I've been doing it. I believe it is a function of female biology. Women wait. From the age of ten or eleven, we wait to get our periods for the first time. Then, for decades after, we wait for them every month, often holding our breath. We wait for pregnancies to take root. We wait, weeping, for the date at the abortion clinic. We wait for nine months to give birth. We wait, fretting, for our children to get home safely. Once the periods start getting unpredictable, we wait for menopause. And along with all of this waiting, from early adolescence on—if we are straight—we wait and wait, and wait some more, for our men.

Historically, we wait while they go to war and kill one another. In the absence of war, we wait for them while they are busy making other conquests. Last year, at a writers' festival in Australia, I sat on a travel-

writing panel with three men. I presumed that all four of us were single
and childless because we each spent long periods of time traveling or living abroad, alone. How wrong I was! All three of them, in their recent
books, thanked loving wives and children—I quote, their "greatest inspi-
rations," their "deepest reasons," "the ones who remind me of my most
important role"—wives and children who waited for them faithfully while
they took off and had their grand, often dangerous adventures in the
world. The youngest one was a few years older than me and had an obvious addiction to war zones. I was fascinated by him, and annoyed. If I have
a child, I will not be leaving the kid behind with Dada while I dodge bullets in the Congo. I won't be able to do that. But men can. That is because
they know the woman will wait, and will perform waiting's corresponding duty: she will take care.

It is no coincidence that I think about this as I wait for a man who
comes to me from no fixed address and who will depart from me, in all
likelihood, for an equally unspecified location.

I walk out to the entrance of the property so that our initial greeting won't
be witnessed by anyone who is working or staying at the resort, especially
Zoë. In the roadside shelter, I sit watching a troop of large ants detach the
wing from a yellow-and-iridescent-blue butterfly. Now they are dragging
the wing away—to eat? to decorate their apartments? I try not to look up
too often at the two-lane highway.

Some dry, angry voice in me repeatedly whispers, "He's not going to
show up." And then adds sarcastically, "And if he does he'll have the bodyguard with him." Several songtows pass. He will be a passenger in a similar vehicle, eventually, come from the bus station in the nearby town.

Provided that he was on the bus from Chiang Mai.

After the ants start dragging away the long, plain body of the butterfly, a songtow signals and slows down, then pulls onto the shoulder just

past the shelter. There he is, sitting on the end of the songtow bench and grinning enthusiastically. Maung. He hops down from the back of the truck and pays the driver, who zooms off.

Maung lifts his small pack up over his shoulder and takes a long look at me. There is no rush to touch. We begin as we ended in Chiang Mai, regarding each other from a distance. I step out of the shelter. He observes, "You're wearing a dress."

"To remind you that I'm a woman."

"Ah, thanks. I forgot about that."

I give him a saucy grin. Yet my pleasure at seeing him is accompanied by an unsettled stomach. I honestly thought that he might not come. I look from the glinting eyes to the heavy black hair hanging just above them to the full mouth, which I seem to know too well, considering that I've met the man only three times. It is a praiseworthy and memorable mouth. I clumsily open my own. "I thought you might be too busy. To visit. How are you?"

"Happy." He finally steps toward me. "I am so happy to see you." Then his arms take me in, enfold me. He hugs me hard, almost lifts me up with the strength of his embrace. He smells wonderful: clean cotton and cigarettes and the spice of male sweat. We remain in the embrace for a long while, stunned. His heart hammers against mine.

I show him the lake before dinner. Walking back, we hold hands. Our swinging arms propel sexual electricity—*zing zing zing*—through us both and out into the dark: dozens of fireflies wink on and off among the trees.

"There are so many of them," Maung says, delighted. "We don't even need a flashlight!" A few steps later, he stumbles on a tree root and I bump into him. "Maybe we do need a flashlight," he amends. "A broken ankle would be hard to explain to my men."

"Do they know where you are?"

"Not exactly. But I think one or two have an idea."

. . .

When we get back to the resort's bar and restaurant, Zoë is a model of discretion. She shakes Maung's hand in welcome, asks about his trip. Then she leaves us alone. We drink wine and eat dinner, talk some more, with openness and humor, about our lives.

How to compress a courtship of months into the space of a few days? We don't have much time—he can stay only four nights. In a week I will return to Bangkok to get a visa for Burma. He's not sure if he can see me again before I leave for Rangoon.

"Let's not think about it too much, when we will say goodbye," he tells me. "I arrived today. I will see you tomorrow, and the next day, and the next. Before, I did not know you at all, but now we're here, together. Compared to before, we have many hours. I've learned something important in my strange job, doing revolution."

"What's that?"

"Patience. There is no substitute for it."

"I've never been very good at patience."

"That doesn't surprise me. You have little training."

I consider this. I want to defend myself, say that I have had training. (What, waiting in airports?) But there's nothing to defend. I cannot comprehend his patience, nor that of the other men and women working on the border, through rainy seasons and dry seasons, through malaria, through jungles, through deaths.

"It's true. I'm quick to act, quick to feel. That's part of my nature."

"Yes, I know." His eyes meet mine. "That's why I am here."

CHAPTER 21

CHOICE

.　.　.　.

Appropriately, he rented his own little cabin. After dinner, and drinks, and tea, he walked me through the lit gardens, talking. At regular intervals we listened to a night bird make a low-pitched trill—like an owl on a harmonica. We were both tired but didn't want to part. Eventually Maung declared that he had to go to sleep, so he walked me along the orchid-lined paths back to my little house. At the door, he gave me a depressingly chaste kiss—on the lips, yes, but dry and restrained nevertheless—and walked away.

The sound of my own voice surprised me, a hoarse whisper unrolling over the grass and flower beds. I called him back. The woman says yes. She begins it. Yes. Come back. Come in.

I write by candlelight. And try not to look at him too much—I don't want my hungry eyes to wake him. But I could look at him for hours—the slopes and roundnesses of the face, the body, half curled, the slack hands. The white blanket is pulled halfway up the smooth expanse of brown back.

I would like to keep touching him, but he's sleeping. He looks seventeen, eighteen—a boy, for all his thirty-six years.

I try to hear the sound of his body inside me. I hold on to the details, the shock of ease—the ease of us undressing, shy and serious, his face close to me. We kept our eyes open.

Two strangers meet in the dark and share hunger. It won't be sated. There is nothing better than that kind of lust, except for more of it. We eat and eat and still the flesh wants to consume more, and can, and does. Shh. Shh. The walls are made of rough wood; cries of lust travel through them. Once, in our hurry to change positions, we bumped our heads together— which reminded me of stumbling on the path—but Maung did not laugh. I was smiling already, with the gratification of my hands on his skin. I could not stop smiling.

"Do you think I am funny?"

"No. I'm just smiling because I'm glad you're here." He looked doubtful, but kissed me.

Is he less of a stranger now, or more of one? We lit the candle afterward, and talked for a long time, released from our bodies, claimed by them. Already sleepy but questioning what we're up to. In the early stages, I actually asked him, "What am I doing?"

He answered, "You are having your clothes removed. By me. Is it all right?"

"It's not all right. You're going much too slowly."

He laughed. And continued doing what he was doing, more slowly still.

Lying in bed, talking and talking, I fell asleep between sentences. My response to the last question he asked me was lost, drawn down into a cave of dream images. Zoë's six-year-old daughter was splashing in the lake. I sat on the bank, glancing from her to the ants as they pulled a butterfly's wing over a tree root. But the wing was actually part of a scarf my cousin gave me, threads of blue, green, yellow woven through black cloth, a scarf I use all the time here, as a sarong, a wrap, a soft talisman of home. I was worried that the ants were taking her gift.

Maung whispered, "Karen. Karen?" But I couldn't pull myself out of the dream.

Was that fifteen minutes or an hour ago? Now I've woken, and he's asleep. What did he ask me, as I fell asleep? I can't remember.

I follow the bones in his wrist rising into his forearm, the naked shoulder, the neck. Sadness sits tightly in my throat. I already want to use the word *love*. That must be the result of long solitude and months of celibacy. Is it reasonable to fall in love after just a few meetings? Since when have I been reasonable?

I think of the half-dozen white women in Chiang Mai and Bangkok in love with Burmese men. Passionate love takes root easily in a place full of exiles and extremes, even if the extraordinary circumstances have become habit. Maung seems the least desperate of men; he is even-tempered, calm, blessed with a good sense of humor. How else could he manage his life? Over dinner, he explained that he moves around almost constantly. The ABSDF offices in Bangkok, Chiang Mai, and Mae Sarieng are under threat of raids by the Thai police, whose tolerance of Burmese dissidents changes constantly. When that tolerance plummets, policemen descend on the makeshift offices and confiscate computers, printers, paper files. Sometimes they send people to immigration detention centers. Maung told me about the five-thousand-baht rule: most of the dissidents try to carry around that much money at all times, in case they are stopped by Thai police and have to pay a bribe to avoid detention.

People live as well as work at the ABSDF offices, Maung said, their few belongings tucked into market bags, bedrolls on the floor beside their computer tables. The offices themselves shift location regularly. "Most of us live between arriving and leaving."

"That's the definition of a refugee," I said.

He shook his head. "The real refugees are in the worst situation. Their lives have been stolen from them. It's bad for refugees from Burma because Thailand isn't a signatory nation to the U.N. convention on the status of refugees. So, officially, they don't exist. The Thai government doesn't have to care about what happens to them. If they work, they can be exploited, beaten, killed. Have you ever been to a refugee camp?"

"No, never."

"You will have to go, if you want to learn about Burma." He turned his head to light a cigarette and added, "Soon they will be burned down."

"What do you mean, burned down?"

"It happens every dry season, to the camps that are close to the border. Burmese soldiers come across in the night and set fire to the camp. Thai soldiers guard the camps, but they are useless. They run away." He paused. "So you see, our situation is not so bad."

In this place and time, facing the world and my ignorance of it, everything has become sharper. When I look at Maung, I see someone who has given himself over, completely, to a cause bigger than his one life. The shadow of his eyelashes on the sheet rises, flutters, falls again. The eyes slide, pearl-like, under the closed lids. What is he dreaming?

For years he slept in a hammock, in the jungle—they all did—to keep off the insects and the damp. He says he can sleep through mortar explosions, if they're not too close. Here there is only the sound of crickets.

The next morning, on the restaurant deck that overlooks the pond, Maung and I have hard-boiled eggs and fruit and steaming cups of Nescafé with condensed milk. We watch fish jump in the water. Fog hangs in the gardens, shrouding the trees and the bird-of-paradise flowers. Zoë is already up and about, chatting with other guests as she makes tea and changes the tape in the machine to some hypnotic Indian tabla music. I catch only one of her curious looks. When she approaches with a coffee mug in hand, I ask her to join us. She sits next to me, comments on the cool morning weather, and takes surreptitious glances at Maung. Eventually she asks us about our plans for the day.

Maung and I look at each other bashfully. I say nothing, but I'm all for spending the day between the lake and bed.

Receiving no response, Zoë continues, "We're going into town later. Didn't you say you needed to go to the bank, Karen?"

I blink. The bank?

Then I remember: "the bank" is a euphemism for the pharmacy. I'd told Zoë that I had a single condom in my overnight bag. Gone now. Maung brought some—in battered-looking packages. Also gone now. "I forgot all about that. What time are you leaving?"

"Around noon. I have some errands to do, but you could go to the bank then have lunch. We'd be back by two. Plenty of time after for a swim."

"You are so thoughtful, Zoë."

"Just trying to help. And Maung can have a little tour of the village."

The best noodle shop in town is situated beside a big machinery and mechanics shop. It smells not only of garlic and chicken but of diesel and grease. There's oil on the floorboards. Spiderwebs hang thick in the corners of the ceiling. I love the place. Young grease monkeys and old men and betel-nut-chewing ladies from the market are in and out all day long, eating, talking, gossiping. On the weekend the tables are packed with teenagers, who come for the good cheap food and for the fancy Sony TV that sits at the back of the concrete room, beside the Buddha altar.

Maung pauses at the threshold. "This is your favorite noodle shop?"

"At least in northern Thailand."

"Hmm," he responds doubtfully. "If you like this, you will like Mae Sot. Everywhere in Mae Sot is like this place. But with more dust."

When he leaves here in two days, Maung will stop in Bangkok en route to Mae Sot, a border town farther south, where many Burmese migrant workers make their entrance into Thailand to work in factories and on building sites. A good number of dissidents live there, too; some of the men and women I met at the Christmas party talked about the "Mae Sot office." Refugee camps of Karen and Karenni people are also situated close to the town. I don't know why Maung is going there, and I don't ask. I've understood that he doesn't want to talk too much about his work.

So we talk about mine instead—the series of interviews I'm conducting with former political prisoners, the people I met in Burma, the people I would like to meet here, in Thailand.

Maung says, "I will help you to make contacts."

I thank him for the offer, thinking that I'll have to be careful about accepting it. I've already figured out that there are a lot of rivalries between different groups of dissidents and revolutionary organizations on the border. I don't want to alienate other contacts by seeming to be too connected to the ABSDF, or to him. Nevertheless, we talk about various well-known dissidents and activists. Maung tells me which ones are living in Bangkok. One man, a well-known musician I'd heard of in Rangoon, emigrated to Norway a few months ago.

"It's too bad I missed him."

"You should have come sooner. More people leave every year. They go to one of the U.N. holding camps and they wait to become official U.N. refugees. They get tired of the instability, the poverty. If they have children, it is more difficult. They have to choose: Thailand illegal or somewhere else legal. There is not so much here, for some people." He looks at me searchingly.

I stare into my noodles and reply, "I'm beginning to see the Thailand that so many Burmese people live in—safer than Burma but still a brutal place."

"Not compared to Burma, though. And we get used to it."

"I don't know if I could. I would probably leave. Though leaving Asia can't be easy, either. In Canada, it's really tough for new immigrants."

"And so cold."

"That's why I've spent a lot of time in Greece."

"Is that really the reason?"

"It's not just the physical weather, it's the mental weather. I'm more comfortable in Greece. My character fits the Greek character. I'm happier. Canada feels too stiff for me. When I'm there, I'm always thinking of somewhere else. I would like to settle down at some point—just not where I was born."

"You are lucky! You don't have to choose a country. You can belong everywhere. I think that is the sort of person you are, naturally. I had to learn to be that way. Most of the Burmese people had to learn to be that way. We always miss Burma. But you don't miss your country."

"That's because I left freely. And I can go back if I want to. Besides, I'm not sure that belonging everywhere is a lucky trait. I'm sick of moving all the time."

"Then you will stay somewhere. You have a choice." His eyes contain the obvious question. "All you have to do is make it."

On our drive home from town, Zoë's kids are in the back of the truck with us, giggling and bickering in Thai and English. Earlier in the day, they refused to believe that Maung was not Thai, and kept saying all sorts of silly things to him in that language, trying to make him laugh. But to every one of their jokes and jabs he replied to the extent that his Thai would allow him: "Hello" and "Fried noodles" and "Grilled chicken" and "Omelet with pork." The kids laughed until they couldn't breathe.

The older boy and girl are ten and twelve. They're talking with him a little in English. As we get closer to home, they lapse into long silences, and sit with their heads turned toward the green fields and hills rushing by. Five-year-old Lennie, though, continues to be chatty. Cuddled up next to me, she addresses Maung in Thai. It's the easier language for her, and she still can't grasp that someone who looks Thai can't speak it. She turns her beautiful face up to mine and asks, "Is he your boyfriend?"

Maung smiles. Interesting, that he understands that particular phrase. He regards Lennie tenderly.

I take a deep breath and exhale, "He is."

Lennie takes my hand, snuggles closer. "Do you love him?"

I hesitate. And think, Why not? Why not say it? "Yes."

"Are you going to get married?"

Maung laughs. He understands more Thai than I thought. He leans out the back of the truck, unable to contain a whoop of joy. The other two kids look over. The boy yawns.

I say, "Out of the mouths of babes."

Lennie touches the back of my hand. She is a naturally gentle child, almost too softhearted. "Will you marry him?"

"I don't know, Lennie. We'll see."

That is enough to satisfy her. We'll see. My mind is reeling. When we pull off the highway and into the turnoff for Zoë and Sawan's place, Maung is still gazing fondly at the brown-skinned, green-eyed child.

Suddenly I remember the question he asked me as I dropped into sleep last night. "Do you want to have children?"

No wonder I fell asleep before I could answer.

CHAPTER 22

GIVE YOUR HEART TO ASIA

.　.　.　.

That first night, I called him back to me and he came, but the truth is, I lag behind him. The body—oh, I am good at the body, the joys of skin and food, the open mouth, the eating. That's always the easy part.

This morning he said, almost casually, "I want to love you forever." He was rising from the bed. He stood and stretched, then stepped out the back door of the little house. Down two stairs is an enclosed outdoor shower room, with orchids growing out of the bamboo walls. He laughed as he lathered soap over his torso, under his arms, his chin. "What you don't understand about me yet," he said, "is that I am a child. I am a child!"

Tears jumped to my eyes.

He is a healthy, happy child, declaring his love because he's sure that he will be loved in return. So simple, so romantic. And unbelievable? We have spent almost four days together. Despite my attachment to Southeast Asia, I disappoint myself, because I am a cynical Westerner when it comes to the realm of emotions. Sure, I dream of real and long-lasting love, but the idea of sacrificing anything for it gives me pause.

I did not expect this man. Do we ever expect love, even when we are hungry for it? My emotions for him are tangled up with my thoughts and feelings about his country. The dream of love has become enmeshed with a much larger dream, of political change in Burma. Am I just a parasite, falling in love with this man because he brings me closer to his country? I don't bother asking Maung this question. He would think I was being too hard on myself. Besides, he's in love. He can't be properly critical of me.

I am trying to be critical of myself in an effort to control the strength of my feelings. When I see him, that perfect, clichéd phrase happens: my heart goes out to him. Some essential part of me literally pulls toward him, cleaves to him. Why? Because he is himself. A remarkable person. Who makes me laugh. And surprises me. I often have no idea what he is going to say next—a rare and useful quality in a mate. I want to meet his ability to give. And to change. And I love the way he smells.

I was telling him over breakfast about Greece, my wish to go back to the island for a while. He understood. "You need to go because that place is also your home." He moved my coffee cup out of the way and took my hand, lightly, lightly. That is part of his power: he doesn't hang on too hard. His fingers moved from the tips of my fingers to the top of my wrist. "I know you may leave Thailand. There may be separations, sometimes long ones. For me, too, because of my work. Moving around is part of our lives now. But I hope you give your heart to Asia."

I heard those words all day long, as I watched Maung swim far into the lake and wave to me from the place where I had shivered and dived down, seeking a ghost in the green water. Give your heart to Asia. As we made love, again, in the hot silence of midafternoon. And fell asleep easily, then woke to the children home from school, their voices rising and falling in the garden.

"I hope you give your heart to Asia." He said it once, smiled, and talked of something else, but here I am, awake on our last night, watching Maung sleep as I turn those words over and over in my mind. They have a built-in rhythm, and a weight to them, like prayer beads.

.   .   .

In the morning, the warm brown body, the voice, the deep-lidded eyes, with irises so dark they look black: these disappear. The generous mouth is gone. In the past four days I've lived a life out of time, sweet and heady and held, protected within the bounds of the gardens and the lake, Eden in the middle of rice paddies. Zoë and I dropped Maung off at the bus station early this morning. My lover and I barely embraced in public; we'd said our goodbyes earlier, in the privacy of the room we shared. We both felt exposed at the bus station—a rough spot beside the busy marketplace—and reverted to the physical reticence that is part of intimacy in Thailand. To restrain the obvious gestures. To smile only. To touch hands briefly. Look, my heart. This closed bud contains the whole flower.

On our way back to the resort, Zoë and I keep our eyes on the road. "So, are you in love?"

"I think so."

"He's handsome. He's obviously intelligent. Of course you're in love."

"I admire him."

"To be dedicated to a great political cause is admirable." There is something in her voice that reminds me of a corkscrew. It turns. "He spent a lot of time on his cell phone."

I can't help being impressed—she was observant without ever seeming so. I think it's motherhood; it makes women hypervigilant. My mother used to say, "I've got eyes in the back of my head."

"Yes, he's attached to his cell phone. But a businessman would be, too." I laugh, lightly.

"So. What else do you think?"

"Well. It's very sudden. He's a serious person. He would be, wouldn't he, given his day job. He's already asked me if I want to have children."

She exhales sharply, blowing the blond hair off her forehead. "These men!"

"You can't blame him for asking." I refrain from mentioning my non-response. "They all want kids. Those guys I met at the Christmas party, the dissidents I met last year in Bangkok—they all talk about wanting to get married and have a family."

"To replace the families they've lost."

"Well, isn't that what most people do?"

"Yeah, sure, most people do get married and have kids if they aren't waging a revolution. Do you know if he has any money? Or where he gets it, for that matter?"

Now I exhale sharply. Her hard-nosed approach pisses me off: I didn't ask for her opinion. "No, I do not know where he gets his money. NGOs, probably. It's not something we talked about. Obviously he's no millionaire, but I've never been all that interested in money anyway."

"Well, poverty is fine when you're single, but if you get knocked up you'll need to be interested in money." She's smiling. But I know she's smiling to soften the gravity of her words.

I remind myself of what I like about her: her practicality. I hate it, too. The bitch. Here I am, high on romance, blissed out on fabulous sex, and she's lecturing me about the responsibilities of having a family.

"Zoë, I just met the man. In case you're wondering, we used those condoms, okay? I feel as if I'm talking to my mother. No, actually, my mother will be thrilled—she'll be, like, 'Oh, and I'll get to come to Thailand every winter and look after the babies.' " I laugh, too shrilly, and then bark, too loudly, "Fuck!"

For a few minutes we drive on in silence, each sequestered with her private thoughts. Then Zoë lifts one hand off the steering wheel and waves it in the air, a flag of surrender.

"Karen, I'm sorry. I don't mean to upset you. And it's none of my business, really. I know that. I'm just . . ." The sentence remains unfinished. "I know that everything changes after children come. And you're an artist. You're a real writer, it's part of you. But here that wouldn't matter so much. To . . . to them. You're a white woman with a Canadian passport, and if you have kids here you'll have to support them. And him, too, possibly . . . if the NGO money gets thin. The money to raise a hypothetical family won't come from the revolutionary coffers—I can't imagine they're too deep."

I turn my head and glare at her, willing her to meet my eyes. But she just keeps driving, competently and rapidly, passing the slower vehicles. I work to keep my voice steady. "So, what, he's after me for my Canadian passport? He's not interested in moving to Canada; he wants to live in a free Burma! That's all his life is about."

"That's what I mean."

"But what you said was . . . It sounded like something a racist would say!"

"Karen, come on. You know me better than that. You know my life better than that. Just remember how heady and exciting any affair is, in the beginning. The complications come after. That's natural. But his complications, his world—there's a lot you don't know yet."

I fear that I will either scream or burst into tears. Ferocious words rush through my head: You're just jealous! Of my freedom, my pleasure. You're unhappy, that's why you always talk about other people having wild affairs that mean nothing. Maybe you want to have them yourself! Go ahead! Getting properly laid might relax you!

I raise my voice slightly. "Why do you say that? How do you know what it would be like for me?" I watch her steadily, thinking I see the whole of her in that narrow jaw, clamped down. When she turns to meet my eye, it's a shock. She's crying. Tears spill freely from both eyes.

"Oh, God, you're so young. There's so much in you that you think you can just give it away forever." She gasps as she cries—ten seconds, twenty—then wipes her face and stretches her mouth open to turn off the saltwater faucet. She grabs a tissue from the console between us and blows her nose.

We're close to home when Zoë speaks again, in a voice that's almost back to normal. "How do you think I know?"

CHAPTER 23

THE FIRST UNION

. . . .

"Do you miss me?"

"You are a major distraction to my work." I hear Maung smiling through the words.

"Then both of us are distracted. Where are you, anyway?"

"Mae Sarieng."

"I thought you were in Mae Sot."

"The meeting was canceled. Have you ever been to Mae Sarieng?"

"No." But I know it's a border town, with various Burmese organizations stationed there: the ABSDF, DPNS, and another one or two groups I can't remember.

"We have a house here. It's a nice town. Quieter than Mae Sot."

I wonder who belongs to this "we." "Do you live with many people?"

"It depends. Five or six. Sometimes more. We have a military camp a few hours away from here, so when people need to go to Chiang Mai or Bangkok they always stop here for a day or two. You'll have to visit sometime."

"I will, probably. Sooner than you expect. Maybe I'll come tomorrow."

"I thought you were going to Burma soon."

"Ah, that's my big news. I didn't get the visa. I'm on the blacklist."

"Oh! Congratulations!" He laughs.

"I don't think it's that funny."

"No. But to laugh is to make it smaller, not so important."

But it is important. To me.

"I'm happy you didn't get the visa."

"Why?"

"Because you will be closer to me this way. I can protect you."

"I don't want your protection, Maung. I want to keep doing my work. I need to spend more time eating, drinking, and breathing Burma. And I need to work on my Burmese."

"You can do that in Thailand. This is the Burma outside of Burma, so don't worry about the visa. It can be easier here, too. People will talk to you more openly. And you have a Burmese dictionary now."

"What has that got to do with it? I've had a Burmese dictionary for months. Not a very good one, but . . . What's so funny?"

"Sometimes you are so serious that you miss the joke. I don't mean a paper dictionary. I am the Burmese dictionary."

"Oh." This softens me. "Right. My handsome talking dictionary."

"Who misses you. I want you to read me."

"I need to memorize the alphabet first."

"You know my alphabet well already. You are fluent in my alphabet."

This charming innuendo acts on me like a tonic; my bad mood shifts and longing pours in to fill its place. "So when will I see you?"

"Now that I know you are not running away to Rangoon, I will come down to Bangkok in a week or so. Ten days at the most."

" . . ." The sound of disappointment.

Which he hears. "Remember. Patience is important. What are you doing now?"

"I'm just lying here." I skip a beat, then add, "Naked." I roll over on the bed, stretching out. Let's have phone sex with the man of the velvety voice!

There is a long pause. When Maung speaks again, the velvet has been replaced by bewilderment. "Why did you tell me that?" he asks, but doesn't give me a chance to explain. "If you are not too busy now, you could make some phone calls. I will give you numbers of people who would like to talk to you." He pauses again. His voice drops to a whisper. "But please do not talk to them while you are naked. Put some clothes on."

I roll my eyes and sit up. "All right, then. Who are these new people you have for me to meet?" I still prefer to meet people through other sources, but the thing is, Maung knows everyone.

"Two women. Though only one is a member of ABSDF."

"Oh! This is exciting. I was beginning to think that you guys never let women do any of the talking."

"That is unfair. You know it isn't true."

"But it's true a lot of the time. It's often the men who do the talking. The women do the cooking, or watch from the background."

"You don't understand Burmese culture. The women are more shy. Not like Western women."

"In Burma the women didn't seem very shy."

"That's part of the problem. The women are more shy here because they are not in a familiar place, and sometimes they can't speak English well."

"The way to solve that problem is to give them the same opportunities that the men have, for training and education."

"Karen, there are not so many opportunities." I hear the admonishing tone.

But I don't care. This subject has been festering in my thoughts ever since I met my first group of Burmese dissidents here in Bangkok—all men. "That may be true, but women should get half of those few opportunities. They shouldn't be left behind just because they're women."

"We're doing what we can. I know women need more chances, and they will get them. But it is not so easy. Sometimes, if the women have children, they want to stay in the camp. And if they come into the cities and towns there is the problem of the immigration police. There's also the problem of money, and where to live, and what work they do if they come out. We bring people to the towns and cities for short periods of time, to do computer classes, to do diplomacy training, to learn about documentation—all workshops run by different organizations, sometimes for a few days, or a week or two. Then they go back, both women and men." This is an honest response, I believe, but it's also mollifying.

He's a natural politician. I'm still thinking of how to bring up the much thornier issue of why there are no women in positions of power within the ABSDF. Does a revolutionary organization mean any revolutionary changes for women? From what I've seen so far, no.

I've read Aung San Suu Kyi on this subject, too. In interviews, she says she's not a feminist. I wish there was a less frightening word for declaring, "I care about women's lives." She believes that change needs to come for all Burmese citizens before it comes for women in particular. I know she has to be careful of what she says; the SLORC is always looking for ways to undermine her. But waiting for larger systemic change does nothing for women. Whether in a democratic country like India or under a dictatorship like the one in Burma, millions of women and girls in the developing world have to fight for education, for reproductive freedom, for pay equity, for protection against domestic violence—and for justice after that violence is perpetrated, if the victim survives it.

If the women who came before me had waited to improve women's lives until "democracy" became a better system, I would not be a writer, because I would have started having children at seventeen, like my mother. Instead, I had an abortion, left for Thailand, and found my subject matter. And my mother might have died in childbirth, as she almost did, hemorrhaging out her last baby. But because women fought to change a lousy law, and won, she finally had the right to have a tubal ligation without my father's consent—something he had always refused to give her.

What the ABSDF does when it comes to women is none of my (white, foreigner) business, I know. Except that it frustrates me when the men do all the talking while the women are in the kitchen frying the noodles.

"Are you upset with me for asking these questions?"

"I am not upset. But I want you to understand our situation."

"I'm trying to. That's why I ask so many questions."

"Ah. I see."

"Remember, patience is important. So who are these women you want me to meet?"

Aye Aye Lwin says little, at the beginning. She ducks her head down and lets the conversation proceed without her participation, saying that her English is not very good. Yet when a discussion of age comes up she offers her own, proving how carefully she listens. She is thirty, almost thirty-one—three years older than me—but she looks sixteen, partly because she is small and slender but also because her pale face is framed by short, uneven black bangs, which add to the girlishness. The rest of her long hair is tied cleanly in a straight, gleaming ponytail. She sits across from me at the small square table.

We eat peppery cold noodles and *let-phet,* the delicious tea-leaf salad I've become addicted to, plus a Thai dish of green curried beef that I contribute—from a famed street vendor on Phaholyothin—and copious platefuls of rice. My hosts kindly offer me a spoon, but I decline and eat with my right hand. I'm still a mess-maker, but more skilled than I was in Rangoon.

The dinner takes place at the apartment where Aye Aye Lwin, who is an ABSDF member, lives with Ma Tu and Chit Hlaing, who are English teachers. Though Thailand has surpassed Burma in every area of development and education, it still needs the skills of Burmese men and women who learned colonial English as children. With their fluency and fine accents, they make excellent teachers. Chit Hlaing, a quick-humored yet earnest man with thinning hair and a round face, puts up his hands in a gesture of defeat. "I didn't want to come! But the money I make here teaching is many times what I make in Burma."

Ma Tu adds, "There are not many chances in our country. It can take years to get the visa arranged, but if people can get out they will go. My best friend's children are in Germany, Switzerland, Singapore. It's sad for Burmese people, who love the family so much."

Chit Hlaing puts another dollop of curry on my plate. "The foundation of our Burmese culture is caring. On the street, if you see an old lady struggling with her parcels, or a boy who is lost, you say, 'Daw-Daw— Auntie—can I help you?' or 'Nyi Lay—Little Brother—what's wrong?' We can address strangers as though they were part of our family. That is what a country is. But now the immediate families are broken up; they go away from each other. This will happen more and more, until the regime changes. And if the first family is broken it disrupts the bigger family, too—the whole country."

"You don't mention the military intelligence networks. Doesn't that disrupt the family?"

Ma Tu shakes her head. "People in immediate families still trust each other. Usually. The MI makes it difficult for those who have one son or daughter involved in politics—they will punish the other children, even if they are not involved. You always have to be careful of who you bring into the family. There are informers everywhere. Even if there are not informers, we believe there are, so we are afraid. But Chit Hlaing describes the public forms of caring—the worry for strangers, the kindness. Gestures that are cultural, or just human. They should not be political. They are part of being Burmese, part of our Buddhism. But those kinds of gestures will be destroyed also, because the MI creates suspicion and fear among our people. It can make life lonely."

"It reminds me of a line by a Greek poet: 'The world becomes a limitless inn for strangers.' "

Chit Hlaing says, "Yes. Like the West."

"Do you think the West is like that?"

"It's what I observe, from television and the newspaper. People in the West are not committed to anything, and they do not believe in sacrifice, so they are lonely."

I agree with him to a certain extent, but the generalization irks me. "Western cultures are different from Asian ones," I say. "Westerners are committed to different things."

He gives me a stern look, which makes me want to laugh—it's so teacherly! He snappily asks, "And what are you committed to?"

I calmly reply, "I'm committed to writing a book about Burma, which is partly why I'm here."

"Ahh! Please write a good book so that it will become a bestseller and bring much attention to my little disaster country." He gets up and disappears into the little kitchen. Water splashes into the sink, clattering on loose cutlery.

Ma Tu's voice takes on a confiding tone. "He is shocked by Western consumerism. And the children can be so disrespectful to their parents. Even to their grandparents. We have seen tourists . . ." She shakes her head. I expect a woeful tale of rampaging white fifteen-year-olds, but she proceeds in a different direction. "Thailand is more Westernized than Burma—the Thais have lost their culture. Or they have sold it. We are afraid this will happen in Burma, too." She cranes her head over the table—Chit Hlaing is still busy at the sink—and turns back to me. "The prostitution here bothers us a lot. There are brothels in this neighborhood. The girls sit outside. There is prostitution in Burma, but not like here, like a factory. Burmese girls also come to Thailand and end up in brothels.

Sometimes they live like slaves, but their families are too far away to help them. Or the families are desperate for the money. When we talk about the things that the SLORC has damaged, not even the family is safe."

"I don't often think of the damage in terms of the family, but it makes sense. Every other civil institution has suffered."

"A family is the first union. And all the unions in Burma are outlawed."

Chit Hlaing returns from the kitchen and rejoins the conversation. "The journalist and lawyer and doctor organizations, they are also illegal now, because people are not supposed to meet together unless it's for the SLORC's purpose. If an organization is allowed to have a big meeting, you can almost be sure that some of the people are friends with the generals."

Ma Tu quickly interjects, "Except for the monks, the holy Sangha. The regime cannot own them. A few abbots have accepted big gifts from the SLORC, it's true, but they are exceptions. Most of the Buddhist Sangha are good. They want to help the people, and they're able to help because they can travel around and communicate, not only with each other but with the people in the villages and towns. And these people truly love and trust them. The people take care of the monks, and the monks take care of the people.

"Some people believe that political change needs the Sangha. They were very active in the 1988 demonstrations—thousands marched with their alms bowls upside down to show they wouldn't accept any merit-making gifts from the SLORC. It was like a spiritual punishment for the generals. But some people believe they will do more. Did you know there are as many monks as soldiers? Close to four hundred thousand of each."

"But why would it be the monks who do something?"

"Because soon they will be the only ones left. The students can't organize because of university closures, the unions are illegal. The NLD is constantly harassed, and Daw Suu is back under house arrest."

"But it's hard to imagine that monks could lead an uprising."

For the first time since dinner began, diminutive Aye Aye Lwin speaks up. "Was also hard to imagine students could lead an uprising. But we lead an uprising."

It's taken her awhile, but she's ready to talk. Like so many others, she left Burma in 1988, joined the ABSDF, and has spent most of the past decade in a jungle military camp. "I trained in the field. After training, I carry gun, very heavy," she says proudly, then adds something else in Burmese.

Ma Tu translates, "With the bayonet, the gun was as long as she is tall." Ma Tu asks her something, and again translates the answer. "She could carry this gun all through her watch, sometimes eight hours long. She says living in the jungle made her strong."

Aye Aye Lwin smiles sweetly.

"What's it like, in the military camps?"

"Now is not so hard. We know water collection, we know gardening. More rice. We not getting sick. Sometimes we getting sick, but is not the same in the beginning—sick all the time, with malaria. You get it first time, you sick, then it goes away. Then is back, every month."

"Recurrences every month?"

"Before. But not now. We get recurrences only when we get sick with flu or hurt. Then malaria comes again because we are weak. But when we first come living in the jungle we are sick all the time. That's why I am skinny. Eat and eat but always the skinny."

"How does malaria start?"

She looks at me in surprise. "Mosquito bites."

"Oh, yeah, I know. I mean, how do you feel with the first symptoms?"

"You feel sick. You get fever. Then cold. The cold is more bad than fever. So cold the teeth move—what is this?" She clacks her teeth together.

"Chatter."

"Teeth chatter. Then you throws up—you throws up, with fever and cold, and you don't have to do any work. That is the one good part. Vacation time."

I shake my head in awe at how people live through such hardship—for years—and then joke about it. "Don't you need to take some kind of medicine?"

"You have to break fever with the paracetamol and take the quinine, or you can die. Some people die."

Chit Hlaing has been watching me. He observes, "You are also committed to malaria."

"Just curious. It seems like a basic experience when you live on the border. I don't want to be committed—that would mean getting it!"

As Aye Aye begins to remove our plates from the table, she says, "Don't get committed. Malaria is not good."

One of the reasons Aye Aye has left the jungle camp is to improve her English. We chat for a while longer about life in the camp compared with life in busy Bangkok. I realize that I have an ulterior motive in wanting to meet women. I just miss women's company, their conversation, the shared experience of being female. Talking with Aye Aye and Ma Tu makes me happy.

I ask Aye Aye, "Will you return to the jungle camp?"

"To visit. I hope. Not to live. I go to the Norway."

"Oh, Norway! It will be cold."

"Not always cold. But always far away from Asia." After Aung San Suu Kyi won the Nobel Prize, Norway began to regularly accept Burmese immigrants, especially those actively involved in dissident politics. "I go to the Norway, and later come back here to work for Burma."

"How do you want to work for Burma?"

"I want to work for women. Help them learn, help them educate and grow up. I don't know how to do it yet. That is why I'm here. I am member of Burmese Women's Union. And we will be getting help from NGO in Europe, in America."

"But if more NGO money is going to start coming to women's groups, like the Women's Union, then why do you still want to go to Norway?"

She takes this question and holds it for a while, her eyes full of trouble. I've touched an open sore, which makes me regret asking the question so forthrightly. "It is hard, in Thailand, with no papers. Or illegal papers. So better for to go to the Norway, and get citizenship. It is not easy, to be no country." She quickly corrects herself. "To have no country."

CHAPTER 24

TREASURE

. . . .

~~Maung is coming~~ to see me, so I walk up to Soi Dang to buy food. Crammed with treats of every description, Soi Dang leads to the best dead end in the world, a market and a temple. I say hello to the people I know as I pass them, and promise the Esaan woman that I'm coming back within the hour for her chicken. Hungry young couples sit at tables devouring rice and curry or thick noodles; children in their pyjamas are running around with skewers of meat and pieces of fruit in their hands. The withered pharmacist has emerged like an iguana from his dark, narrow shop. He gives me a quick reptilian nod and lights up a cigarette. I walk along the market's edge, buying orchids and the other bits for the temple, the whole ritual package. I could do this every day for the rest of my life.

Inside, I light the joss sticks and the candles, place the flowers, sit there breathing in front of the old gold man for half an hour. Other women are sitting here, too, and two men. One of the women near me has her small boy beside her. I try not to think, thinking: There is no reason to feel so choked up. I want to cry, which is unreasonable, Maung is coming home.

So much for meditation. Through most of my sitting I can't help but notice that the six-year-old boy sits stiller than I do. I comfort myself with the pathetic notion that perhaps he's handicapped—he actually cannot move. But then, as if infected by my mind, he gets fidgety and begins to pester his mother.

Outside, shoes slipped on, I realize it's the word that gets me. *Home.* It's not right—the bed on the floor, the cardboard-box altar. I do the dishes in the bathroom sink. Will I ever, in my life, buy curtains?

An hour and a half later, eight o'clock, I'm here, in the big room where I live, and the darkness has arrived in this city that is never dark. I spread the tablecloth on the floor, put down the grilled chicken and noodles and curried eggplant—it's all in plastic bags. Home? Not home—me. He is coming to me.

I'm hungry, but I won't eat without him. I take off all my clothes and lie on the mattress. He will arrive soon, I will touch him. Now I have to put my clothes back on, because it would be anticlimactic to masturbate before Maung arrives. Besides, I can't answer the door naked; that would embarrass him.

I lie here and will him toward me. The gecko sings—*"Too-kay! Too-kay!"*—as I draw him out of meetings, tasks, away from other people, through traffic lights (they turn green as he approaches), past stray dogs, beggars, dripping air conditioners. Before I see his face, I will hear his feet on the echoey concrete landing, walking past the scuffed walls. He will have to decide if he should take the left hallway or the right. He chooses correctly, and now he coughs outside my door and I have to restrain myself from leaping up before he even knocks.

Knock knock. Who's there?

I expect the stilted words after absence, but when I open up he steps toward me so quickly that I'm taken aback. I think of the lake that first hot afternoon, the boyish grin as he dove into the water. He wears the same smile as our bodies press close. The door slams behind us.

"It's nice to see you, too," I say. More quickly than I undressed myself, he undresses me again, the wraparound skirt a rectangle of ocher cotton on the floor, the black shirt up and over my head, and my hands on his belt as we turn around in a graceless polka, the small clank of the buckle and then his trousers and shorts, now the bare skin of his chest. "Are you in a rush?" I ask, walking backward toward the mattress.

"Not too much," he whispers, and stops, and kisses me. That mouth! *Vive la révolution!* His wetness turns into my own—his tongue in my mouth pulls liquid silk between my legs, I slide as he maneuvers me around again, throws me off balance. I push him backward onto the mattress and fall down on top of him, messing the carefully straightened sheets. With me weighing him down, he must feel the lousy coils under the foam pushing into his back. He lifts me deftly, a rapid reversal, and he's on top, right there, at the drenched edge of me, ready to dive in.

Then, a pause. He whispers, barely audible.

"What?" I'm listening too hard to our genitals to hear words. I don't even notice the mattress coils.

"I am not wearing. A condom."

"I don't fucking care." Slightly sobered, I amend, "Just this once."

Then he's in, in, in.

We drown in skin. No surprise, to think of him diving into the lake, my cunt. The human body is an inland sea, all our salts and minerals churning in perfect order. There is no turning away from these depths, only longing to make them deeper. To pull him into me is to have him push through me, find something else below, beyond me. Fucking as deep-sea diving. The divers acknowledge that it will be impossible to make it back to the surface, they must keep going in, to the treasure.

Where is it? Here, love. You are the treasure, and me: these bodies, alive, peeled open in nakedness. Oh, happy, serious, wild frenzy!

Later, we're almost sleeping as the world floats back to the surface. The sound of the gecko returns. *"Too- kay! Too-kay!"* And traffic growl.

Sweat on the skin, the smells. I love you, we murmur. The old promise is as delicate as a sea horse.

More treasure drifts up on the tide. An uncomfortable, attractive, worrisome understanding. I realize what he was searching for, inside me. For the first time in my life, I feel it hovering around us like a little fish. Gold seed, brown eyes. The bright minnow of a child.

CHAPTER 25

THE STORY

.   .   .   .

In the middle of the night, I wake up to him sitting on the mattress with his back against the wall, smoking. Watching me. Our positions reversed. A different glow shines in the balcony doors.

Maung says, "The light is so bright."

"It's the moon."

He sounds offended. "It is not the moon. It is neon—someone turned on a sign. Strange light. But it makes your face look beautiful."

"It's the moon. Go on. Look at it."

He goes out on the balcony with his Marlboros and I fall asleep again.

A week later, at dinnertime, we walk along Soi Dang, not holding hands. But my knuckles graze his as we swing our arms. Our elbows touch, our shoulders. A week of this, touching, and talking, seeing each other every day. Except for Wednesday. He couldn't come. He was on the other side of the city and it would have taken two hours to get here on the bus. But today he came early and there is time for a walk and street food before sex and falling exhausted into sleep. It's lovely to be out with him, in the life of the city, to see the same things—a child walking across the overpass with a birdcage, the piles of fruit on the stands in Soi Dang.

His knuckles, my knuckles, his hand on my waist as I sidestep a motorcycle that passes too closely. The street is so full of people that only local traffic comes through, usually at a snail's pace, though sometimes the boys on their bikes can't resist zipping through a gap in the crowd.

A brown man with a white woman incites a certain amount of curious staring in this neighborhood, especially when the white woman had been shopping and eating alone. The pharmacist looks up from the counter in his grotto. The big Esaan lady who sells grilled chicken and *som-tam* is all eyes and lascivious smiles. The curry woman is reserved as usual, but after we pass by I feel her eyes boring into the backs of our heads. I know they want to know if he is Thai. Later, when I return on my own, that will be their first question. I will answer honestly, and they will express their negative opinions.

Over dinner, Maung tells me about the latest round of talks the ABSDF has had with other armed groups on the border. "When we are together, we are revolutionaries, fighting the Burmese military, discussing strategy—where to put the troops, thinking about where the SLORC troops are. Strategy and maneuvers. Then I am a different person for the other talks, with NGOs, and sometimes not exactly NGOs, but like NGOs—European, American groups that might give us funding. I can never say 'revolutionary.' Some of the NGO people were French. They especially don't like the word 'revolution.' Why not? They had their big revolution!"

"Maybe that's why they're not so keen. Their own turned out to be very bloody."

"I cannot help that the French killed each other so much. It doesn't mean Burmese revolution would be like that. We are Buddhists. We don't want to cut off the generals' heads. We just want to build a democratic government. The generals work so hard, they need a long vacation. In prison. How can we do that without revolution? All right, I find out more about diplomatic means—I have to, because the Burmese military is so big. We cannot win at armed conflict.

"Everyone, all the ethnic leaders—Karen, Karenni, Shan, Pa-O, Wa, Kachin—for all, it is just time. More time passes, everything will change. There will be more cease-fires. The SLORC will make deals with the ethnic leaders. It's already happening. The generals have so much money. And they have China, Russia, Israel. The world is happy to sell them guns and tanks and airplanes. But if I say 'grenade' to a Western NGO they have a heart attack."

I can't help laughing at this, though the joke is too true to be genuinely funny.

He responds to my laughter with a rare physical gesture: a big flourish of his arm, hand aloft. "You think I am kidding with you! I am not kidding. We are supposed to be good dissidents. Be polite to the land mines. Work with the white people." He pushes his untouched plate of food away from him.

This is the first time he has expressed frustration with . . . anything. Even so, he holds it easily. And lights a cigarette for his second course—not that he has eaten much of his curry.

"Maung, five minutes ago you said you were starving."

"My stomach is bothering me." He has an ulcer. That's why he was awake the other night.

"We shouldn't talk about NGOs over dinner. They make you feel sick."

He takes another drag. "You know, we need them. Revolutionary or dissident, we need them. This makes me crazy sometimes." He takes my hand and looks deeply into my eyes, as if about to make a declaration. Which he does. "I am so glad you don't belong to an NGO."

"Oh, you're so romantic! I'm glad, too. It's my fate to belong to nothing. That's a writer's job."

"To preserve your objectivity?"

"No, not at all. That's what journalists say they do, though I don't believe them. I'm glad I'm not a journalist. My job is to preserve my subjectivity. I have to keep my biases safe. I celebrate them."

"But you do belong to something." He frowns. And squeezes my hand.

"You," I say, raising my bottle of beer. "And the revolution!" I turn his warm hand over in my cooler one and kiss his palm. I trace the lifeline, the work line, the love line.

"What do you see?"

"In the future, you will live in Burma. And you will be a politician. You will never be rich."

"I know," he says. "I would like to give up politics, but I cannot. I will be an opposition politician, too. That is my job. To oppose the ruling party." He sighs. "Do you see children?" He looks at me so seriously that I literally squirm.

"Maung, I don't really know how to read palms."

"But whatever you say, I believe you."

"Then I will say that you need to eat more. You've had five cigarettes and half a beer for dinner."

"You are like my mother."

"That is not a sexy thing to say to your girlfriend!" I toss his hand away from me, happy to change the subject. "You must never again say I'm like your mother. It's forbidden!"

"But it's a compliment."

"Eat some food!"

"See? Just like Meh Meh."

I push his plate in front of him. He puts out his cigarette, sheepishly picks up his spoon. "I will try."

"Try." My pleasure, as I watch him eat his food, is smug, even carnal. And deeply motherly.

. . .

He goes back to the office tonight—the Bangkok office, that is, where he sleeps on a mat on the floor—to prepare for an early meeting with some NCGUB guys: the National Coalition Government of the Union of Burma. And the NLD-LA: the National League for Democracy—Liberated Area. Meetings, meetings, meetings. They are endless. Maung doesn't tell me what they talk about. There are more than a dozen different groups to interact with, at least, and a few hundred egos to negotiate in order to proceed as some kind of united front. Though I'm not sure how united that front really is.

Within its own ranks, the ABSDF has had serious problems. The two sections of the organization represent a serious split in the leadership, with Maung on one side and Moe Thee Zun, the prominent student leader, on the other. I've also discovered that an execution took place in the jungle a few years ago, of an alleged spy, which outraged those who believed the man was innocent. An ABSDF member told me about that incident reluctantly, in confidence, and I didn't press him for details: an execution was not the proposed subject of our interview. I would like to ask Maung about it, but I'm not sure how to, or when.

Maung wants to know what I'm faithful to, what defines me, the way revolution and being Burmese define him. What do I belong to? Why on earth did I say I belonged to him?

Because that's what he wanted to hear. But it was a romantic feint. I don't believe that lovers belong to each other. He doesn't belong to me. His work owns him; it's the center of his life. I respect him for that, as I respect all those who are involved in Burma's democracy movement, both the armed and the unarmed fighters. But I also understand those French NGO people who don't like the word *revolution*. Recent history is drenched in the blood of revolutions. They have always been such a good excuse for mass murder. Even the word makes me suspicious. Doesn't the revolution simply revolve, coming back to what was there before in a disguised form?

And yet. I believe that some wars need to be fought. But most of them should never begin, and too many of them—in Africa, Central America, the Middle East, not to mention the jungles of Burma—lead to the slaughter of innocent civilians.

But to return to the first question, which should be easier to answer than ones about revolution and war: what do I belong to?

A code of behavior—morals. I believe in acting when I see injustice. I believe in speaking out against violence of all kinds, especially if it means risking my own comfort. But that's too noble: my big mouth never thinks of comfort; it has its own designs. It's hard to know when speaking out makes a difference, or if the course of action chosen is the right one. But it is wrong to do nothing. It is criminal to be silent in the face of an outrage. The pathology of the bystander pretends to be a minor, forgivable pathology, but it is the mildest, most common face of evil.

Daily I meet people who have lost everything because they acted and spoke out against injustice. They insisted on their right to protest, to demand better from their abusive leaders, and they paid dearly for it. All the former political prisoners I've interviewed have had staring contests with death. A man I spent a few hours with last week, Win Naing Oo, was interrogated, tortured, and, once he had healed from the torture, beaten unconscious in prison. After the beating, he watched as his whole body turned blue and swelled with septicemia. It is a miracle that he did not die, or that he was not crippled by the beating. He has made it his mission to document the various prisons and work camps he lived in. My writing about the Burmese prison experience will depend on his book *Cries from Insein*. My work will come, in part, from his memory. This tall, slender man with shaking hands sat across from me (there was no table between us) in a dirty room with a broken tap dripping behind him, and he said that it was worth it, his suffering, his exile, his loss of health, the nightmares, the pain—so many different kinds of pain. It was all worth it. Not because he had survived but because he had acted, and his action took the form of resistance.

And I have fallen in love with a man who does not question the sacrifices he makes for the cause he believes in. Do we match? Maybe I should join an NGO and do real humanitarian work in the field—build wells in the refugee camps or help in the Burmese clinic in Mae Sot, an extraordinary place run by a Karen Burmese woman named Dr. Cynthia Maung. Maybe I should just teach English. The most useful thing I do around here is interview people about their experiences in Burma and on the border. Even that is beginning to feel more useful than actually writing a book.

The people I interview want to talk, even if they don't want to talk about everything. By listening carefully, by asking questions, I become a mirror that reflects their lives back to them. They are here illegally, set apart from the dominant culture, existing in a long, difficult limbo. To tell his or her own history is one way for a human being to reclaim legitimacy. The power of story gives both ways, to the teller and to the listener. It is literally life-affirming.

Brutality makes no sense. It ravages the senses; it takes apart meaning. To be survived, it needs to be integrated into the larger context that is the story of a life, the story of community. If something else came before the cruelty, something else can come after the trauma it leaves behind.

When I have finished an interview with a former political prisoner, I feel a mixture of emotions: a closeness to someone who, an hour or two before, was a stranger; a deep weariness, from taking so much in and holding it; and a sorrow that is not always sad. Maybe a better word is *tenderness*—an anxious tenderness for this person who has entrusted me with his story. Tenderness for his family, from whom he's been separated, usually, for years; tenderness for my own family, from whom I've separated myself willfully. Tenderness for the human condition—how we struggle, how cruel we are to each other, how deeply we want to love and to be loved. I think I feel *metta,* to use the Buddhist term, which carries with it an appropriate formality: loving-kindness. It is a specific feeling, but also a kind of atmosphere that I move around in for a few hours or days after talking with the person.

It's not easy to separate after these interviews. Too much has been said, too much has been given, for a hasty departure. The desire to remain in the same room is almost physical, a magnetism between myself and the people I've spoken to. We want to return together to this other world of the present, in Thailand. Usually I end up staying at the house or apartment for an hour or two afterward, talking with the larger group of people, drinking tea, chatting. And laughing. We return to the present and usually find a way to laugh. Often the group ends up eating together. The ubiquitous food vendors of Bangkok make it easy for me to contribute to a communal meal. And I talk about my other work, or show the photos that I often carry around with me, of Greece and Canada.

What do I belong to?

The story.

Such a small word. And not an answer Maung would understand.

CHAPTER 26

ENGLISH LESSONS

.   .   .   .

On the weekend, I took Aye Aye Lwin shopping for clothes to keep her warm in Norway. She doesn't know when she's leaving—the paperwork is still moving through the labyrinth of United Nations and Norwegian bureaucracy—but I'll miss her when she's gone. I've returned to the house where she lives perhaps half a dozen times; Aye Aye, Ma Tu, and Chit Hlaing have taken the place of a small family in my life. They help me with my Burmese and tell me stories about Burma.

On our shopping trip, I got to be the expert on cold weather, searching for skirts that were thick enough, socks with real wool in them, a good-quality winter jacket. Late in the afternoon, near the end of our spree, she said, "I am older than you, but you are just like my mother!" A few minutes later she said, "And Maung, he is like my father."

"Is he?" She always refers to him as Ako, which means "older brother." They seem to be very close. They were in the same jungle camp together for a long time, and I think he protected her. Early on, in the military camps, the ratio of women to men was something like three to two hundred. She's told me that she has a boyfriend, but he's still in the jungle.

I don't know if she knows that I am involved with Maung. More than once, we've arrived at her house together, as we did this evening. Maung came in to say hello to everyone, then went to the ABSDF office, which is not too far away. I'm not sure when or how romantic relationships are made public. People must figure things out on their own, but surely, at some point, we will be more open about being together. At present, I have the feeling that we're sneaking around. Maung is a private man, discreet, though that was not my first impression of him. Chiang Mai was more of an exception than I realized. I've gone with him to another party, in Bangkok, but I attended as "the writer who is writing about political prisoners." Maung didn't stick to me as he did in Chiang Mai, which was a relief. Of course, he doesn't have to woo me now that we're sleeping together. But I don't think he would have wooed me anyway—too many older political figures were there. Maung was serious throughout the evening, drinking little, murmuring a lot on his cell phone. Once, he disappeared for half an hour. I eventually found him outside, deep in conversation with one of the other men.

We see each other sporadically, and spend our time together in a room without a kitchen. To share a home you must be able to cook food together, not pour curry and som-tam out of plastic bags. I love the street food, but I miss cooking. For that matter, I miss sitting at a dining table. I contemplate buying one but always have better things to do. I bought a work desk for one of the communal dissident houses, but a table for myself seems an extravagance. One of the reasons I love visiting Aye Aye is that the little townhouse provides a domestic haven. It's comforting. It's comprehensible, though much of the conversation goes on in Burmese.

Tonight, after we eat together and have a discussion about the mysteries of skiing—Why would anyone want to ski, really, in the cold, covered with padded clothing? Why?—Aye Aye asks me in Burmese if I want to go to "[Burmese word I don't understand]" with her. I'm so pleased to understand half the question that I say, "Yes, let's go," without knowing our destination. Typical. Somehow I think it has to do with Maung—his house, which I take to mean the ABSDF office. But I'm not sure.

She picks up her knapsack, which suggests that she's going to a computer training or something, but they're usually on the weekends. We say goodbye to Ma Tu and Chit Hlaing, but we don't leave the little street in the usual way, by walking out onto the big road; we walk back down the lane for two minutes, then turn into a narrow passageway between buildings, the kind of path you would miss altogether unless you know it's there. Obviously the locals use it often, to get from one *soi* to another without having to go to the main street. Aye Aye glances at her watch and picks up the pace. "We have to hurry. I'm going to be late for English."

"English?"

"English class. I'm going to school."

That was the word I didn't get. School.

We leave a vacant lot and pass into the next soi, walking up the street past good-sized houses with small compounds. "That building. Classrooms are upstairs."

A big dog begins to bark. Louder and probably tougher than the dog, a woman yells in English, "That's enough! Stop! You know everybody. Stop that barking!" She sounds Irish. Or Scottish.

Aye Aye says proudly, "Is Miss Nola."

"Your teacher?"

"Headmaster."

"Oh." Through the chain-link fence I see the woman turn sharply into the doorway, her dark red hair swinging. The screen door slams behind her.

"Her house is our school." Aye Aye opens the gate. The dog—a German shepherd—resumes his barking, which is pure canine welcome, accompanied by tail wagging and stolen licks of hand or leg.

"But, Aye Aye, why did you bring me to your school? My English is pretty good."

"Your English is perfect! I bring you because Miss Nola wants to meet you."

I suddenly feel nervous. Marla must know Nola; Marla seems to know everyone. And I know that she has probably told some of her friends how untrustworthy I am, problematic, inexperienced. It can be worse than high school around here.

"Hello, Miss Nola! I brought my friend, the *sa-yeh sehyama*."

I smile, touched. Aye Aye has used the respectful Burmese term for "woman writer."

"Oh, it's great to meet you. I'm Nola." A woman with big blue eyes comes toward me, her hand out. The eyes are enlarged by the roundness of her face, a freckled, smiling moon. "Aye Aye—and a few other people—have told me so much about you."

"Yes, it's a small world, isn't it?"

Nola turns to a few more students, young men, who have just sauntered through the gate. The dog starts again. "All right, hurry up. It's seven, your class has probably already started!" Aye Aye and the others step out of their shoes and disappear into the house. "And you shut the hell up right now, you bloody rogue!" Scottish, definitely. The dog puts his head down but looks up at us, maudlin, full of longing. The heavy tail begins a cautious wag.

"He's a real love, but he just can't stop barking. It drives us mad." The accent is soft around the edges; she hasn't lived in Scotland for a while. She holds the door open for me. "Can you stay a bit? A friend of yours is here. You could have a drink with us when the classes are over."

"A friend of mine?" My voice comes out high and reedy.

"Yes, a friend of yours. From the party. I'm sorry I wasn't there; I heard it was quite a good one. And you were very popular, weren't you?"

I laugh awkwardly. I can't think of anything to say but, "Yeah, we all had a really great time." And I call myself a writer.

We're inside now, passing through a short hallway and into a large sitting room—sofa, TV, all the regular stuff except for the piles of English workbooks piled tidily along one wall. Happy to shift focus, I ask, "So you run a school out of your house?" I sneak a peak through the partially open kitchen door—someone in there, banging cupboard doors. I grit my teeth and smile as Nola talks.

"I guess I do run a school, though I still keep thinking that there are just a few classes going on upstairs. But we're always full, all levels. You see how many shoes are at the door? We have to find a bigger site, because there are so many people who need to learn English.

"It's not political work," she says ruefully, "except that Burmese people need the English if they're going to keep doing the politics. Or just about anything else, for that matter. It's like computer training—necessary for communications. It's great to have these people come out of the jungle and start sending emails. Some of them have already taught themselves Web design."

I refrain from mentioning that I've never sent an email myself.

"I don't teach the classes, unless one of my teachers can't come in. But I organize the whole thing, work on funding. It's crazy to be doing all this from a kitchen table, but I'm not quite ready for an office yet. I'm still getting used to being so sedentary. I used to move around all the time. I worked on the border, delivering rice for the BBC."

The BBC. Rice?

She sees my puzzled look. "No, not that BBC. The Burma Border Consortium."

Of course.

A drawer slams hard in the kitchen. We both turn around just as a woman cries out, "I found the fucking corkscrew!"

The voice does not belong to Marla. I feel physical relief, and happiness, for who emerges from the kitchen but Charlie the Kiwi filmmaker, bottle of wine in one hand and elusive corkscrew in the other. Her China-red lipstick complements an ear-splitting grin. She walks straight into the conversation. "Yes, Nola's given up all her wild frontier ways and is practically a married woman now. To the most handsome man on the border, too." She raises the wine bottle, which is not yet opened, and gives Nola a mock toast. "I think I should crack this bottle right now. Why wait?"

"Charlie, behave yourself. Don't touch that corkscrew until all the kids go home." With this admonishment, the Scottish accent becomes sharper.

"I'm already touching it, and besides, they're not exactly kids." She gives me a wink and starts twisting through the cork. "Come on, Nola, I'm a guest in your home and I desperately need a drink." She looks at me. "I just got in from Phnom Penh, where I was visiting my lovely brother. But he had a sick roommate in his house, and we both had a ton of work to do, and I caught this weird stomach bug. You can't even brush your teeth with Cambodian water, it's so lethal. Ah, Thailand! Civilization!" The cork comes out with a jovial pop.

Nola responds, "Well, I need a drink, too, so it's cruel to start without me. At least give me a cigarette, would you?"

Charlie puts the bottle on an end table. She sprawls on the sofa. "We'll let the wine breathe while we have a smoke."

Almost three hours later, long after the students have left, we've finished the second bottle of wine and have made it halfway through the third. The fourth is looking like liquid wisdom. Charlie and Nola are engaged in a detailed, intense discussion about vomiting.

I started it, by quizzing them about malaria. Nola is telling a grim tale about being on a visa run in Malaysia and coming down with an attack while she was on a train. Now that she's been drinking, she sounds like a Scottish miner. "When I got outta the station, I was so ill I could barely walk. I was delirious. But I didn't want to get stuck in some Malaysian hospital in quarantine. I just hadta keep going, to catch the next train and make it back. Then, of course, I started puking up me guts. And there's nothing you can do to stop it. I hadta change trains, too, so I walked from one flower planter to another on the platform, puking into every one of them. I'm sure people thought I was a heroin addict on a bad trip. 'Twas bloody awful. But I made the damn train."

"What if you'd passed out or something?" I ask. "There was no one to help you. You could have died."

"Well. I wasn't pleased. When you first get malaria, it's uncomfortable, but by this point in time I was used to it. You kind of develop a sense about just how sick you are. If I'd really thought I was dying, I probably would have gone to the hospital." It's the "probably" that sticks in my mind. Nola lifts up her hands, shrugs. "Here I am, I survived."

"How does it feel?"

Charlie guffaws. "What do you think, Kaz? It feels like shit!" Kaz. That's what my favorite cousin calls me. "And sometimes you know you're so sick that you have to take the damn pills. I was on a march on the Burmese side once, with some ABSDF guys and the KNU. It was the monsoon; we had leeches all over us. I've never been so fucking sick in my life. But Nola's right—you understand when it's critical to have drugs. And I knew, so I took my last pill. But the timing was wrong. Five minutes after I took the damn thing, I threw up. I had to have that pill in order to make it out, so I dropped down on my knees and scooped through the puke until I found the damn tablet and swallowed it again. Thank God I managed to keep it down."

"Malaria's not all bad, though," Nola says in a philosophical voice.

"Really?"

"It's the best diet going. I always lose ten pounds at least."

As Nola drinks, she gets funnier and sharper and sweeter at the same time. She sees the doubtful look on my face and laughs. "I'm perfectly serious! Just think how much money the Burmese resistance movement could generate by organizing fat farms for Western tourists. Overweight white people could go out to the military camps in the jungle, get malaria, and lose ten or twenty or even forty pounds. Medics would have to be there, of course, dispensing Fansidar and quinine, and making sure no one died or went cerebral." Her nostalgia-soft eyes quickly focus on my face. "The falciparum strain of malaria can get into the brain if it's not treated properly. And then, well"—she wipes her hands one against the other— "the brain swells and the person usually dies."

"But falciparum seems to be rarer these days," observes Charlie as she pulls the elastic from her hair and scratches her scalp. Her gold hair rises and shakes under her fingers. I can't help thinking that underneath it all is the miracle of her unswollen, non-malarial brain. She flips her hair over her head. "I love the fat-farm idea. We've got serious potential there. The tourists would get skinny, experience true adventure, and further a noble cause at the same time. If the rates were competitive, imagine the AK-47s and grenades the guys could buy. A Southeast Asian guerrilla war won with American fat—that's got a nice ring to it, don't you think?"

"There are more and more fat English people, you know," Nola interjects. "I think we could market it in Britain, too. Why not Britain? At least they have a vague idea of where Burma is."

After pouring me the first glass from the new bottle, Charlie yanks her thick hair up high on the back of her head and forcibly restrains it again with the elastic band. "You'll have a chance, Kaz, at some point, to go out to the camps. If you want to."

I snap back, "Are you calling me fat?"

We all convulse with laughter. I'm happy to make them laugh so hard.

In a surprisingly lucid voice—almost her no-nonsense, smart "headmaster" voice—Nola says, "We'll have to find the right person to take you to one of the military camps. And the right camp." She rattles off the names and numbers of battalions ranging from the south to the far north. Presumably, she has visited them all, even as they've shifted through hills and valleys, because of the work she used to do for the BBC.

I sit up and try to shake some of the fuzz out of my head.

Charlie says, "Well, it always depends on what's going on, who's doing what."

I insist, "I'll find my way to a military camp on my own."

Charlie yawns. "Well, make sure you watch out for land mines."

"I don't mean I'll go by myself! I will be accompanied."

Nola is quick on the uptake. "What d'ya mean? Who's going to take you out?"

Why be cautious? I'm at home with these two, everything's fine. A secretive smile unfolds on my face.

Nola sits up on the edge of the sofa and howls. The dog lifts its head. "One of them has already got to you! I can't believe how fast those guys work! It was the Christmas party, wasn't it?"

This conversation will cause me some anxiety later, but in the moment it's as good as flirting. My mouth remains closed. Except to take a huge swallow of wine.

Charlie lights another cigarette and happily sucks on it. I've never seen such a keen smoker. She raises her finely plucked eyebrows. "Of course! It was at the Christmas party. It's all coming back to me now."

Nola looks at Charlie. Then at me. She sits on the actual edge of her seat, close enough to me to grab my hand. Though she doesn't do that. "You have to tell me. Who is it?"

I smile.

"Tell me!"

There is a long and, for me, confused pause. I'm drunk. This is not how I should tell anyone about my new relationship. But it's too late to change the subject. At least I can lower my voice and vacuum it clean of drama. It comes out like a verbal shrug. "Maung."

Nola lurches backward. She is astonished, and clearly not by joy. Her big blue eyes gleam; the generous whites are full of tiny red veins.

Suddenly I feel depressingly sober.

"Karen, that's . . . I'm sorry to say this, but I—well, I like you a lot, so I want to be honest with you. I think it's awful. He's not a good man."

In a markedly noncommittal voice, Charlie says, "I thought Angie was his girlfriend."

The hostess of the Christmas party: machete eyes. "He said that they're only friends."

Charlie sounds indulgent. "Kaz, he's been staying at her house for years." Isn't it possible that you can stay at someone's house a lot without sleeping with her? Charlie again, reading my mind: "A lot of people more or less understood that they were together. He allowed that to be understood. Both of them did." Charlie savors another drag and says, with the exhale, "Even if they weren't. Exactly."

Nola is hardly over her shock; she still looks bug-eyed. She glares at Charlie. "But he's not with Angie. He's just been using her for her house." Then she glares at me. "He's got a rich Burmese girlfriend here, in Bangkok. Daughter of a gem dealer or something. Money's very useful, as you can imagine. The family supports the cause."

I'm the one who should be bug-eyed. But I just say, "Really?" as though I'm talking about an unexpected change in the weather. I'm not surprised, just stung. It's like a blister, at the beginning, before you've walked very far.

Charlie, at least, seems to be reserving judgment. She cracks several one-liners, the most memorable being, "Women of all nations must sacrifice for the cause!" But Nola is solidly angry, even offended. Not with me but with Maung. I am puzzled. Why is she taking it so personally? After one more cigarette—"If only I could smoke in my sleep!"—Charlie excuses herself and goes to crash on a mattress in one of the classrooms.

Soon afterward, Nola walks me out to the gate. I walk through, she shuts it. We look at each other between the metalwork. Her eyes shine under the streetlights. "A lot has happened on the border that you don't know about. People have histories."

I stand there, waiting for her to say more, but she shakes her head. "It's so late. We're all going to be tired tomorrow." Her official, taking-care-of-business voice returns. "The soi's quiet, but the main road's full of cars. There are lots of cabs. We'll see you again, okay?"

"Good night. And thanks, I had fun."

"Until the end."

"No, even that. It's better to know than not to know. I'll talk to him."

She replies, "Yeah, you do that. See what he tells you."

CHAPTER 27

BELOVED

. . . .

As I haul my ass up the filthy stairs at two in the morning (the elevator is broken), I think about the blister. I reach my floor feeling the painful pressure of it. Exhaustion and the depressing effect of alcohol spread through my body, compounding the ache. Ouch. The blister of love, honey. It's good that Maung doesn't have a key. I would hate to walk through the door and find him in bed. I mean, on the mattress. I bet she sleeps in silk sheets on a teak frame.

But what if I've just heard some malicious gossip? I wish. I believe what Nola told me. Truth often has an unsettling familiarity.

I try to see the bright side. If your lover must cheat on you, shouldn't it be with the daughter of a rich gem dealer? Anything else would be too dull, and therefore insulting. I bet she has long, black, luxuriant hair. And a twenty-four-inch waist.

That fucking bastard.

Ha-ha. Literally.

I consider escape. I will pack up a bag of clothes, grab my passport, and go to the airport. I will fly back to Greece. The island in spring is my beloved.

I don't know why Jung made such a big deal about dreams. The important ones are obvious. They are the adolescent poetry of the subconscious.

I dream that I'm in an enormous bed with red tie-dyed sheets. Above the bed is a watercolor painting of an elephant in the jungle. This painting is owned by a man I've never met.

Across the room is a teak armoire with two high shelves at the top. Out of reach, hanging from the upper shelf, are a series of keys on separate key chains. They belong to the French writer Colette. I wonder if I'm allowed to touch them. How? They're too high anyway.

Then all of a sudden I am rock-climbing, splayed on a broad back of stone, trying to hold on to a rope and a sheet of red canvas at the same time. (The canvas is the same color as the bedsheets, but the material is much coarser, like an old-fashioned sail.) Far away, people shout commands, but I can't hear properly; I don't know if they're above or below me. I see only perpendicular angles of rock and vaulting space. Though I'm in danger, I feel no fear. The shouting mountaineering types are more experienced than I am. I worry that I'm going to do something wrong. That's where the considerable anxiety in the dream comes from: not that I'm going to fall to the ground and break my back but that I'll do something wrong. I *am* doing something wrong: I've got twisted up, entangled in my efforts to hang on to both the canvas and the rope.

I wake up with my arms crossed under me, stiff. The left one is asleep—I can't move it. It's like a severed arm in the bed with me. It takes more than ten minutes for the pins and needles to melt away.

Then the phone rings.

.   .   .

"I already told you: I don't want to talk about it on the phone."

"But why not? What's wrong? You are upset."

"Yes, I'm upset. I'm pissed off at you."

"Do you want me to come right now?"

It's ten in the morning. I don't often see Maung during the day. If he stays over, he leaves in the morning, like Dracula. I've never had lunch with the man.

"Let's have lunch," he says. Asshole.

"I don't know if I'll feel like eating."

"Oh, this is bad." Given the merest permission, he would laugh.

I say nothing.

"Do you want me to come now? Is it an emergency?"

Is it? In the great scheme of things? Refugee camps. Guerrilla skirmishes. Detailed histories of incarceration in my head, my notebooks. Malaria swelling the brain.

"No. It's not an emergency. Just come over tonight."

I hang up in his ear.

I try to meditate in front of my humble altar.

I bow down three times.

And laugh, with a ragged catch in my voice. I need to change the flowers: the water stinks. It's all a bit silly. A real Buddhist would be scandalized by the Buddha on a cardboard box.

Only enlightened people can meditate with this kind of angry hangover. For a while, slouched in the half-lotus position, I think about how badly I want to have sex with Maung. Which just makes me angrier. And it's not that I want to claim territorial rights over his body, either. Well, maybe just a few territorial rights—but that's not the conscious motivation. I'm suffering attachment, as the monks would say. The lovely, aggravating thing about making love is that that is exactly what happens. You do it enough with one compatible, friendly person and you make love. You create affection, not just orgasm.

Instead of meditation, I read some of my Buddhist texts. As usual, Ajahn Fuang, the beloved Thai abbot, is being wise and reasonable. I resist the impulse to heave the book across the room.

> You can't even sacrifice your grudges, your anger? Think of it as making a gift. Remember how many valuable things the Buddha sacrificed during his life as Prince Vessantara, and then ask yourself, This anger of mine has no value at all. Why can't I sacrifice it, too?

Truly pathetic. I'm trying to forgive Maung before he has even apologized for being a dishonest cheat.

It's a challenge to argue in a small, unfurnished apartment. No place but the mattress to sit on, and no barrier props—no tables or sofas to stand behind, no chair backs to clutch. There is nothing upright in the room but us, and the fridge, which can't participate in any useful way.

I sit at the head of the mattress with my back against the wall, and Maung sits at the end of it on the floor. We've been facing each other for a while now, talking in fits and starts.

"Who told you about this?"

"What does that matter? I want to know why you didn't tell me."

"It is not a simple situation. It is not easy to explain."

"Try."

"I was seeing her. And it's true, her family has money. They support the movement. That's important. But it wasn't working out. They wanted me to marry her."

"No big surprise there, Maung. She's their daughter."

"She's been married before. She's divorced now."

"Jesus! Because she wasn't a virgin, she didn't have a right to expect a serious commitment from you? That's great news for me!"

"That is not what I said."

"But it sounds like that's what you meant."

"That is not what I meant. I meant she is an adult. Her parents cannot plan things for her." His voice lightens into familiar explanatory mode. "You know, not all Burmese girls are virgins when they get married for the first time. The Burmese are not so crazy about this virgin thing."

"Apparently."

"Why are you being like that?"

"Like what?"

"So cold when you speak."

"Because I'm angry. I'm hurt."

Long pause. "Karen, I am sorry. I didn't tell you because the relationship I had with her is over. I still see her sometimes, because I am still connected to her parents."

Meaning money. Zoë was right. The revolutionary coffers are not that deep. Do you know where he gets his money? I've thought a lot about that tense conversation I had with her in the truck. It seems like years ago, though barely six weeks have passed since I was at the lake. And the first thing she asked me about him was whether or not he had a girlfriend.

He looks at me beseechingly. That is the only adverb. "Karen, it is a delicate situation. I have to . . . what is the word? Withdraw. I have to withdraw slowly, because of the political involvement."

Slow withdrawals! That should be hilarious. I would like to explain it to him, and make us both laugh, but I just sigh.

I'm already getting tired of politics as the excuse for lousy behavior. A lot of people around here do that—Marla is the perfect example, along with other icy, finger-wagging people I've met recently. I'm being politically astute and savvy, I've joined the revolution—that's why I treat people like shit.

"What about Angie?"

"Angie?"

"Yes, Angie, your Chiang Mai girlfriend."

He smiles. "You were talking to someone who does not like me."

"I bet Angie doesn't like you much, either."

"Angie is my friend. She is my friend for a long time."

"Am I really supposed to believe that, when everyone else thinks you've been a couple for years?"

"If we were a couple, we would be married now." No laughter here, and no beseeching. "I've never had a sexual relationship with her. She is my friend. I told you that from the beginning. So that you would understand. I don't care about gossip."

We regard each other in silence.

It's hard for me to look at him. What does it mean to love a man's body? Will I love this man in five years? In ten? In twenty? Why do I love him so intensely right now, when I know that he has betrayed me? I don't really believe his explanation about the Burmese woman. About Angie? Maybe. Even now, he might continue the relationship with his invisible, gem-laden compatriot because ABSDF needs the money.

I am angry at myself because I don't really care.

I don't know him, not really. How dare I say I love him?

Yet what is this feeling, if not love? How else do you do it except by doing it, by wading into the swamp, mouth-deep?

I recognize his clothes now, one pair of jeans or another, a light-green plaid shirt. The cornflower blue button-down collar he's wearing today. I know the feeling not only of Maung's skin but of his clothes, the way his body has imprinted its shape into the materials. I think that's what happens with love: you wear the beloved, and he alters your form, as you alter his. Despite my drunken talk of flying off to Greece, there is nowhere to go but toward the man in front of me.

Nevertheless, I stay on the mattress, holding my knees. He remains at the end of it, on the parquet tiles. It's good to see him from this small distance.

"Can you still love me?" he asks. I've never heard his voice with so much quiet in it.

I stand up unsteadily and step down to the floor. I stretch my hands out to him. It could almost be that stupid fairy-tale scene of the man on bended knee, proposing. But Maung gets up quickly and hugs me.

"I will think about it," I mumble against his blue shoulder.

"About loving me?"

"Yeah."

"Good. Please think about it carefully."

We pull away from each other. He lights a cigarette. I go to the bathroom. And when I come out he's sitting on the floor again. "I also need to talk to you about something," he says. "Two things."

So much for that Western cliché I was so looking forward to: lustful making-up sex.

"What?" I sit in the middle of the bed.

"I got a phone call from Marla the other day."

"Oh, no!" I launch myself over backward, feeling the mattress springs between my shoulder blades.

"She had a lot to say about you."

"I can only imagine."

"She says that you are not trustworthy, because you are a writer."

I let out a howl and come up on my side, propped on my elbow, head in hand. "Sounds like the SLORC Censorship Board."

Maung speaks as if he's giving a report. "She told me that I should not help you to meet Burmese people and do your interviews, because of what you might do with the information. She thinks you could hurt the movement."

I sit up again, slightly breathless. "When did she call you?"

"Yesterday."

My mouth opens; nothing comes out.

"You see? Some people do not like you, either. It's not so good when they talk about us, is it? When they try to turn people into enemies?" There is nothing smug in his voice, just the usual resonant thoughtfulness, and something new—a cunning I've not heard before.

"She was a real a bitch to me when I first back from Burma. But this is unbelievable. That she would call you. Fuck! Does she know we're together?"

"I don't think so. She called me because she knows I have many contacts. She knows I could send information out to everyone in Mae Sot, Mae Hong Son, Mae Sarieng, every border town, every camp. Just a few phone calls and faxes, the news gets out, no one would talk to you. She may have called some people herself."

"What a fucking bitch."

He makes a face at the nasty language. "People want power. They do many strange things to get it. If they think someone is stealing their power, they do bad things. They do violence. Or they do small bad things. They make excuses. Or lie. I am also like that. We are all like that. You, too. It is the human problem. That is why it is important to be diplomatic with people. To be careful, to not offend. You reassure them that you respect their power."

"Oh, come on. To not offend! Isn't the SLORC offended by all of you?"

"I am talking about the people we work with. You know, the NGOs, the journalists, the foreigners. They need us. Marla needs us. She has been involved with Burma for a long time. It is a big part of her life. If we were not here, she would not be here, either. This is a relationship. We are on the same side, but we still need to be diplomatic."

"You know, it's a Greek word. *Diplo* for 'double' and *mati* for 'eye.' The diplomat sees the situation with two different sets of eyes."

"You are clever, you can do that easily."

"But not with people who are jealous control freaks!"

"Yes. Especially with them. You don't need to be a careful diplomat with the ones who love you. You need to be a diplomat with the ones who do not."

"I'm too honest."

"Yes. There is a saying in Burmese: 'It is good to tell the truth. But it is better to tell the truth in a more appropriate way.' "

"But Marla is not telling the truth!"

"I am not talking about Marla. I don't know why she dislikes you so much. Because you are pretty? Because you smile a lot? You are also just . . . young."

I shrug, feeling pissed off at Marla and petulant with Maung. "So what if I'm young!"

He reaches over and kisses me. "Don't worry. It's a problem that goes away with time."

"What else do you have to tell me?" I hope some other deeply humanitarian NGO type hasn't been gouging me in the back.

He holds my gaze. One two three four five six seven. The long stare is the preface: This will be unpleasant. But I don't want you to be upset.

"I have to go away. To America."

"What? Forever?"

He lights another cigarette. "No, just a trip, not very long. To meet with Burmese people. And lobbyists." Takes a drag. "Diplomacy trip."

"So, how long is not very long?"

"About two months."

"When are you leaving?"

"In a week."

I shake my head. Such crappy news, and I'm still hungover. "I think we should go out for a drink. And some *gwiteo*." Nothing like noodles for comfort. "There's only one beer in the fridge, and I've been in this apartment all day long writing about an imprisoned man and thinking about my cheating boyfriend. Let's go."

Furious, I throw on some dirty clothes. Why bother looking beautiful? He's leaving in a week! For two months. I'm not going to ask why he didn't tell me sooner. I don't want to hear the diplomatic response.

CHAPTER 28

THE SITE OF A WOUND

·   ·   ·   ·

Last week Maung left for the United States. I didn't cry—we try not to do that around here—but I left Bangkok as soon as I could. I've been in Mae Sot for three days, staying at a scruffy little guesthouse. The walls between the rooms are made of thatch (the holes are stuffed with toilet paper), the mosquito nets have gaping tears, the mattresses stink of mildew. I love it. The town's a bloody mess—roads ripped up through the center, too many mangy dogs, and two-stroke engines belching fumes. The dusty streets exude the faint yet distinctive odor of criminality, along with an overripe whiff of seediness. Crime does nothing for me, but seediness is attractive. I have a nose for it.

Consequently, I spend a lot of time watching the men in the gem-trading street. My cover is photography. The camera is a way to move among and stare at them. Dozens of men hunker down at low tables, poking at the glassy, glittery stones with silver pincers. The buyers are mostly Chinese-Thai and Thai; the sellers are Indo-Burmese and Burmese. Buyers squint through magnifying loops and dubiously thrust out their lower lips. Sellers flash their gold watches toward the sun with insistent gestures.

This is where much of the region's gem trade becomes Thai; just a few days ago, all this jade, all these cut and uncut rubies, sapphires, emeralds were Burmese.

Other men hover at the edges of the business. They usually wear well-pressed, clean clothes, but that doesn't fool me. They have a different look about them. More cautious, a tension in the limbs, an animal wariness in the movements of the head. They appear to be standing around, smoking or reading a newspaper, but they're also doing what I do, which is why we're aware of each other. We watch. Are they the smugglers themselves, or hired thugs who work for the smugglers? Burmese government agents? Informers? I promise myself that I will not ask; I will not allow myself to speak to them.

They attract me sexually. Danger can arouse, heighten sexuality. But I've never been into criminals or physically dangerous men, so I can't understand why these ones intrigue me. Their physical tension could spring into violence; I sense that that's part of their job description. Yet I would like to bring one of them back to my mildewy mattress, get him to fuck me for an hour, then fetch another one after dinner for the evening session.

That is seediness at work on me.

I try to take a photograph of the man with tattoos on his forearms, but he raises his hand in front of his face, palm out. I lower the camera. He drops his hand, too, then holds my gaze as his mouth curves into a good-natured, mocking smile. I saw him yesterday, and the afternoon I arrived. Already we know each other well. His eyes flicker over my face and down, exploring my neck, chest, breasts, until I turn and walk off, toward the other market, fruits and vegetables, deep-fried grasshoppers, pigs' heads on the massive cutting tables. Safer subjects.

In one of his letters, Graham Greene wrote that seediness has a deep appeal because it feeds our nostalgia for something that has been lost. But what? Wildness? The grimy underbelly of civilization, a place where we can still act like beasts and tell morality to fuck off? I'm not so sure. I think certain people are drawn to seediness because it flourishes on the site of a wound. Wounds are like magnets, variously repelled by and pulled to each other. The wound outside draws us because of the wound inside. That is the unsavory attraction.

So. What is my magnetized wound? And why does a wound seek a dangerous, emotionally disconnected pleasure? A pleasure that is also a betrayal (of my lover, of my healthier instincts).

I don't know. I don't know. I don't know. How many ways can you not know something? I think back through my life to times of violation—the attempted rape in Spain, the teacher who used to make comments about my body whenever we were alone together, the man in Paris who stalked me through the streets until I lost him by hiding in a stairwell. A few other minor incidents. Yet each of those experiences undid me—sent me into paroxysms of anger, uncontrollable crying, loneliness. Shame. They also sent me back to another time, an early part of my life that I can't remember. I was too small to remember. Remember what? I don't know.

After turning away from the tattooed stranger, I bought some mangoes and returned to the guesthouse, where I sat eating at the big teak table and reflecting on the weight of morality, of being a moral creature. I wasn't thinking about my promise of monogamy to Maung. I was thinking about Mae Sot. For me, it is wrong to have lustful, mute, slavish sex on the site of a wound.

But it seems to work well for a lot of men.

Every year thousands of Burmese girls and women enter Thailand through the Thai-Burma border towns of Mae Sot, Mae Sai, and Ranong. Agents recruit them from poor villages, sometimes with the promise of well-paying domestic or factory work. When they arrive in Thailand, they're in debt to the men and women who have brought them overland, fed them, smuggled them into the country, arranged their job. But that job is often not what they expected.

The bedroom is the workplace: a curtained cubicle just large enough for a narrow bed where the women are supposed to have sex with a dozen or more strangers every day. There can be as many as thirty to forty clients per day on weekends and during festivals. Sometimes the men refuse to use condoms, making HIV infection an occupational hazard. Even when Burmese women come to Thailand expecting to enter the sex trade, they are often shocked, after they arrive, by how much they have to work and how few choices they have. Brothel owners keep passports. In Thailand illegally, the girls and women are afraid of the Thai police, who sometimes work with the brothel owners to receive a cut of the profits.

If a defiant girl refuses to have sex with clients, she is beaten and raped until she is compliant. This is called "seasoning." A similar term exists in dozens of languages, in dozens of countries where women are trafficked into the sex trade by a global crime network. Human trafficking, predominantly of women and children, is organized crime's third largest economy, superseded only by drugs and weapons. Yet governments all over the world still don't take it seriously; traffickers, brothel owners, pimps, and the local officials who help them are rarely prosecuted according to the severity of their crimes.

I know these facts from talking to NGO workers and from reading human-rights reports from Amnesty International, Human Rights Watch, UNICEF, the International Labor Organization, and so on. How many ways can we know something and still not be able to face it?

I decide I would like to meet some of the women. I begin to make inquiries, phone calls, ask people at Dr. Cynthia's clinic. But something stops me. On the surface, visiting a brothel feels voyeuristic. I wouldn't be able to spend enough time with the women. Second or third visits would be difficult to manage. As the human-rights reports show, many people have already documented the horrifying circumstances of their lives. Do women who work in the sex trade want to talk about the cage they live inside? The brutal enormity of the problem frightens me, and its locus in the individual woman's body makes me feel physically ill. I shy away from the subject because the damage is too immediate, too near, dangerous in a way that arouses nothing in me but fury—a fury that is all the more enraging because it's impotent.

Yet no one can spend time in Mae Sot without seeing the evidence. The little twinkling lights on the house, so pretty at night: that's a brothel. The tea shop beyond the market, where such young girls serve: also a brothel. The decrepit building on the road out of town. The karaoke place near my guesthouse. Even a small café and ice-cream shop run by a local family—the back courtyard is lined with little booths, quiet during the day, busy at night.

Last night I went to a bar often frequented by NGO workers and dissidents. It sounds like a joke: a Canadian writer walks into a bar and sits down to drink with a Médecins Sans Frontières doctor, a Burmese dissident, and an American teacher. But there's no punch line. I'd met the doctor earlier in the day, at my guesthouse, and I'd met Win Myint Aye at the Chiang Mai Christmas party, but he seemed a different man now, with dark circles under his eyes and a haggardness in his face that wasn't there before. Yet he greeted me warmly and asked how my work was going, then told us how glad he was to meet the doctor, because he had studied medicine before leaving Burma and was still interested in medical work. The two of them immediately started talking, so I turned to the strawberry-blond American woman. She'd been teaching English and basic math among Karen and Karenni refugees for almost five years. Though she was a shy, self-effacing person, the way she spoke about her work—with knowledge, intelligent humor, and enthusiasm—was an unconsciously displayed CV of her talents.

Often these spontaneous drinking parties among border-dwellers involve subtle jockeying for status among the foreigners, something the teacher and I discussed. As an independent writer, I'm one of the lowlier white entities, though not as lowly, apparently, as a refugee-camp teacher. She pulled her chair closer to me and whispered, "All those experts who fly in for a week or two and make their pronouncements on the Karen, or tell the medics what they should be doing, they can be really irritating."

Not five minutes after these words slipped into the smoky air, there was a lull in our conversation, and to our joint amazement we heard the Médecins Sans Frontières doctor say, "But the Thai-Burma border refugee camps are an easy gig. I mean, comparatively. The refugees here live in luxury compared to the ones in Africa, who really suffer." We stared at him, speechless, shocked that a doctor could turn suffering into a competitive sport. Win Myint Aye angled his chair away from the table, a look of pained disappointment on his face.

We didn't hear any more of the doctor's pronouncements, because a small drama unfolding behind us interrupted him. A young Burmese woman stood up, talking loudly. She gestured at the end of each sentence with a wild swing of her arms or a raised fist, and she addressed her tirade to the Thai and Burmese men at her table. Another young sex worker sat there, too, but she sucked her pink drink from a straw and ignored her friend, who was so unsteady on her high heels that she had to press her thighs against the tabletop to brace herself. The slippery fabric of her turquoise-blue dress rendered this balancing technique ineffective; twice it looked as if she was going to topple over. She began to shout, her beautiful made-up face contorted with anger.

I had no idea what she was saying. The linen-suited Thai man beside her reached out, laughing, and grabbed one of her arms. On the fingers of the hand he used to hold her, he wore two rings, jade and ruby, both set in gold so yellow it looked orange. He pulled her down toward her seat, but she yanked her wrist from his grasp and stumbled away from the table, losing her balance finally and keeling over. She caught herself with her outstretched hands flat on the dirty floor, her bum in the air. The entire table erupted in laughter, and the Thai man looked at one of his companions and asked, "What the fuck is she saying?"

At that moment, Win Myint Aye stood up so suddenly that his heavy wooden chair fell backward with a loud clatter. Several people looked over at our table, wondering what would happen next. But he had already turned away from the scene and strode across the bar; he pushed through the swinging doors and disappeared into the street. I looked back at the girl and saw that her white high-heeled shoes were at least a size too big for her; no wonder she was unsteady on her feet. As if to follow Win Myint Aye, she walked, swerving and swearing, out of the bar, her voice grown ragged; she was close to tears. One of the Burmese men, still grinning, got up and went after her.

The teacher, the doctor, and I were silenced by the sounds emanating from the table behind us: the men were imitating the girl's gestures and making fun of her. The other young sex worker sat without smiling, her drink empty before her, her face empty, her hands upturned and empty on the littered tabletop. For the first time I noticed how crooked her lipstick was, falling away from the line of both the bottom and the top lip. She'd put it on the way a little girl does.

The American woman and I watched the doctor, as though waiting for him to declare that women in Africa suffer more. But all he said was "Let's get out of here, shall we? I'll ask for the bill."

CHAPTER 29

THE HOUSES

OF SLEEPING CHILDREN

. . . .

Rock Hudson's Asian doppelgänger appears in the courtyard this morning and sits down at the table where I'm having coffee. The massive teak slab could seat twenty people, so the man's presence is not an infringement of personal space. I think he has come for the TV, which he watches while chatting with the Karen housekeepers as they go about their morning tasks.

He speaks Karen—so I can't even try to eavesdrop—but from the camouflage jacket and the furtive manner I suspect he is Burmese-Karen, not Thai-Karen. In another moment I know it, because he catches my eye and introduces himself. "My name is Tennyson. Like the poet. A lot of Burmese-Karen are named after English people." With a casual wave, he asks who I am. I answer with my name and nationality.

"Ka-rén?" He looks thoughtful. "It must be fate." No, I think, just a misplaced accent. He relaxes back into the chair, his handsome toughness falling about him like a loose uniform. "What are you doing here, anyway?"

"I want to visit Huay Kaloke." That's the name of the big refugee camp near Mae Sot.

"The Burmese attacked it ten days ago."

"I know." The photographs have been in the Thai papers almost every day. "That's why I'm here. To visit the camp."

"They burned everything," Tennyson continues in a subdued voice. "The little market was burning, the school, our church, the clinic, all the houses. They burn the camps down to make the refugees go back to Burma. It's crazy."

"It does seem like an insane way to treat people."

"Is someone going to take you into the camp? An NGO or someone? The Thai guards don't always let visitors through the gates."

"I don't know yet. Even if I can't get in, I'll spend more time at Dr. Cynthia's clinic. I've been there a couple of times."

"Did you meet her?"

"Just for a few minutes. She's very busy. One of the medics showed me around the clinic. It's an incredible place."

In 1989, when the soft-spoken thirty-year-old Dr. Cynthia Maung set up a clinic in a barn outside Mae Sot, she worked straight through her own attacks of malaria and dysentery, treating sick and injured Burmese people seven days a week. She used a rice cooker to sterilize her few medical instruments. Now the Mae Tao Clinic has grown into several clean, sturdy buildings that serve a population of more than 100,000 Burmese people, from both inside and outside Burma. Dr. Cynthia and her medics help the sick, train new medics and midwives, counsel women in reproductive and dietary health, and refer the most seriously ill to the Thai hospital in Mae Sot—a reciprocal relationship that the doctor and her colleagues worked hard to build. They also equip backpacking medical teams that enter Burma illegally to serve poor and isolated communities. Though she's Baptist and married with two kids, no wonder the woman is often called "the Mother Teresa of the border."

Tennyson asks, "Why do you want to know about all this, Dr. Cynthia's clinic, and the camps? What are you doing?"

"I'm writing a book about Burma."

He sits up straighter. "Really?"

"Yes."

"And you will write about the struggle of the Karen people?"

"Yes."

He places his palms flat on the teak table and stares at me. "I work for the Karen army. The KNLA. You know?"

"Yes, I know. The Karen National Liberation Army."

"Right! I will take you wherever you need to go. Show you things."

This stranger turning up to offer his services seems too easy. He reads the distrust on my face and shakes his head. "Don't worry. I know who you know. I am a friend. Everyone at Dr. Cynthia's clinic knows me. I know Moe Thee Zun, from ABSDF. And I know Maung." He goes on, naming people I've met or have heard of, declaring his credentials. I wonder if Maung has sent him to help me. Or to check up on me.

"Do you want a cup of coffee?" I offer.

"No," Tennyson replies in a gruff voice. "I want to help you."

In the 1930s and '40s, the minority Karen people fought beside their British colonial "masters" against the Burmese independence fighters. Throughout their long reign in various territories, the British colonizers became experts at manipulating cultural and societal inequities in order to consolidate their own power. By bringing education and medical facilities to isolated, long-neglected Karen outposts, they created a loyal ally.

Many Karen people saw the British as their saviors, because they promised to help the minority ethnic group negotiate for and construct a state of its own—an almost Shangri-la-like land called Kawthoolei. With the crumbling of the British Empire, that grand promise never came to fruition. In 1947, General Aung San negotiated the country's independence from Britain. Later the same year, he and most of his cabinet members were assassinated, plunging the country's future into uncertainty. The shaky new democracy didn't have time to resolve the tensions between the central government and the ethnic groups. Another military man, General Ne Win, staged a coup d'état in 1962 and became Burma's ipso facto dictator for the next twenty-six years. In 1989, he handed power over to the SLORC.

The Karen have never stopped fighting for their autonomy. They are in a similar position to many other ethnic groups of Burma—the Karenni, the Shan, the Wa, the Mon, the Kachin, the Rakhine, the Naga—except that the Karen are the only ones who are still openly fighting against the generals. The others have signed cease-fire agreements with the junta in exchange for a fragile peace and an unobstructed, mutually lucrative opium trade. Thus the Karen resistance—which enforces the death penalty for opium trafficking—finds itself alone, slowly being crushed by a superior military power.

Hundreds of thousands of Karen people are internally displaced within Burma, cut off or shut out from their ancestral lands in the southern delta region, in central Burma and farther north. Sometimes they are forced to live in SLORC-run compounds while they work on government projects, or they hide from the soldiers in the jungle, trying to avoid capture and forced relocation and the labor that comes with it. Every year brings a new tide of refugees into Thailand.

The stories they bring with them are terrifying. I learn one thing, essentially, from the human-rights reports I've been reading. Something is broken in the human race. Is this brokenness another name for Thanatos, the death impulse that battles with and often overrules Eros, the life force? But the Freudian opposition seems too reductive, and does nothing to help me understand the nature of evil.

The most sadistic and psychopathic members of the SLORC's army are not sent to work in the country's jails and interrogation centers, at which the Western world occasionally wags an admonishing finger. The amputation of penises, of breasts, the immolation of live children, the rape of little girls and grandmothers and women in labor—the sickest, most annihilating torture is perpetrated in places that do not exist on Western maps, against people who often know little of the political labyrinth they are trapped inside. They are never mentioned on the evening news. Nothing about them is noteworthy. The child's favorite color was yellow; she often had a cough. The man turned the furrows in his fields just so. This woman wore her grandmother's thin gold ring on days of celebration.

Yet those distant people are so much like us. The small. Unknown except in their narrow worlds; there, and only there, beloved. Unlike us, they live their lives in a time and place that is out of joint.

Suffering is a mystery, the hard side of the bargain for knowing the pleasures of being alive. People often experience too much of one or the other. Crimes will always outnumber punishments; justice sought is rarely received. I must not take it too personally.

But if I do not take it personally, how must I take it? What will the meaning be, therefore, of the human-rights reports, and Tennyson's long, sad soliloquy about his people's suffering, not rehearsed, per se, but repeated, by heart, through the heart?

I walk through the hot air. I see the green lizard on the tree in the courtyard and feel my little happiness. I do not witness my husband having his penis cut off and stuffed into his mouth. I am not the woman whose baby is killed, cut up, boiled; I am not the woman who is forced, then, to eat her baby's flesh. Later, she is shot by a young soldier. I am not the soldier, either. Yet such atrocities have happened. They will happen again, and not so far away from this place and this morning.

I no longer wonder about God. But I wonder about humans. Do I believe in humans? Like other teenagers, I wrote down my obligatory quotations from Camus. I think it was in *The Plague* that he wrote, "There are more things to admire in men than to despise." But are there?

There is no understanding. There is only damage and its wages, its demands, before and after. We wonder how the Holocaust could have happened, how people could have done that to one another, how the civilized world could have colluded in the extermination of innocents, if not by action then by the crime of inaction, indifference. We wonder about that historical barbarity while it continues to happen in other ways, in other places. Not the magnitude but the intent, the system, and the act. Who could throw a screaming child into the bonfire of her destroyed house?

I make a vow. The first half of it is the lazy vow of many rich people: I will accept the bounty, the silk and the fruit, the beautiful mouth of the beloved, the songs, the books, the sea and its islands. I will relish the gift of my life, not squander it. I will live with gratitude.

The second part of the vow is more difficult: I will live also in conscious mourning. The gift should belong to everyone—the woman, the man, the burned child. But it does not belong to them, they are dead.

I will live in consciousness, in mourning.

But what will I give? How will I act? There has to be something more than the vow itself. There has to be a way to measure its fulfillment.

The next day, I walk with Tennyson through the ruins of Huay Kaloke refugee camp. Children trail us, chatting with him and eyeing me, hiding behind each other's shoulders. Once again, my name makes an impression. This time I am glad: give them anything to be amused by, these little ones tossed into the blackened fields like so much grain. How can they grow here?

What is left of the camp is black. The ground is black, or gray with ash, or white with ash like dirty snow. Charred trees stand here and there, offering no shade. A few black house frames still stand, undulating in the forty-degree noonday heat. As it appears, so it smells—of burned-down fire, ash, smoke. Filthy children come to a well and haul water away in cleaned-out gasoline and oil containers.

I am thirsty. Tennyson, I want to say, take me away from here, I am so thirsty. Instead, I photograph the children. Some of them do not smile. Some of them stare into the camera with undisguised anger, their faces raw. When I click the shutter, I feel ashamed.

Seven thousand people had houses here. Small thatched houses, but houses nevertheless. There was a market, a clinic, a church. Gone. Everyone is now living under tarpaulin. The cinder-block school and library is still standing, but the windows are framed in black. I stick my head through an aperture that looks and smells like a large fireplace. Desks, benches, books, scribblers, pencils—burned.

Tennyson tells me, "The school and the library. Where our language and our future go together. They always burn them. And not only at Huay Kaloke. The next day, soldiers attacked Beh Klaw camp. It's sixty kilometers to the north, with over twenty-five thousand people. The soldiers killed some people there, shot them. It always surprises me that they don't kill more people, because they take *myin-say*. You know that?"

"Ya mah?" That's what it's called in Thai. Horse medicine. An opiate-amphetamine, ingested in tablet form or crushed up and smoked.

"It makes the soldiers crazy. And more stupid than usual. How else could they steal from these people? They loot the market first because the people who have shops have some money, sometimes jewelery. So the soldiers go there with their faces painted black, and they take what they want. Then they go to the clinic and get the microscope. It's their habit—they must have a lot of microscopes. Sometimes they take the microscope away, sometimes they shoot it or smash it. Then they start burning. They come at ten or eleven at night, cowards. To burn the houses of sleeping children.

"The other day, a granny was crying. We thought, she is depressed, her house is gone. But it wasn't the burned house—she is used to that. Many times her house is burned. She was crying because no one saved the photo album. She forgot it because she had to get her grandchildren out of the house—the mother and father were away somewhere. The soldiers had already set the market on fire, and everyone's house is made of bamboo and thatch. So it all burns"—Tennyson claps his hands loudly—"just like that. It's gone. It takes an hour or so, and everyone loses everything—clothes and plates and books. And the photo album." He spread his arms and described a full circle, taking in the temporary shelters. "This is the way my people live. Always a war on them, even when they are not soldiers."

Tennyson takes me to the section of the tarpaulin expanse where his friends and family live. They are all worn out and hot. One of them has a serious case of conjunctivitis, the red eye suppurating and painfully swollen. We do not stay long. For the first time I wonder where Tennyson himself lives. Here? No, he must have a place to stay in Mae Sot.

I'm shy to ask about this. It seems too private, and culturally untoward, for a young woman to ask a man where he lives. But I'm curious. Presumably, it would be too dangerous for an active KNLA member to stay in the camp. Tennyson told me that when the Burmese soldiers arrived in Beh Klaw they searched out the hut of an old man who used to be a Karen commander. After he confirmed his identity, they shot him in the chest.

Tennyson and I stop outside the temporary clinic so that I can meet some of the medics and take photographs. He watches as I put new film into my camera. "An NGO told me that you load a camera. Like a gun."

"And we also say you shoot it. You shoot pictures. Or you shoot your subject."

He blinks at the clunky old Nikon in my hands and says, in a voice like cold iron, "It's nothing like a gun. You can't kill anyone with it. And a picture is still there after someone dies." He shakes his head. "A camera keeps people alive."

Moved by his poetic turn of thought, I nod but keep quiet. The empty air feels uncomfortable, but I literally bite my tongue.

Tennyson continues, "When you kill a soldier from the other side, you always try to get to his body and take whatever is worth anything: his gun and ammunition first, but also his money, his watch maybe, his boots, his jacket if you need one. Often they don't have much, just the gun. But once, when I was looking through this dead kid's clothes, I found a letter. Folded inside the paper was a bit of money—three, four hundred kyat, I don't remember. But I remember the letter. To his mother. I read it. He said he wanted her to buy a big pot and start selling noodles on the street. She lived somewhere in a little town; they were poor. He was going to try to send her some money, but Burmese soldiers at the front line make little money. He said he didn't know how much he would be able to send her, next paycheck.

"He just talked about the *mohinga* noodles. The white noodles, for breakfast. I sat there with that letter in my hand and I cried like a child. The mother had lost her son. And she would not get his letter. She would not get the money, either."

He scratches his head and turns away from me. "We are sick of killing each other. But still we do it. I have friends whose chests are tattooed with the words 'We will not surrender.' The Burmese soldiers still burn down the refugee camps."

I follow his gaze into the near-distance: row upon row of colored tarpaulins, and a scattered kaleidoscope of more colors—clothes hanging on the lines that secure the shelters to the ground. He looks me in the eye. "I was shot several times. But I survived."

"That's extremely lucky."

"You must be lucky," he replies, as though some people, for private reasons, choose not to be. "If not, you die. I have a good fate." He walks off as I turn into the clinic tent.

When we drive away from Huay Kaloke refugee camp on Tennyson's noisy Suzuki, I smell charcoal. At first I think it's because we're traveling along the perimeter of burned land, but soon enough the expanse of black field and patchwork tarpaulin recedes. We're on the two-lane highway back into Mae Sot, a short distance away. Farmland, some of it green, some of it fallow, stretches away into small hamlets of Thai farmhouses and trees. I smell something burning, something burned, even on the motorcycle. Then I realize: it's settled into the fiber of our clothes, our hair. I sniff the back of Tennyson's khaki jacket. But there's no scent of the man, no sweat at all. Just ash.

CHAPTER 30

A MEDIC OF MAW KER

.   .   .   .

Today Tennyson is taking me to visit Maw Ker refugee camp. The motorcycle thunders through the hot wind over the hotter road. Dust strikes our faces and rims our nostrils. When I turn away from his back to spit, I feel the sandy crunch of it between my molars. Tennyson yells, "We're eating a lot of dirt, aren't we? Isn't Thai food delicious?"

Maw Ker is some sixty kilometers away from Mae Sot, tucked into the sparsely forested hills, not close enough to the border to be attacked easily by the Burmese regime. It is a barren, messy but also orderly village of almost nine thousand Karen, Burman, and Indo-Burmese Muslims. It's been here for more than a decade, a model refugee camp. Tennyson goes to a friend's hut to sleep off the heat of the journey while a guide takes me to visit the camp leader, the teachers, the health workers. "Educated people," he says humbly. As we walk down the main road of the camp, the guide nods to friends and neighbors with a proprietary air, showing me off. He asks how far away Canada is, is Canada so very far away, is it farther than America? "Do you think you could help me go there and find a job?"

"I'm sorry. I don't plan to go back to Canada for quite a while."

His high, broad forehead wrinkles in doubt. His jowly face is quick to translate private feeling into visible expression. Does he think I'm lying to him?

The narrow lanes off the main road are part open sewer, part stagnant black stream, edged with sticky rust-colored mud. "Hot season," my guide explains. "But yesterday it rain and rain." We detour around a large puddle of water.

The place has the feeling of an abandoned village, yet there are so many people here, hidden in the open. Most of the children were born here. Their eyes glitter from the low doorways, from behind clumps of weeds and small banana trees, through chinks in thatch-woven walls. They are like children everywhere, lively with intelligence and humor, hungry to eat up the world. But this is not the world, and the food here, for both the body and the mind, is neither rich nor plentiful. The place is small and stunted and tightly crammed with people. Men and women sit on the porches of the little huts, idle, or with small tasks occupying their hands. Frustrated energy floats around them. There is no electricity, no TV. How many radio programs broadcast in Karen, their native language? A model refugee camp is synonymous with a model prison. When Tennyson and I arrived, we had to stop at a checkpoint manned by Thai soldiers.

I ask the guide, "Do you ever leave the camp?"

"Not often. We are not allowed to go out too early or to stay out too late."

"Why?"

"The Thais don't want us to take their jobs. They want us at the camp only."

"What happens if someone stays out?"

He shrugs. "Money. The guards want some money from us. Or they might beat you up."

I wonder what happens to the women, the children, not just at the hands of the Thai soldiers but at the hands of their own men. This is a traumatized population without much medical help, with no psychological counseling, in overcrowded conditions. Domestic and sexual abuse must be rampant.

"Is it hard for the families here, to get along?" I ask.

He scowls. "To get along?"

"Are there difficulties between the men and women sometimes? Fighting, problems at home?"

"Problems. What you mean?" His big head pulls back. He knows exactly what I mean.

"I mean, is there violence sometimes—between the men and the women? Because the situation is so hard in the camp, maybe it affects people's relationships?"

He shakes his head. "No, no! Nothing like that here. Only the Thai soldiers violent, and the Burmese soldiers. Not the people, we all peaceful."

Right. As if he's going to tell a white stranger about the personal problems of his neighbors. Or himself. I try to redeem myself by asking a few questions about the school.

But he keeps talking about the cruelty of the Thai soldiers who guard the camp. "It gets worse. In the beginning, long time ago, they respect. Now they don't respect."

"But even the Thai king came here, didn't he, to visit?"

He makes a sour face. "That's long time ago. He come for a little visit. But he does not stay." He looks me straight in the eye. I hold his gaze and walk into a mud puddle.

By the time we get to the clinic, my shoes are heavy with mud. My feet are filthy. I kick off some of the mud as I stand looking at the long, narrow building. It sits on a small rise amid a group of leaf-thatch and bamboo huts. The forests on the surrounding hills are plucked clean of bananas and good wood. The few trees left are naked: their leaves have become walls and roofs.

The stairs into the clinic are made of roughly halved trees. I leave my mucky shoes on the bottom step. On my way up the stairs, I swear as I stumble. A young woman appears in the open doorway. "Hello. Are you all right?"

My guide, still standing at the foot of the steps, introduces me. "I'll tell Tennyson you're here," he says, and waves. "I have to go home now."

The young woman proffers a bamboo bench—the "waiting room" bench—and says, "Please sit down." Pause. "But not fall down," she adds, not smiling at her own joke. She has dark circles under her eyes, but fatigue doesn't seem to affect her lightheartedness. "I'm happy to meet you," she says. "It's always good to have visitors." She wipes the sweat off her upper lip with a small handkerchief.

She is twenty-two, with lovely feet and hands, a black waterfall of hair drawn back with an elastic band, and skin the color of pale clover honey. Flawless teeth. Her name is Victoria. She is a medic.

She became a refugee at the age of three, when her father joined the KNLA and began to fight against the dictatorship. If the Burmese military knows that a man is involved in armed insurgency, it will sometimes torture and kill the rest of his family. So her mother left with her and her two siblings, choosing the insecurity of a refugee camp over the dangers of staying inside Burma.

"How did you become a medic?"

"I took training at Dr. Cynthia's clinic."

"Ah! I've visited there a few times. I couldn't believe how many people the doctor helps. And how happy the atmosphere was. It wasn't what I expected."

Victoria smiles. "You know how it is! I was scared to study there because I thought, It is a hospital, it will be so sad. But at the clinic we learn that, together, we can do something good. Dr. Cynthia is our hero. She is like Aung San Suu Kyi."

Victoria goes to a small dispensary and takes out several rolls of gauze. I watch her cut strips off the roll and fold them into small pads. The rest of the clinic stretches out on either side of the waiting room into two long sections—one for men, one for women. A few men and a few women with children sit or recline on the mats in each room. Some are sleeping; some have glazed, feverish eyes. A few are expressionless, slack with exhaustion and illness. There are no curtains or other attempts at privacy. Saline drips are hooked to the thatched walls. The walls don't reach all the way up to the roof, so I peer out over the heads of the patients to the rest of the camp and beyond, into hills covered with thin trees.

"What kind of illnesses do you usually treat here?"

"A lot of malaria. And the children suffer from chronic diarrhea. Some of the mothers think if a baby has diarrhea it's best not to give him water. So the babies die."

"How is the water?"

"We tell them to boil it, but sometimes they can't. It's hard to find firewood for boiling. So the children get sick easily. They're not strong to begin with. Mortality for the small ones is twenty-five to thirty-five percent. A lot of babies die."

"How many patients do you have a day?"

"Between seventy and eighty. The majority children. Malaria is worst for the children. The adults survive, but the children are weak. All malnourished."

"Everyone on the border seems to get malaria."

She sighs. "Yes. I still get an attack every few months. If I'm working too much. Have you been in the camps a lot?"

"No, I haven't. I want to spend more time on the border. But I don't want to get malaria."

Her face hardens. But she's smiling when she says, "We also do not want to get malaria."

"Of course not, no. I know that. No one wants to get malaria."

Silence. I am, truly, an idiot. The silence acknowledges this and permits me to speak again. "Do you work here alone?"

"Not usually. Another woman medic is often here. We also have some older girls who act as nurses for us, helping out, tending to the patients, giving them food. Our head medic is sleeping in the consultation room. He was up all night with a sick man." She points to the bamboo wall behind her. The entire clinic is made of bamboo.

Another young medic and two nurses join us. They are younger than me, quick to laugh, pleased to have the distraction of a visitor. There is a solemnity about them also, an authority in their hands and eyes as they accomplish small tasks while we sit chatting. They tease me about Tennyson. I didn't tell them that I arrived a couple of hours ago on the back of his motorcycle; the camp grapevine has supplied them with this information. They're so curious about the nature of our relationship that I suspect they have a crush on him. "Is he your Karen dictionary?" asks one of the nurses.

I don't mention anything about my Burmese dictionary. "Unfortunately, I don't have a Karen dictionary! I've never touched a Karen dictionary. Though I agree that they're very handsome." The young women clap, thrilled that I run with the joke. Eyebrows raised, I look around at them. "You are all so beautiful," I tell them, honestly. They loudly protest the compliment. Which makes them more beautiful still. I lean toward the inquisitive nurse and slyly ask, "Is Tennyson your Karen dictionary?"

The other young women shriek with delight. The nurse leaps up off the bench, her cheeks as red as apples, and exclaims, "I already know how to speak Karen! I don't need a dictionary!" We laugh.

In the middle of our laughter, a woman screams.

CHAPTER 31

A CHILD OF MAW KER

. . . .

She's only a few feet away and her cry is loud, but guttural and deep, not shrill. A two- or three-year-old child hangs limp in her arms.

The two medics slide off the bamboo benches and go to her. They want to take her little one to examine him, but she doesn't want to let him go. She holds him tight, safe against her body. The medics talk with her for a few seconds, explaining, cajoling. Then one of them yanks the child away; the mother clutches at his legs for a moment, then gives in and begins to cry soundlessly.

I can't process the speed with which the scene a few feet away has changed while remaining unaltered here, in the waiting room, where the two nurses beside me are still chatting. "It's so hot, isn't it?" one of them says.

The other responds, "Because of the rain. The heat is too wet." Accustomed to the sickness, the births, the deaths, neither of them glances over at the crying mother and the medics, who are now preparing a needle.

I ask, "What's wrong with the woman's baby?"

In chorus, they reply, "Malaria."

"Go and see," one of them says, pointing with her chin.

I step into the women's side of the clinic, where I sit on the floor opposite the medics, out of their way. When the boy's shaved head lolls back, his eyes fall open, exposing the whites and the edges of his brown pupils. I wonder if this ghoulish sign of unconsciousness is what made his mother scream.

Victoria is in charge. She holds the needle while the other medic holds the child. Then, quickly and violently, she pokes it into his upper thigh. The mother gasps down a sob, and I flinch. The two young women lay the child out flat on the straw mat. Victoria tries to slide a plastic tube down his throat, but it's too big. She keeps pushing, but it won't go down. The plastic scratches the inside of the child's esophagus like a small shovel, digging, digging. She jumps up to get a smaller tube.

The clinic is so unlike a hospital. Patient and mother and medics sit on the bamboo-strip floor, their bare feet folded under them. The dull eyes of other patients watch everything but betray no emotion. They've seen this struggle with malaria happen before; they have experienced it themselves. I know that most of the world's people seek medical attention in facilities like these, but that does not help me digest what I'm seeing. It does not help the mother who sits here.

She wipes her face again. She has stopped crying. The child is still.

I look expectantly at the little boy. A clear fluid was in the needle. What was it? A drug. A good drug. It will take effect now. He will wake up. Where is Victoria with the smaller tube?

One of the nurses goes to get the head medic. He comes in rubbing his eyes, his countenance wrapped in the hot skin of sleep, which sloughs off him in seconds. As he kneels beside the child, he wakens fully, gives a series of orders in Karen, and pulls out his stethoscope, shines a light into the clouded eyes. Now he speaks sharply to the nurses. After preparing another needle, he administers it as quickly as Victoria administered the first one.

Victoria returns with another tube from the dispensary counter. Again it's too big and won't fit down the child's throat. She jumps up again and almost runs into one of the nurses, who hands her a smaller tube. The head medic holds open the small mouth and pushes and pokes until the length of plastic disappears into the child's gut.

Victoria attaches an accordion suction to the tube, and one of the nurses pumps the apparatus with her foot. Gray, half-digested rice from the boy's stomach slowly appears in the clear container. After his stomach is empty, the head medic performs cardiac massage, pushing down with his large, splayed hands on the boy's narrow chest. The rhythmic pumping sends new blood, new oxygen, into the little body, making it writhe and contort before falling still again.

Now. The little boy will wake up and cry out. The limbs shudder. And go still. Shudder again; the legs kick the air and fall.

The head medic swats a fly away from the child's face then sits back on his heels, his hands spread on his thighs. He sits there for a while, looking down at his hands. Then he swats another fly away from his own tired face. The child's expression is also one of weariness, the deep sadness of sick children. But he is no longer sad. I don't understand until Victoria begins to unravel the gauze from the IV bandage, which is big and thick. When the mother sees the gauze being unwrapped, she, too, understands.

She makes a sound I've never heard before and hope never to hear again. Her voice rises from the core of her body and fills the long room, and pours out, into the rest of the camp, into the hills. She howls; her head tilts up. I close my eyes, incapable of looking anywhere. The insult is that life is already taking over her child's death. I hear the medics and nurses go about the business of cleaning up, rattling stethoscopes, pulling the suction apparatus apart.

I open my eyes. The woman gathers her son, limbs akimbo, off the mat and into her embrace. One of the nurses pulls the tube up from the child's stomach, through his throat, out of his slack mouth. Victoria is still unraveling the gauze from the small, bruised arm. It comes away easily, layer after layer. Low sobs wrench out of the mother. She clasps her child close to her body again and rocks back and forth in rhythm with her cries.

Refugee children appear at the front and back entrances of the clinic to see what's going on. They come inquisitively up the steps, two almost smiling, others with apprehension in their eyes. Victoria clenches her teeth against the woman's crying and reaches past her, carefully pulling the thick IV needle out of the boy's arm.

I look down. Beneath the bamboo slats, the scrawny chickens of the Maw Ker refugee camp scrounge for any edible thing. The nurses giggle at some private amusement known only to them. How strange their laughter is to me, how awful their ease with the child's death. Yet death is normal, especially here. Every day they live with it on the bamboo doorstep, waiting to barge in, barging in often enough, and departing with the lives of innocents. The nurses and medics cannot allow every tragedy to devastate them.

I realize that I am crying. I've been crying since the woman howled. But it's out of place. No one but the mother shows her emotions. I rub my eyes and stand up just as Tennyson appears. The medics explain to him what has happened, but he seems to know already. He nods away the explanations and turns to me. "Did you take photographs?"

"No."

"Why didn't you? Why didn't you take pictures so people can see?"

"I couldn't, Tennyson."

"But we need pictures of this. This is the truth, this is how our children die. This is murder. This is the way the Burmese regime kills our children. Why didn't you take pictures?"

"I'm not a good enough photogra—"

"Yes, you are, you are. You have a good camera, you take good pictures."

I'm surprised by how angry he is. "Tennyson, I couldn't take pictures. I'll write it down instead."

But the promise of the written word makes little impression on him.

In the propaganda fields of the world, the image is all-powerful. He speaks briefly with the head medic and looks with concern at the child and the mother.

I, too, look at the little boy, and think, numbly, Now he is a body. A corpse. I'm trying to convince myself. I've never seen the life go out of a human being before. I'm unprepared for how small death seems, how its inevitability has stripped it of importance. Not for his mother, of course, nor for the medics who struggled to save him, nor for me. I am shaken.

Tennyson still looks furious. "They have no oxygen. No oxygen tanks. And not enough drugs. So the babies die of malaria. For nothing. Stupid malaria." He spits out the last word. Then he opens his wallet and places two hundred baht—about ten Canadian dollars—in front of the mother.

This gesture seems callous only to me, because I have no need of ten dollars. To the others, two hundred baht signifies generosity in a moment of need. The grief, common to them all, cannot be paid off. If only it could be.

Tennyson growls, "Let's go." I say goodbye to the medics and the nurses at the dispensary. The head medic returns to the consulting room to go back to sleep. Another medic, a young man with a ponytail, comes into the clinic without asking why the woman is crying. She rocks the boy in her arms. The nurses move around her, taking care of what has to be taken care of.

Tennyson points down the stairs and says in a tone of reprobation, "Your shoes are all mud." As I put them on, the last of the camp children scatter. They know the boy is dead.

I walk behind Tennyson, who walks beside his friend, my guide from earlier in the day. Tennyson speaks rapidly in Karen. His friend grunts or murmurs short responses. Past the first row of thatched huts, the woman's crying remains distinct, clear in its rhythm. It would be hard to live near the clinic.

Her crying mixes with the sound of a child crying somewhere near the main road. It weaves through the rising voices of early evening and blends with Tennyson's greeting to a woman washing dishes. A few huts later, he stops to talk to a man layering dried leaves into a roof. I can still hear the woman.

When we arrive at the guide's house, I sit outside in the falling light of dusk. Children nearby play a game with stones. Years ago, I played a similar game with my Thai schoolmates. But these are such different children, tossing the little stones. The darkness slowly eats away at their features; in every child I make out the small boy's face. I still hear his mother's voice, faintly, through the voices of the children, though that seems impossible.

A while later, Tennyson calls me in to eat. The family have killed one of their chickens in my honor. I sit to eat with them, and they tell me their stories. Their hospitality demands politeness and genuine engagement; I have to put the events of the day aside. We talk, we laugh, sometimes until tears come to our eyes. In the midst of an anecdote, I think about what happened this afternoon. The woman and her child occupy a place beyond the glow of candlelight that illuminates the bowls and plates, the pot of curried chicken.

For me—and for Tennyson, too, I think—the evening becomes a secret echo of her and her boy. Our journey back to Mae Sot through the unexpectedly chill air is part of that echo. Tennyson does not yell a single time into the blasting wind.

When he drops me off at the guesthouse, he offers some curt advice. "Sleep now. Don't think. I'll come to check on you tomorrow. Try not to think." Then he tramps away under the lurid blue lights on the guesthouse fence.

Before leaving the courtyard, he stops abruptly, turns around, and takes a few steps back toward me. I can't see the expression on his face, but I hear the strain in the whispered words: "It doesn't matter. About the photographs. We have too many photographs already."

I stand beside the big teak table until he starts up the motorbike and drives away. I wonder where he's going. Where does he take his grief and anger? Where does he store year after year of grief and anger?

I'm too tired to bathe, so the sweat and dust of the day lie down with me. I am so tired and so awake. "I want to help you," he said a week ago. "I'll show you whatever you want to see," he said. But, Tennyson, I didn't want to see that. I'm stretched out under my torn mosquito net, but the thin woman is close, still crying, her child dead in her arms.

Outside the nearby temple, the street dogs of Mae Sot are fighting. It's a savage, wild sound. Repeatedly attacked, one of the weaker creatures yelps in the lane that Tennyson has just left. "Shh," I whisper, and turn on my side, inhaling dirty skin and mildewy mattress. Finally alone, my throat constricts.

I don't know the child's name.

I forgot to ask his name.

Tennyson will come in the morning. To see how I am. Ha! I am fine, fine. I've never been anything but fine. Tennyson will come, he won't want coffee, he never wants coffee or a soft drink, he never wants anything to eat. Tennyson will know the boy's name. Won't he?

The dog in the street whines. The other dogs attack again, and the yelping crescendoes. "Shh," I whisper, a beggar for silence. But the sound doesn't go away.

CHAPTER 32

THE SCARF

. . . .

~~Tennyson is sitting~~ at the gleaming teak table when I come out for my morning coffee. "How long have you been here?"

"Ten minutes." He looks back up at the TV. An action movie. *Rambo?* Mercifully, the sound is muted.

I nod and stir my Nescafé, admiring Tennyson's profile. He really does look like Rock Hudson. He feels my eyes and shakes his head as if to rid himself of a wayward insect. Still staring at the TV, he asks, "Did you sleep okay?"

"I slept like shit. I had bad dreams."

"Ugh." Male Asian grunt of vague acknowledgment. He drags his chair closer to the TV.

"Tennyson?"

"Ugh?" Male Asian grunt, more responsive.

"Do you know the name of the child who died yesterday?"

He turns his big head toward me slowly. Gazes into my eyes. Incredulous? Disgusted? Monumentally annoyed? I can't read the unhappy look on his face. As slowly as he turned his head, he asks, "Do you think I remember the names of all the dead children?"

Resisting the urge to crawl under the big table, I squint into my coffee and take a sip. So. He also feels guilty about not knowing the child's name. "No," I eventually say. "I guess only God can do that." I say this to make him feel better. It seems to work.

In a mild voice, he asks, "What do you have planned for today?"

"I'm going to go back to the Muslim part of town and take some photographs. Visit the tea shops. And the mosque."

"What about tomorrow?"

"I don't know. Why?"

"Maybe you want to go to Umphang, a town about three hours from here. Some ABSDF guys are there, but also a lot of Karen. Because there is a meeting. You take a songtow truck to Umphang, with other passengers, mostly Thai. Sometimes the journey is more than three hours. Depends. Four sometimes. Someone will fetch you when you arrive. Don't be afraid."

I make a face. "I'm not afraid of riding in a songtow, Tennyson," I say, as though fear is ridiculous. Which is obviously not the case. But, like many other vulnerabilities—sadness, exhaustion, confusion, longing—fear is beginning to seem like a luxury. I am allowed to be afraid if my house is about to be burned down. Particularly if I am still in it, with my children. Or if I am about to be raped or murdered or sold to a brothel. Otherwise, normal human fear is an indulgence. I've always secretly suspected this. Now I know that's true.

"I have to go somewhere for a few days. So I will not be here to take you places and make introductions. In Umphang, you can meet Moe Thee Zun. Do you know who he is?"

I nod just once, immediately more interested in faraway Umphang. Moe Thee Zun was the famous student leader who organized and led some of the most significant antigovernment protests in 1988. He came to the border before the MI could find him and is now a leader of the other ABSDF section.

Maung has told me almost nothing about this rift. Early on, I innocently asked him what it meant when people talked about the two "sections" of the ABSDF. I didn't yet understand that there had been a literal break, and that both factions insisted on keeping the same name. He told me there were personality conflicts between various people, so the two groups separated, each taking supporters with them. "The revolutionaries got divorced?" I said, eyebrows raised. But trying to bring levity to the subject was a mistake. Maung shrugged himself out of bed and went to smoke on the balcony.

"Does a songtow go to Umphang every day?" I ask.

Tennyson replies, "I will find one for you. For tomorrow. They usually leave in the morning."

I'm heat-dazed, riding shoulder to shoulder with fifteen people crammed into the back of the small covered truck. Like the Thai women, I hold my scarf over my nose as dusty wind gusts through the long side apertures. We hurtle through the thick stands of trees, almost jungle; labor up and careen down parched hills, almost mountains, through sun-stunned fields burned black by farmers. The passengers sit facing each other on two benches. Several bags of vegetables, a big sack of chilies, and two long, misshapen boxes shift and slide on the floor between us, sometimes bumping us in the shins. We sway together, silently, helplessly pleading: Despite the driver's unwise choices, his lack of sleep, his probable amphetamine use, let us survive this journey. With amendments when he pulls out to pass other laboring vehicles on the steep hills: But if we are to die in a head-on collision, please let death or painless unconsciousness come as quickly as possible.

.   .   .

The truck lurches to a halt at a small roadside hut. Two dark-skinned men approach and wave their hands at the driver, trying to negotiate payment for the trip. They don't speak Thai very well.

The tension rises as my fellow passengers glance at them, then survey the cramped songtow. The woman across from me pulls the scarf from her head and whispers sharply to her neighbor, *"Kohn baa-maa."* Burmese people. The other woman yells at the driver, "There's no room!" Interested only in the extra fares, he shouts back, "They will ride on top, they don't care." The women grumble to each other.

One of the men easily swings up to the roof; the other man throws him their bundles, then walks to the back of the truck and peers in at us. There is a third passenger with him, unseen until now, a small girl, maybe ten or eleven, with a full-lipped red mouth and kohl-drawn owl eyes and long curling lashes. She blinks and the world wobbles. What a face. A gold-and-crimson glimmer pierces her nose. I wiggle, shift my knees to the side; there's always room for a child in these trucks. The Thai woman opposite me snaps, "She can't sit with us."

I glare at the nicely dressed woman. She's not a peasant. A peasant would make room. Sometimes, in tense situations, I lose my vocabulary. Or just don't know the right words. How do you say "callous racist bitch" in Thai? Darn, I don't know. But other words jump to my mouth. "What are you talking about? She's a child. Of course she will ride with us."

The woman is taken aback; her face softens in confusion. Then hardens again. "She can ride with her father. Or in the front with the driver. Not with us." But we all know there's no space in the cab, either. He already has two passengers up there.

I throw my only punch immediately, because the father and daughter are getting nervous, the songtow driver impatient. The other passengers won't meet my eye. They're just waiting to see who wins; this is good entertainment on a long trip. "We respect the Buddha's ideas, don't we? Compassion and kindness. Even for foreigners." Being the one who is most obviously a foreigner here, it's as though I'm making an appeal for my-self. Which I suppose I am.

Not even the racist will argue with the Buddhist card.

"The little girl will ride beside me." I smile at her father first, then at her. "Come sit here." The moment she hears Burmese, she looks up at her father and grins. I twist my knees away and move one of the vegetable bags to make space for her. Other passengers signal their agreement—or acquiescence—by helping her into the truck.

Thin gleaming girl child! I ask the man beside me to shift the bag of chilies. If she sits against them for a long time, they will burn her skin, even through the cotton sack. I once saw that happen on another long songtow journey. Her father thanks me and clambers up onto the roof of the truck. She folds herself down onto the floor as the truck pulls onto the highway. I pat my leg, showing her that she can lean on me; she is obvi-ously tired. The hair that frames her face is black, but the long braid is gray with dust. Her three layers of clothes are filthy, especially at the edges, where the material touches her skin. When I ask her name, words pour from her mouth.

I explain, "I can't understand, I only speak a little."

"Oh, that's not a problem, I just want to talk." She talks and talks, self-possessed, laughing at her own jokes, asking me questions. I stumble along behind her, picking up phrases I recognize. She is to be married soon, un-believably enough; her mother is dead; she and her father and uncle are going to the refugee camp near Umphang to see a sick aunt. I think. She lives in Maw Ker. "I have been to Maw Ker," I tell her. "Then you must come again," she says. "To visit us."

When she is all talked out, she molds her skinny body to my legs, wor-ried about sliding toward the open end of the vehicle; everyone holds on tighter when the truck goes up the steep hills. Soon she begins to nod off. "Here, take this." I pull my scarf from my neck and ball it up into a pillow.

But she doesn't want to touch it. *"Ayun hla-deh,"* she murmurs, and shakes her head.

She's right: the silky black material woven through with bright threads is beautiful. For an old traveling companion, it's still in good shape. "Don't worry," I tell her, patting my thigh. "You're tired." After a few more refusals, she puts her head down on the pillow-scarf and drops into sleep, one arm over my lap, the other curved around my shins. The Thai woman's upper lip lifts in disgust. I gently stroke the girl's hair away from her face.

After two more hours of numb bum and aching knees, the truck grinds to a stop. Below us, and stretching toward the hazy horizon, are thousands of thatched roofs, brown dominoes fallen in a complex pattern up and down the hillside. A refugee camp. We are close to Umphang. The girl's father and uncle jump down onto the dusty road; they look sandblasted. The father calls out. Calls again. I touch her back, the scapula like a blade under my palm. She wakes and rubs her face. Blinks. Lifts her head to me and smiles.

Goodbye, dark eyes of the world.

"You will come and visit us?"

"I will try." As she climbs out of the truck, an inordinate sense of loss, or regret, rises in my chest. I lean over the chilies and push my scarf into her hands. "A present for little sister."

I'm relieved that she doesn't refuse. When the truck pulls away, she is still oohing and aahing, showing her father. She waves with one hand and holds the colorful fabric to her cheek with the other. I wave too, smiling, wondering what will happen to her.

Do the light touches leave a clean trace, a thread of kindness to weave into suffering, that endlessly unraveling bolt of cloth? This notion is a Buddhist tenet—in essence, to be kind for the sake of kindness, to step gently through the world. But what I do is small. Even what I think is small; my mind is not big enough to understand what I meet here, to absorb and to know it. The little girl needs much more—a guarantee of protein and rice, a peaceful country, an education—so many things that are impossible for me to give. What is a scarf?

CHAPTER 33

ONE WOMAN

. . . .

A shirtless man waters the bougainvillea in front of the wooden house, which is built on stilts in the old Thai style. I lean out the window and watch a piebald dog pee against the outer beam. A flip-flop flies in the dog's direction; someone under the house shouts in Burmese. The bougainvillea waterer laughs and sprays the farther plants. Muscle flares over shoulder bones and extends into excellent arms. He turns and grins at me. "I'm the gardener!"

"I see that."

"Did you do your interviews?"

"Some of them." In fact, the man who spent the most time in prison didn't want to talk about prisons. He wanted to take me for a walk through the verdant fields here, on the outskirts of Umphang.

"It was like an Indian film," says the shirtless man.

"What?"

"When you went for a walk with Thet Mu. I thought he was going to burst into song and you would run across the field to each other, like Bollywood. So romantic." He drops the water hose, spreads his arms, throws back his mop of curly hair, and runs toward an invisible woman at the other end of the fence. The man under the house giggles and makes a comment I don't understand.

I laugh, too. "I didn't know you were watching, or I would have danced."

"Oh! More fun!"

"What's your name?"

He opens his mouth in mock amazement, then puts his hand to his heart. "I'm not insulted. But I'm well known in my circle. A Burmese circle."

I realize that this is the famous Moe Thee Zun.

A few hours later, a few of us sit on the large porch at the front of the house, a bare lightbulb over our heads, lizards running around on the insect-crowded roof beams. Moe Thee Zun's voice is sharp, commanding. "We were trying to think of ways to get more regular people to join the protests. Students are good, but a whole country is not just students. The demonstrations had to include everybody, working regular people, the ones we knew were also sick of the government, just like we were. We knew they were our comrades also, but they were afraid." He shakes his head. "So I went to the monastery. I wanted to ask the monks if they would help us. If the people saw the monks join the protest, then they would become more brave—they would join us, too."

He lowers his voice to an urgent whisper. "I was respectful. I asked to see the abbot and explained to him what we were going to do. I said that the students wanted to invite the monks to join us, to show that we had their support. Most Burmese people love the monks, they know they are wise, they listen to them. And, to my amazement, the abbot agreed to join the protest.

"Our brother monks followed me out of the monastery carrying their alms bowls upside down. That means they would not accept any gifts from the generals or perform Buddhist ceremonies for them. This is a serious thing and everyone would see it, that the Sangha did not support the government.

"As we walked along, more and more people came out of their houses to join us." He conjures up masses out of the air with a sweeping gesture. "There were thousands, then tens of thousands, walking down the road together, and the crowd continued to grow even after we reached the pagoda and gave our speeches.

"We had a lot of power through these rallies, but we lacked political experience. The older politicals who knew more about the government did not want to help us. They did not want to form some kind of coalition with us. They thought we were too young to be involved in politics. This was the big missed opportunity. The Burmese BBC radio station announced that we would be having a rally on August 8, a strike rally, and none of the students realized how big that strike would get. Millions of people heard the BBC broadcast and went on strike. Imagine that! We could have brought down the government—just a few more days, the country would have stopped functioning, no one was working! But we had no real plan of action and not enough unity, not enough direction."

He drops his hands in his lap. A heated exchange follows, in Burmese, between him and the other men. I see that he is not as young as he looks. None of them are students anymore. Like Maung, this man is pushing forty and living by his wits in an unstable political exile.

Two of the men go back inside the teeming house. The political meeting that Tennyson mentioned will take place tomorrow, and a dozen people have arrived to spend a couple of days here. One of them is Win Min, whom I first met at the Christmas party. He has a dapper mustache, a quick sense of humor, and a talent for computers. Earlier in the day he promised to show me how to send an email, but at the moment he stares into the screen of a laptop; he's busily finishing a report. A couple of guys stand behind him like hypnotized sentinels, watching his fingers fly over the keys.

With the house so full, I suggested that I get a room at a guesthouse in the town, but Moe Thee Zun said no, I could have the bedroom. Two more men have since shown up, making me regret my presence as an overnight guest; I'm taking up badly needed space. But it's too late to leave. And it's probably the only chance I'll have to talk to Moe Thee Zun alone. His comrades have left us out here on the porch together. "Ko Moe Thee, I have a difficult question to ask. You don't have to answer it if you don't want to. Of course."

He puts his elbows on his knees and rests his head on his hands, an expression of longing on his face. He will be disappointed: I'm not going to ask him if he's single. He's been flirting with me steadily. Many of the Burmese men on the border flirt subtly, or charmingly, or obviously, or ingratiatingly, each according to his means. It's a condition of life without women; a new woman in their midst must be tried. Is she single? Is she available? Will she love me?

"I still don't understand why there are two parts, two sections, to the ABSDF. Why did the organization split up?"

He sits back and bites his lower lip, puts his head to one side. Grunts. His hesitation makes me feel the depth of my duplicity. I've asked him about a rift that involved him and Maung. If he knew about our relationship, he would answer the question differently; he might not answer at all. I feel like a spy. Though I am spying only for myself, in an attempt to understand what's going on. At least, that's my rationalization.

I wave my hand. "You know what? I'm sorry, never mind. It's a private matter." But it's also a tendency of secrets: we want to tell them and they want to be told.

"No, it's all right. It's not so difficult to explain. There were conflicts between people. Disagreements. If two groups do not get along, they split up." I wait. He steeples his hands together. "But we were right to part ways."

"Why?"

"Many reasons. Some people on the other side do not respect."

"Don't respect what?"

"The law. After we split up, I was very glad." I wait again. "Because in 1992 there were executions in Kachin territory. I was thankful we had nothing to do with that. Maung gave the order."

"What order?"

"For the executions."

I immediately think, It's a war. People have to die in a war. "Were they SLORC soldiers?"

"No." His forehead wrinkles in consternation.

"Well." I can hear the defensiveness in my voice. "I thought . . . I heard there was just one. Only one."

Moe Thee Zun looks at me, puzzled. "No. That's not true. It was a group of people."

"Who were they?"

I know. I know before he says it. The gooseflesh rises up my arms, down my back.

"They were members of the ASBDF. Some were students, like us. Some of them were tortured."

The words reverberate in my head. "Like us." The voices inside the house, and the Burmese music on the ghetto blaster, grow faint. "But they must have been . . ." What? What could they have been? "Did they commit crimes?"

"The men in command said they were spies for the SLORC. But I don't believe that. Many people don't believe that. It's almost impossible that they had any communication with the SLORC, especially so many of them. It wasn't just one or two. It was a group, and at least one woman. One of them had been a political prisoner. He had already suffered enough. He would never betray the movement. There was no trial.

And there was no place to confine them. So they were executed. Maung was responsible."

"He did it? He killed them?"

"No. He wasn't in the camp. One of his men did it. Or maybe more than one. I don't know the details. I only know it was wrong. Many of us think it was a power struggle within the organization." He takes a cheroot out of his breast pocket, tamps it against the floor, and snaps off the end. But he doesn't light it.

I remember Maung talking, before he left: "If people think someone is stealing their power, they do bad things." And Nola, that evening outside her gate: "A lot has happened on the border that you don't know about."

One of the men comes out onto the porch again and announces that dinner is ready. Moe Thee Zun puts his cheroot behind his ear and gets up. I stand too quickly and almost lose my balance. Moe Thee Zun walks into the house, and I wait for the dizziness to pass. Do I know anything at all?

A large group sits in a circle on the wooden floor; the steaming bowls of food begin to arrive from the kitchen at the back of the house. Someone gives me a stack of chipped plates to hand around. Win Min the computer expert asks if I'm still excited about sending my first email. We laugh about the Westerner learning computer skills from the man who has spent years living in jungle camps.

Maybe the story I've just heard about Maung is meant to discredit him. It could be a lie, a fabrication by a rival who doesn't like him.

Moe Thee Zun returns to his flamboyant, talkative self. As we reach out to take spoonfuls of curry and soup, he makes jokes in English and Burmese. People chat easily through the meal. I listen from a distance, half my mind on what I've just been told. I need to speak to Maung. Why didn't I know about these allegations? The woman is always the last to know. About the other woman. About the executions.

I glance at Moe Thee Zun throughout dinner. His colleagues are indulgent or deferential toward him, but consistently affectionate. Along with his charm and earnestness, an essential element of his character is a persistent innocence. He's like the teenager who has dared, and fought, and beaten himself into the mold of manhood. Has, in fact, become a man. But remains boyishly transparent.

Late in the chilly evening, Moe Thee Zun and I talk about the mental and physical benefits of yoga—of which we are both practitioners—particularly of Sirsasana, the headstand. He's about to demonstrate his agility in this pose when, fortunately, we're interrupted by footsteps and voices on the porch stairs. Two men announce themselves just as they come into view. Moe Thee Zun greets them and asks if they're hungry. I see their guns even before they take off their jackets—gleaming gray and black machines.

Moe Thee Zun whispers, "They're semiautomatics," though they look automatic enough to me. "Here," he murmurs confidentially, and pulls a small handgun from the back of his jeans. "I carry one, too." He puts it down beside him on the floor and gives it a few pats, like a pet turtle. The Karen men who carry the bigger guns place them on the same table where Win Min, indefatigable, continues his light clatter at the computer keyboard. The cell phone that has been ringing intermittently throughout the evening rings again. Someone answers it in a low voice. The gun, the computer, the cell phone: all the elements of modern guerrilla warfare are here. I'm the only woman and the only Luddite in the house.

The newly arrived visitors aren't hungry, just tired. A young man comes out of the shadows of the back bedrooms with a pile of mats and blankets. There's already a row of sleepers farther back in this large main room. Another row forms, to be followed by several more during the next hour, until the spacious floor is lined with sleeping bodies, or wakeful bodies shifting on the hard, cold planks.

"I will go to bed now, too," I say, nodding at my host.

He gives me a long, probing look, to which I cannot reply. Finally he says, "I understand. You are also tired from your journey. Your things are already in my bedroom, yes?"

His bedroom? I'm sleeping in his bedroom? Bloody hell.

I get my toothbrush and return to the main room a few times, but the bathroom is continually in use. I forgo brushing my teeth. Wearing a nightshirt and clean shorts, I cringe as I get into the cold bed, which makes me want to pee even more. Never mind. Exhausted, I go to sleep with a full bladder. But a few hours later, when I wake in the pitch-dark room, I have to pee so badly that it hurts. I hop out of the bed and fumble for the switch on the wall. It takes a long time to find. My watch reads 4 A.M. I open the door. Men everywhere, snoring, snuffling, slumbering. The bathroom is on the other side of the main room, near the kitchen. There is hardly a path to be found through the bodies. Then someone gets up and goes to the bathroom before me. I hear each foot shuffle. A double-nostril sniffle. A yawn so long that it becomes suspenseful. The bathroom door creaks open, creaks shut.

I hear the first tentative dribble as it falls into the squatter toilet. Then comes a good hard spray, steady on, which reverberates through the whole house.

I quietly shut the bedroom door. I will not walk through the collection of sleeping bodies and perform water music for the revolutionaries. Legs squeezed shut, I look around. A man could pee out the window. A man would not be worried about this.

I open the wooden shutter and lean out the window. Impossible.

Could I just go out the nearby front door and down the steps? To pee in the bushes beside the house? But scorpions hunt at night. And spiders. What if one of the armed Karen men thinks I'm a dangerous intruder and shoots me as I'm ascending the stairs?

I open the bedroom door again, wide enough to let a swath of light fall across the first two rows of sleepers. I walk out, determined to go to the loo. But I just can't. My feet pad down too close to their faces, sometimes almost touching the tousled black hair. It's a dreadful combination in Buddhist culture, where the lowly feet must not come near to the esteemed head. I gingerly creep back into the bedroom.

I have a water bottle in my pack. It will have to serve as a traveling chamber pot. I get out my scissors and hack away the plastic top.

When I pour out the urine, it falls to the ground with an unexpectedly hard thud, then a splash. I crawl back into bed, mortified.

In the morning when I get up, the first thing I do is look out the window. The splotch of wet dust is still visible—not soaked in and faded, as I hoped it would be. But no one will ever know.

The big main room of the house is full of sunlight and glittery dust motes and sleepy men drinking tea. One of them gives me a familiar movie-star smile. "Tennyson! When did you get here?"

"Early in the morning. Still dark. I slept in the hammock under the house. I think you pour some water out the window. Why you do that?"

I wave my hands and quickly ask, "Why didn't you tell me you were coming? I thought you had meetings to go to."

"Yes, Karen. This is one of the meetings. Today." He blinks slow panther eyes at me. Of course, he would be here. Naturally he would not tell me he was coming. It's like that. Before Mae Sot, I took a weeklong trip to Mae Sarieng, where I met the same people I'd interviewed in a safe house in Bangkok. In a bar in Mae Sot, I drank a beer with Bo Saw Htun, the man I met at the Chiang Mai party who reminded me of a Mexican composer. People are fluid, I am fluid—we move and bump into one another.

So I learn the assumed normalcy of having no home. The exhaustion goes underground, underskin, into the blood and bones. I, too, can sleep on a mat, a mattress, in a stranger's bed. To be honest, I have led a vagabond existence for years, but here, as I follow the dissidents, cross paths with them, wander through the tarpaulin-and-bamboo camps collecting the faces of ash-dusted children, my sense of homelessness deepens as it expands. This is the way of the world. Fragmented populations of people live at the edges, their clothes getting thinner and dirtier with each passing day, their eyes yearning toward a center they cannot reach. That center is a safe home. Not a safe house, which denotes danger, but a full domestic world, its known pleasures, its rich containment and simple beauties. Even nomadic peoples enjoy that containment, which arises partly from comforting routine, partly from familiar, beloved objects: the set of spoons, the enameled plate, Grandmother's hand mirror. The largest embodiment of that containment—the biggest container—is the community that envelops the cherished home.

No wonder the men here live in obvious longing for women, for wives, for mothers. It's erotic in the sexual sense, certainly—there are more young men than young women, many of them are single, and they don't want to be—but it is erotic in the larger sense, too. Home is an extension of the human body. The first human home, the original safe container, is the womb. Women are the mistresses of containment, the holders, the absorbers. Men can be this too, of course, but homemaking itself remains a womanly art.

I used to find the word *homemaking* vaguely embarrassing. As an occupation, it was an uninspiring potential fate. But being among Burmese refugees and exiles in Thailand has taught me that it's no small act to make a home. Making a home safe enough for a child is the ordinary miracle. How many refugees on this earth can only dream of it? The tendency— perhaps from television images, news clips—is to envision the displaced as herds, flocks, haunted masses carrying children and possessions on their backs, walking away, arriving in makeshift camps only to leave again. And they are that. But they are also individual men and women and children with the old human longing: to be held safely in their world. Each one of them has a name.

Some of them even have the same name as a certain beloved English poet. Tennyson is wearing his bulky army jacket that smells of ash. Does he sleep in it? I wonder. Last night, he must have. I'm so happy to see him that I want to hug him. But I only smile.

CHAPTER 34

GOOD PEOPLE

. . . .

The reason I keep thinking about home is that my period is two weeks late. Or three. I don't know exactly. I thought I wrote down when my last cycle started, but I'm back in Bangkok and my wall calendar and notebooks yield no information. Has it been a month?

Time is deceptively elastic. A week stretches into long days filled with intense experiences and conversations, so that seven days can be as replete as twenty. It feels as though I've lived here for years. Where? Around. Bangkok, Mae Sot, Chiang Mai. After Mae Sot, I spent a week in another border town, Mae Sarieng. Next week I will return to Mae Sarieng to interview more people from the DPNS and the ABSDF.

Marriage, children. Home. The other ordinary miracle, of course, is pregnancy.

One thing I know: if I am pregnant, I will not have an abortion.

I could not bear an abortion in this place, at this time. I don't regret the abortion I had when I was seventeen. I mourned it as a loss but also recognized that it was the only way to keep my own life intact. Now something else is at work, something more powerful than my need for self-definition. Evolution, I think. To become fatly, healthily pregnant is the female body's most positive response to the near-scent of death, illness, and loss. Life is here! sings the belly. The future is suspended in these upside-down flower pods full of eggs.

Maung and I haven't been overzealous with the condoms. Each time we made love without one, part of my brain scolded, What are you doing? while my body opened wide and swallowed.

"What are you doing?" I ask.

"Traveling too much. And sleeping only a little. There are many people to see, a lot of meetings. Talking. I talk a lot. That's part of the work."

"So how's it going?" He has not told me exactly what he is doing in America—"Meetings, meetings," he always says, explaining nothing. I think he might be working on the sanction lobby. Many Burma activists in the U.S. have been trying for years to massage the American administration toward economic sanctions against the junta. I ran into one of Maung's colleagues in Mae Sot, and that's all we talked about—what the U.S. can or cannot do for Burma and the movement.

"It's going slowly. The cigarettes are very expensive. And it's freezing. My feet are always cold."

I don't know what to say.

"Are you all right?" he asks.

My darling, I recently heard allegations that you were responsible for executions in the jungle, the deaths of people who may have been innocent of real crimes. Is this true, my heart? But I know that we can't talk about it on the phone.

"I'm fine. Also tired."

"Is something wrong?"

"I just miss you. I'd like to see your face again. It's been a long time."

"It's only a month!"

No. It's been six weeks.

His voice takes on enough buoyancy to keep us both afloat. "We're almost halfway. I know it's not easy over the phone."

"No." Why do upwelling tears affect the voice? I don't want him to hear me crying. I can't tell him what I'm crying about, because I don't know. Sure, I miss him. I feel such skin-hunger these days, lust and more-than-lust, an animal desire to be in a dark place, burrowing down in the present of our bodies, that shimmering privacy surrounded by the large, complicated mess of Burma.

"Something has happened. Something is wrong."

"Maung, I love you. That's why I'm upset." An accurate if incomplete statement.

He laughs. I laugh back.

"Are you going to be okay?"

I inhale a lungful of air and speak while holding it. "If I were pregnant, what would you want me to do?"

As I hear the verge of tears in my words, I hear the pleasure in his. "Bear it. Bear it! Are you pregnant?"

I exhale, "I don't know."

"How late are you?"

"Two or three weeks."

"But you've been traveling a lot, Karen. Mae Sot, Mae Sarieng, Umphang. So maybe your body is confused." I keep forgetting that Maung is also a doctor. "How did you like Mae Sarieng in the end? Did you warm up?" At the beginning of my stay there, I, too, was cold all the time.

The town was more northerly than I thought, and I didn't have warm clothes. "I bought a sweater and a blanket and everything was fine. And I interviewed Ko Lwanni, the poet."

"And ex–political prisoner. Was he nice to you?"

"A true gentleman. I also spent a lot of time with the DPNS guys. One of their members was injured by a land mine and needed money for the operation."

"You paid?"

"That's what the book advance is for, my dear. Expenses in the field."

His voice drops into its familiar seriousness. "Do you feel like you are pregnant?"

I close my eyes and stir a spoon around my gut. "I have no idea. I just know that my cycles are usually like clockwork. When I'm really stressed out, I might be a week late, but never more. So . . ."

"Maybe you are!" The elation in his voice sets my teeth on edge. "We could announce our engagement."

Announce. Make the engagement public. Follow it with a marriage celebration. Am I old enough to get married? I recently turned twenty-eight. I'm old enough to have a young family and baby food in my hair.

"You have to get enough rest. Eat properly. I'm sorry, Karen, but I have to go, the card is running out. I'll call you again in a few days. I'm sorry I can't give you a number; I keep changing places. Do you want to talk some more?"

"No, I'm fine. Call me in the evening or the morning, Thai time, to make sure you get me. I'll be in Bangkok for at least a week. Then I think I'm going up to Mae Hong Son."

"I love you," he says in his deep, steady voice.

Vexed, I deliver my fond, echoing reply and hang up the phone.

Bear it. He said that twice. To me the phrase suggests not the beginning of a family but some kind of punishment I'll have to endure alone. I chide myself: it's the English thing. If I could speak Burmese, his response would have felt different. I cannot get angry about words spoken from thousands of miles away. He was happy. Thousands of miles away. Bear it.

.   .   .

I catch a motorcycle taxi and careen through Bangkok wearing a back-pack loaded with precious liquid cargo.

Nola's dog is happy to see me. He picks his way around the students' shoes on the floor and sticks his wet nose into my hand. Nola stands behind him, eyeing me shrewdly. "What's wrong with you?"

Is she one of those people who can magically tell when a woman is with child? I hope not, because that means she might suggest that I have a cup of water instead of five glasses of wine.

"Everything's different. I met Moe Thee Zun in Umphang. He told me about the executions."

Nola raises her eyebrows. "Someone was going to tell you sooner or later."

"Why didn't you tell me?"

"Why didn't Maung tell you?"

"Fuck, I don't know. I don't want to think about it."

"Most people don't want to think about it. It's a big wound. A shameful thing for the whole movement. None of us like to talk about it." She leads me into the house. I hear some of the younger students upstairs chanting lines of English back to their teacher.

"Moe Thee Zun told me about it the first evening I was in Umphang. Only because I asked. It was like he opened a box, let me look inside, then shut it again." I take off my backpack. "Can we have a glass of wine and discuss, oh, I don't know, the joys of Mae Sot? Or whether Clinton will invoke sanctions? Or how about books? Have you read any good novels lately? Novels about anything other than Burma."

She lets out a low whistle. "Wow. You're really stressed out, aren't you?"

"I brought two bottles of not-bad Italian red. I didn't want to start drinking alone."

She nods. "You're so wise. The alcohol will be safe with me. The students'll be leaving in about half an hour."

.   .   .

Days pass. Maung will be back soon. I think and I do not think about the executions, the ones who died. One woman. Rumors of torture. I distance myself from the gooseflesh that rose on my skin in Umphang, and the feeling that came after I left. Not that I didn't know and couldn't trust Moe Thee Zun, Win Min, the men from the other side. But that I didn't know Maung. That I don't know him.

At the same time, I'm anxious to see him again. In the welter of days, I place my confusions aside, though I cannot put them outside myself. I know. I know. Unknowing is impossible.

But I can be busy. Writing. Meeting more people. Reading. I interview several more former political prisoners and meet people from the Burmese Lawyers' Association and the NLD-LA. I ask questions, listen and make notes. I don't inquire further about the split in the ABSDF, reluctant to touch that raw nerve.

But it lifts up of its own accord and touches me. Every secret is at odds with itself. It seeks entrance into the open field of human discourse. One of the men I interview tells me a story.

Soon after he arrived at a Karen military camp for training, he watched a weathered Karen guerrilla herd a man and a woman out of the safe area. The soldier wielded an AK-47; the couple wore manacles and had signs around their necks that the Rangoon student couldn't read—the words were in Karen. When the young man left his hut and followed a few steps behind the captives, the soldier turned to him in anger. "Go back, go back. You don't want to be near these two." The woman began to cry, to sob, holding her hands together as though in prayer, supplicating the armed man. The student saw that she was pleading for her life.

The soldier pushed the people away, onto a path through the trees. The young man watched until he couldn't see or hear them anymore, then he went around the camp asking people about what he'd just seen. Some shook their heads and turned away; some told him the couple had done bad things and were to be punished. Finally, an older woman explained that the two had been caught having an adulterous affair. The guerrilla took them to a cliff a couple of kilometers away from the camp and shot them.

Did the signs say Sinner? Adulterer?

The Karen guerrillas, remember, are fighting the good fight against a superior military force that persecutes and kills the most vulnerable and innocent of their civilian population. The war against the Karen has been called protracted genocide. The Karen are the good guys. They are also a predominantly Christian people. The KNLA reserves the right to execute its people for drug trafficking, for violent crimes—and for adultery, as proscribed in those authoritarian, law-bound Old Testament books Deuteronomy and Leviticus, where all adulterers and adulteresses are put to death, no questions asked. Such a punishment was a barbarity two thousand years ago and it is a barbarity now, but the good people continue to do it.

I'm afraid of the good people. Goodness makes us smug. From smug to dangerous, the distance is minuscule, the step small, a stumble. I like to believe that I'd never take such a step, and that is precisely where the danger lies.

All the revolutionaries, young and old, carrying guns or redefining themselves as dissidents, each one of them grew up under a political system predicated on violence that could and sometimes did result in imprisonment and untimely death. Murder, torture, lies, threats, betrayal, isolation, distrust—these have been the working tools of political and social life in Burma for half a century. Thought control and intimidation are built into neighborhoods, village councils, schools, universities. It would be naïve to think that fighting a war in the jungle would make young men wise and peaceable.

I'm not making excuses for Maung—if the allegations against him are true. I'm not making excuses for the person or people who pulled the trigger. Nor do I suggest that goodness itself is an illusion. I'm trying to understand what might have happened. In that jungle camp, wherever it was. I will ask him about it. He will tell me. But I will never know.

I imagine my way to some kind of answer because I love him. Because my body may be irrevocably involved with his. Suddenly his admonition to me doesn't seem so ill phrased at all.

Bear it.

If I love him, I will bear it, whatever it is.

CHAPTER 35

SHELTER

WITHIN BROKEN SHELTER

. . . .

"Don't come inside me," I whisper. He pulls his head up and finds my eyes, questioning. But I don't want to interrupt with more words. I thrust my hips against his, holding on to the rhythm. I have waited for this and I want this, now, I don't want him to stop.

We've been shy with each other, maladroit. Though he slept comfortably in the plane for hours, the vastness of the ocean remains between us. After two months apart, sex is hunger, an appetite to satiate urgently, forcefully. But it doesn't deliver us over to each other.

That comes only after sex. To let my eyes rest on his body is to return to him. What is more lovely than the beloved, come back? His arms gleam in the half-light; I would like to lick them. I peer at the thick black line of eyelashes. He didn't get his hair cut in America, so it's too long in the front and back. The thick black sheen falls like a helmet over his head.

The darkness that is not dark spreads into the room, along with the noise of people below, laughing at the noodle stand in the parking lot.

"My period came. A few days before you got back." More than six weeks late. I was convinced I was pregnant. A quarter exultant and three-quarters terrified.

"I understood." His voice is soft, ever so slightly resigned.

"It's better. We're not ready for a baby."

"I know." He turns on his side toward me and opens his eyes, fixes me with a steady stare. "But I want one."

"Yes. I feel that, too."

For the first time in my life, the appearance of the blood made me sad, and the sadness confounded me. When did I begin to feel this intensely physical desire to have a child? A few days after that poor Karen woman in Maw Ker lost her boy to malaria. The body cried out, "Make another child, make sure we have a child; we must have children to replace the ones who slip through our fingers, out of time." No wonder the refugee camps are teeming with babies and toddlers. Maung has been here since 1989. He is soon to be thirty-seven. I'm not surprised that he wants to stand in the light of a new baby.

I'm about to voice some of these thoughts when he startles me with an observation of his own. "You are like a man."

"How so?"

"You are so sexual. You want so much."

I pull away from him, hurt. "Maung, we've been separated for two months."

"It is not a criticism. I don't complain. The Burmese woman is not usually like that. She is more quiet. She does not know what the orgasm is. If she has the orgasm, it frightens her."

"I'm sure she would enjoy the orgasm once she got used to it. It's natural to be frightened if you don't understand what's happening to your body. Even if it feels good." I wonder who "she" is. An early girlfriend? The gem dealer's daughter?

"But you like it."

"Yeah, I'm definitely into the orgasm."

"Every time?"

"Why not? It's not the be-all and end-all of sex, but I'd rather have one than not."

"I see." He sounds perplexed.

"Don't you like having an orgasm every time?"

"But I'm a man."

"Meaning what? That men should have them and women don't really need them?"

"We have the sperm. The orgasm is . . ." The doctor appears in his face, searching for the right word. "Functional."

I whip the pillow out from under my head and hit him with it. "And women have the womb! We grow the babies and make the milk. How functional is that? The least we should get in exchange is a lot of orgasms. Trust me, after not having sex for a long time the orgasm I just had was extremely functional."

He takes the pillow hits with equanimity and replies, "I see only that you are very aggressive. The orgasm makes you aggressive."

I crawl on top of him, growling. "Here, let me show you aggressive." Take that, and that.

And I'll take some, too.

My lover has been back in Thailand for almost a week. It's already hard to remember what it was like without him here. That may be because the two states—with, without—are not so different. My longing for him is greater now because he is closer, but we haven't spent much time together. Still, I am happy. The promise of him provides a flesh-and-blood center to my days.

Maung leaves in the morning like any working husband, kissing me quickly, whisking himself out the door. I may not see him tonight if he is too busy, or works too late, or cannot face the trip back across the sprawl of Bangkok traffic. I can't stay in the communal ABSDF house, so there's no question of my going to him. I try to look on the bright side: wanting but not receiving enough is an aphrodisiac.

The yearning suits me. Our relationship is only one of Maung's obligations; perhaps the least of them. The anxiety this provokes is familiar. I've had other relationships with unavailable men. Does this have to do with my past—the emotionally stunted father and the little girl I was who craved his love? I'm sure it does. But knowing that doesn't help me.

This world is more real and more pressing than my past. Political exigencies make my personal concerns seem indulgent. I grasp that outwardly, but I whine about it inwardly. I want to rest. I want my lover to rest. I want us to go to a movie (*The English Patient* is playing) or spend the day in bed, making love, eating, and reading the newspapers. No, I want us to spend two whole days doing that. But such desire is unseemly; I would not admit it to anyone. Why should he and I have such bliss when ABSDF battalions are engaged in active combat on the border?

This is a serious question, but if I asked it at every moment joy would become a sin. One needs balance, but I don't know how to find it in a climate of emergencies. In the past six weeks, several thousand more Karen refugees have poured across the border into Thailand, their SLORC-attacked homes and fields charred and smoking behind them. An ABSDF safe house was ransacked by Thai military intelligence and every computer was confiscated. Several members of a battalion at the front line sustained serious injuries; one of the men's wives had just had a baby. The two-year-old child of a dissident was diagnosed with cerebral palsy, a condition likely caused or at least worsened by the malaria she suffered as a baby.

Tragedy is a climate; I have acclimatized. My eyes are open and they ache. One day I went to help out with some paperwork for the Burmese Women's Union. After doing some editing and typing, correcting English text, I guiltily confided to one of the activists that writing a book wasn't enough. She sighed. "But we all feel that way. No one can do enough. Just write your book."

I do. I continue to collect stories, talk to people. While I try to control my personal longings and berate myself for being too soft, they remind me that my yearnings are as basic as cooked rice. Though the Burmese dissidents have exiled themselves in the name of political activism, they usually talk about their families and their friends. The former prisoners often describe more about the relationships they forged with the small animals in their cells than they do about their political convictions. That is partly because the political convictions are common knowledge between us, almost taken for granted. But it's also because they've sacrificed the personal world in order to do political work. It is the personal world they crave; they recognize that it sustains them. They reconstruct it as best they can out of a few photographs, music tapes, memories told and retold, grafting the past onto the present to keep it alive. The politics is the road and the method. It is the fraught journey. But the personal is the only shelter.

Forced to live in a prison, under a piece of tarpaulin, in one place then another, and another, the mind struggles to build an interior freedom, or even the possibility of freedom, a new life relegated to the future. And the mind succeeds. People can build their lives on a fracture.

A shelter within broken shelter is another version of home. I can live there, if I want to. In some ways, I already do. And the company is fine.

CHAPTER 36

THE BEGINNING OF JUNGLE

. . . .

"Karen, I need to spend some time in Chiang Mai. Then I have to go to Mae Sarieng and the jungle for the rest of the month."

I respond to this news with measured nods, hypnotized. We're in a noodle shop with steaming bowls of gwiteo and a TV in front of us. A Hong Kong melodrama lays bare the political machinations and the lusts of an old, well-powdered dynasty. Unaccustomed to televisions, Maung and I sit on the same side of the table and stare at the topknots of the men and the long embroidered robes.

He raises his voice above the Thai dubbing. "I am a leader. I have to go see everyone."

"I know." I push chopsticks laden with noodles into my mouth. A woman in an elaborate wig screams at her lover—he seems to have failed to garner the favor of some important lord. I think. I don't get all the words. I fill in the gaps by guessing. At least I'm not like that woman. Teeth bared, eyes bugging out. So un-Buddhist.

I'm calm because I was expecting Maung to announce his departure.

I take another load of noodles. Chew. Swallow. "You'll be going to the camp from Mae Sarieng, right?"

"Yes, Camp One and Two. I'll divide my time between each of them."

"When are you going?"

He swivels his head away from me, mumbles.

"What?"

"In two days."

I nod again. If I were pregnant, would it be different? If a child were to arrive in a year, would we have a house by then? Where? I don't think I could live full-time in the noise and pollution of Bangkok, though I know that's where Maung needs to have a base now. I also don't know if I have enough money to rent a proper house in Chiang Mai. If I did that, would five or six comrades live with us, because they had no other place to go?

We watch the Chinese lovers fighting. The long sleeves of the robes fly; the braided black hair flies, too; there's a lot of whirling around. I suppose I should ask Maung if he's going to stay with Angie in Chiang Mai. But I prefer not to know.

Other women manage, year after year. The Burmese women, the white women who live with Burmese men on the border, in the various towns, here in Bangkok. Their revolutionary husbands go off to clandestine meetings, they make dangerous border crossings, they leave for weeks, months at a time, and the children stay with the mothers. Nola says she wants to have a baby, too. Soon. Sometimes other women help take care of the children. There's that—cheap child care. I could hire a poor Burmese woman to be a nanny. That is, if I had enough money. How long will it take me to finish my novel and get the rest of the advance? Maybe it would all work out.

I push my stool back, then turn to Maung, who still stares at the television. "You know what?"

"Ungg." Male Asian grunt: willing to listen.

"I'm going to come with you."

He turns to me. "Oh! I would like that. I'm glad you want to come."

For a moment I think I've misunderstood. Maybe he invited me and I missed it because I was watching Chinese actors fighting in shrill Thai.

"But in Chiang Mai I'll be in meetings a lot."

"I don't want to come to Chiang Mai." I need to keep writing, uninterrupted. And I don't want to pay for my own accommodation there. No matter where he stays, I wouldn't be able to stay with him. "I need to keep working on the book. But I'll meet you in Mae Sarieng, and come with you to the camps. I'd like to see them."

"It's not very comfortable."

"That's fine. I've done a lot of camping. We're not staying for three months, are we?"

He raises his hands in a "Who knows?" gesture. "Maybe we will. It's nice in the jungle. We'll be able to spend some time together."

Two weeks later, on a sweltering April morning, we leave Mae Sarieng in the back of a pickup truck with ten other ABSDF members, both men and women, and a load of supplies. It reminds me of a school trip: we're giddy with excitement when we start out, talking to one another loudly over the laboring engine. It's a hired vehicle driven by a burly Thai man with one eye. We don't drive on a paved road but on a trail used by water buffalo and motorcycles, through vegetable fields and fallow rice paddies. Bumping along, the morning air already hot, we begin to rise into hills without houses. We pass village hunters who walk barefoot on the dust track, smoking wooden pipes, old thin-barreled rifles slung across their backs.

Maung is the first of my Burmese companions to nod off. This gift for sleeping has been bestowed upon many Southeast Asian people, but no amount of cultural immersion changes my general insomniac state. Instead, I lose myself to the entanglement of green and dust-washed plants by the trail and to the more richly shining greens far beyond it. To extend my vision over the land makes me remember what a balm nature is. Green stuff. Dry yellow chaff. Deep blue sky. Birdsong flutes up when the truck slows for potholes. The dry heat huffs in our faces.

Bumping along the track dislodges the sadness in my body. Sadness for those who have told me their stories. For Aung San Suu Kyi, who is once again under house arrest. For the Karen refugees in their camps, rebuilding shacks that may be burned down again next year. The air smells of dust and vegetation, a wilder and richer scent than that of fresh-cut hay. I breathe in, my eyes on the hills. As we drive farther and farther away, toward the beginning of the jungle, I give myself over to the living strength of the color green.

Hours later, we arrive at a wide stream. Someone tells me that if I followed it I would reach the great Salween River, which divides Thailand from Burma. Along a stretch where the banks widen into a stony beach and the roots of a banyan tree hang in the air like sailing lines, the earth rises up and buckles into a high hill. "The camp is on top," Maung says. "Getting water is a real drag." He has returned from the land of the free with some useful slang and more contractions in his everyday speech. "But don't worry. We won't make you work too hard."

"I don't mind working hard," I respond, and hop out of the back of the truck. The bamboo huts are invisible from the stream, but a stairlike path up the incline signals human habitation. The steps are so newly cut they look wet.

They *are* wet. People begin to descend the steep hillside to meet us, slipping and sliding. Everyone jumps out of the truck and we splash through the stream. I know a handful of people here, having met them elsewhere along the border. The greeting on the rocky beach is full of affection. The men clap each other on the back and let their arms remain around each other's necks and waists; the women take each other's hands. Everyone talks or embraces or opens their arms in greeting; older children have come down, too, and they smile and jump in the water. It's a power-ful moment of homecoming, but something about it strikes me as odd, un-expected. Maung swings bags of gear and provisions to his friends. People shout from the top of the hill.

When I go back across the stream to get my bags, the distance allows me to realize that it's the first time I've ever heard Burmese people make so much noise in an uncontained space. They are outside; they are not be-hind compound walls. In the cities and towns of Thailand, these men and women move carefully and quietly in public. Despite the hard living and the danger, no wonder dissidents in the cities and towns of Thailand often express nostalgia for the jungle camps.

A man I recognize but cannot place comes loping through the water, insisting in Burmese that I can't carry my own bag. "I can," I keep saying. "I can!" When I refuse to give the backpack over, he turns and lifts his hands toward Maung, who yells, "Just give it to him! He wants to help you!"

Then I know who he is. Maung's bodyguard, a thin, dark-skinned man who often wears the baseball cap he is wearing now. I haven't seen him since before Maung went away. He has small, glittering eyes and betel-dark lips, which upturn in a smile as he lifts the pack off my back and slings it over his shoulder. In gray shorts and a khaki T-shirt, he blends into the trees as he tramps away with my bag.

I'm not allowed to help unload supplies from the truck, let alone carry so much as a package of batteries up the hill. Instead, a young man leads me up the slippery clay steps, turning often to make sure I'm all right. We reach the plateau, which is ringed by thatched huts in two sizes, small and slightly larger; several more rise up an adjoining slope.

It feels hotter here than it was in Mae Sarieng, though that seems im-probable. I smell the woodsmoke of cooking fires. The young man deliv-ers me to a hut not far from the edge of the hill and introduces me to a pretty young woman who has just lit up a cheroot. A Burmese paperback is splayed open against a rock beside her. "Oh, hello!" she says, putting the cheroot down on another rock. She stands and brushes out the wrinkles of her sarong. Her bobbed hair is pinned in a little curl at the nape of her neck. "It's nice to meet you," she says formally. "I am Khaing Lin."

"I am Yee Yee Cho," I respond, which cracks her up.

"Yee Yee Cho! Who gave you such a nice Burmese name?" It basically means "sweet smiler."

"Members of ABSDF." Maung, actually, but there's no need to mention that. I smile. "See?"

"I see! You have the—" She twirls her index fingers in her cheeks.

"Dimples."

"Dimples! *Ayun cho-deh!* So sweet!" She laughs and plucks her cheroot off the rock. She draws on it quickly, but it has already gone out. "Please come in. I will show you everything." Once inside the two-room dwelling, she glances around with a scowl and laughs again. "Somewhere is my lighter." Then louder, as if she were calling to the missing object, "Somewhere in this universe, my lighter!"

Within a few minutes it's clear that I will be staying here with her, her daughter, and two other women. This is the single women's hut, she explains. Oh. Obviously that means I won't be staying with Maung. He and I have repeatedly referred to *our* trip to the jungle. Thus I had it in my mind that we would stay together. Not just in the same camp but in the same hut. Khaing Lin chatters on. I try to listen, but the only words I hear for a minute are booming in my own head. Why didn't Maung tell me about this?

My hostess leads me into the second room, where a little girl sits on the raised bed platform, a hairbrush in her hand. She holds the brush out, bossily, to her mother; as Khaing Lin begins to fix her daughter's hair, the girl talks like a four-year-old version of her mother, propelled through language by curiosity and sparky irreverence.

I interrupt her to tell her that she's cute. She looks at me as if I were trying to give her a headless doll. Khaing Lin chides, "Say thank you!"

Dutifully, without feeling, she thanks me.

I try again. "What's your name?"

"Decembaa."

Khaing Lin tugs the brushed hair smooth, parts it, and expertly divides it into two long pigtails. December throws herself off the bed platform and runs outside to play.

"Why did you call her December?"

"Oh, because it's such a beautiful word. Isn't it?" She pats the bed platform. "You can leave your bags here."

I move to put my bigger pack on the dirt floor, but she shakes her head and nods at the bamboo platform. "Up, up. To avoid bugs and snakes."

Ah, right. I lift the bag.

Two platforms are built on either side of the entrance, which has no door, just a curtain. They double as shelves that hold large, striped market bags. I've seen so many of these nylon sacks in exiles' rooms and offices—containers for people's clothes, books, and personal effects.

"Let's go out to check the fire. I'll make some noodles, then prepare your sleeping place. Are you hungry?"

I follow her out the back of the hut to the cooking area, where a large aluminum pot sits in a fire. With sure movements and a blackened fork, Khaing Lin rearranges the scarlet embers.

"I forgot to look for the lighter!" The cold cheroot is stuck behind her ear. "Never mind!" She pulls a twig out of the fire, blows out the flame, and uses the live coal to light her cheroot. "Ahh. Very good, the cheroot. Do you smoke?"

"No. I love the smell, though."

"Be careful! That means you may smoke soon."

As she cooks our noodles, we compare notes on the people we know in common along the border, moving through ABSDF members, NGO workers, and English teachers. Then the conversation drifts to Burmese writers and poets. Khaing Lin shows me her small pile of books inside the hut. Several novels, collections of Burmese poetry, and a few recent literary journals make up the treasure.

I pick up one of the novels. "I met this writer when I was in Rangoon."

"Really?"

"Yes, I interviewed her, and we had lunch together, too. She's a good talker."

"Yee Yee Cho, you are so lucky! I would love to talk to other writers. I write poetry, too, and some journalism. But it's not easy to do that here." She gently takes the book from me and presses it between her palms. "Who else did you meet there? Did you talk with other writers?"

I describe my dinner with Sayagyi Tin Moe (she shows me a dog-eared collection of his poetry) and the ship captain who talked like a professor. I tell her about two afternoons I spent with Ludu Daw Ah Mar, the famous fiction writer. "I thought it would be hard to find her house, because I didn't have directions, but when I showed the address to a si-car driver he knew exactly where she lived."

"Yes, everyone would know her house. The people love her books."

"That's what he said. He'd read everything she'd written."

Back outside, using two rags to hold the handles, she lifts the pot and takes it to the hillside. She speaks through billows of steam as she pours out the water. "Burmese people love books. The country used to have the highest literacy rate in Asia. Before the dictatorship. Even the women, hundreds of years ago. The monastery schools taught boys *and* girls to read. As for me, I used to love going to the library. I was always involved with a book."

The noodles congeal in the pot as Khaing Lin and I talk, jumping from one literary subject to another. Eventually she stands up, flattens out her sarong in a businesslike way, and asks, "Do you like chilies? I put them on everything because the food here is boring."

She gets some bowls and sets aside December's portion before dousing the noodles with chili oil. "She will be home soon. She always knows when the noodles are ready."

We eat quickly, then go back into the hut to get my "bed" ready. This consists of a blanket and an elusive mosquito net.

"I wonder where I put it," Khaing Lin says. "You have to use a net."
She pulls a bag off the platform and unzips it. "Aha!" The gauzy white
mass unfurls under her hands. "Even if it's very hot, make sure you use the
net, okay?"

"Some people say that it's hard to get malaria in the dry season."

"It's true, we don't have so many mosquitoes in the dry season. But
one mosquito is enough."

CHAPTER 37

GORKY

.   .   .

I ~~see Maung~~ at dinnertime, in a communal kitchen shelter. He is obviously happy, surrounded by talkative men who fall silent when he speaks. He has also changed into a longyi and jettisoned his Marlboros for a cheroot. He's in such high spirits that I don't want to spoil it with my disappointment about the sleeping arrangements. I smile as he introduces me to everyone. In due course, I discover their various titles and jobs: information officer, military strategist, radio operator, commanding officer of such and such battalion. Apparently a group of soldiers are here from the front. Right now they're bathing in the stream, and soon they'll come up the hill and devour all the food in sight.

The information officer says, "The soldiers are always hungry. They work hard and the food out there is not so good." He smiles at me enthusiastically. He has a thick scar through his upper lip, which emphasizes his fine teeth. "Maung says you are a writer. Do you know Gorky?"

His tone suggests that I may know Gorky personally. "Well, I know his name. And that he was Russian. But I haven't read him."

The radio operator is thrilled. My ignorance provides him with a marvelous chance to narrate Gorky's life story, from his humble beginnings to his revolutionary activities in czarist Russia, from his great friendship with Lenin to his eventual disgust with the Bolsheviks' savage disregard for human rights. A couple of times the other men join the conversation, but his love of Gorky is the star, and it speaks, and through that love shines his knowledge.

I presume he also knows a lot about radio systems.

I sit back to listen, saying, "Hmm" occasionally and "Really?" at the appropriate spots. Sometimes he interrupts himself to ask his companions in Burmese for the right word in English. He reminds me of the qualities I most admire in Burmese people: their love of literature and art, their openness to the world, their ability to bring the world into their own experience, their intellectual generosity, their enthusiasm for learning and for teaching. Because, of course, he is teaching me. Just as I realize how serious my Gorky deprivation has been, he asks, "Would you like me to lend you one of his books? I have a photocopy of *My Universities,* in English."

I thank him for the offer, genuinely pleased. I'm always short of reading material.

After dinner, Maung walks me back toward Khaing Lin's hut. We walk slowly because it's not that far. It's also dark, though the froth of the Milky Way glitters above us. A moon glow shows above the treetops in the direction of the stream.

"Khaing Lin says this is the single women's hut."

"Yes. Though you are not a single woman."

Teeth clenched, I nod. It's so hard to speak sometimes. I feel needy, and feeling needy makes me mad at him. "Maung, I promise I will ask you this just once. Then I won't ask again. Do you think we might have a chance to spend any time together? Alone?"

"Difficult. It's communal life here. You and I are not married, so we cannot stay together like we are married." I don't bother pointing out the obvious hypocrisy of this behavior, considering our usual conjugal relations.

"Why didn't you tell me that before? I know it's stupid, but I thought . . . I just . . ."

"You thought we would stay together?"

"Why didn't you explain that we wouldn't? At least I could have prepared myself."

"I'm sorry. I was busy in Chiang Mai and I did not think about it. For me it's obvious."

"For me it wasn't."

"Do you want to declare?"

"What do you mean?"

"We publicly announce our engagement so we can act like a married couple."

I roll my eyes. "That's almost as bad as . . . Christianity! We should declare our marriage plans so we can sleep together!"

"I am a Buddhist, not a Christian. I told you it was not so easy in the jungle."

"I didn't realize you were talking about us."

We have arrived at Khaing Lin's hut. I hear her inside, murmuring to December in a mellifluent voice, half spoken, half sung.

I sidle closer to Maung. "Will you kiss me good night?"

"It is better to be private."

"Maung, who can see us? Most people know that I'm here because we're a couple. We've been out a lot together in Bangkok. It's no longer a big secret."

"But it doesn't have to be a big public."

"All right. Fine. I'll see you tomorrow. Maybe. If I'm lucky, I guess." I duck into the little house before he can say another word.

Do I care that I am being childish? Not at all. Like a child, I enjoy my petulance for the illusion of power it gives me.

CHAPTER 38

A LOCK ON INSPIRATION

. . . .

During the next week, I visit briefly with Maung and his colleagues over lunch or dinner; we spend one long afternoon in the radio-operations hut. With a copy of *My Universities* in my hand, I learn about how far the signals reach, how often the operators are able to listen in on SLORC radio communications, how the SLORC sometimes decodes their signal and listens in on them. Sometimes the two sides find themselves on the same wavelength and talk and swear at each other.

Throughout these visits, I inwardly congratulate myself on my maturity. At meals, Maung and I occasionally slip off a flip-flop and touch our feet together under the table. What a thrill. It seems we are engaged in a chaste, public courtship for the benefit of his comrades. It is natural, in this world, that my behavior will determine their approval of me. They are a family, after all, formed and bonded through experiences I can only imagine, no matter how much I may know of the details. Part of me strongly rejects the notion that I need to be approved of, that I need to satisfy an entire group's requirements in order to show my love for their leader.

I remind myself that if I were a Burmese woman I would probably be more accepting, more patient—qualities that are valued in every Theravadan Buddhist culture. Women are expected not just to exhibit those traits but to embody them. I pride myself on my ability to adapt, but in fact this pride is false: I don't like adapting when it means acting out some kind of charade. I don't like adapting to celibacy when my lover and I have been apart for two months already. On several of these hot afternoons, I daydream longingly of Greece. I wish I could teleport myself out of this bamboo camp to the edge of the Aegean, blue water spread out, waiting to be entered by men and women who live more easily in a conjoined realm of body and heart.

What a load of romantic crap! But I indulge in it as I sip my warm water and wonder when constipation becomes a serious problem. (It's been two days since I've had a meaningful visit to the stinky latrine.) Romantic crap or not, the extrovert's tendency to intertwine emotion and body works well in Greece, land of loud talkers, big huggers, passionate hand-wavers.

I shake my drowsy head back and forth. Snap out of it. I'm not on the edge of the Aegean, I'm on the edge of Burma, with cheroot smoke in my nose, in my mouth. Why not? An information officer offers me one and I tamp down the tobacco and snap off the end as if I've been doing it all my life. We light up and smoke as he shows me a few snapshots of his battalion's first few months in the jungle. He explains how people move from one camp to another, from camp to town or city, from city back to camp, bringing books, mail, supplies, job assignments, and news.

Though he never states it directly, I understand that there is a slow drain of people out of the jungle. As the SLORC buys more weapons, swells its ranks continuously with young, destitute soldiers, keeps troops near the border into the rainy season—which traditionally has been a period of détente—the ABSDF armed battalions grow smaller, worn out. Without more new recruits, it's hard to keep a guerrilla force alive.

Besides the soldiers fighting in the jungle and the undercover agents sent back into Burma, the ABSDF's other powerful battalion consists of people whose weapons are made of words. They are public-relations people and record keepers, clipping and sorting and keeping notes for Burma's unofficial history. It is a curious thing, to enter a small house in a dusty Thai town and discover dozens of metal bookshelves sagging with carefully labeled files. Political events. Business deals. Overt and subtle shifts in the regime's chain of command. The names of the dead, the missing, the presumed dead. The names of the imprisoned. Records that no one inside the country can keep. The men and women who build the files and fill the metal shelves believe that someday there will be a place in Burma for the truth they have so carefully preserved.

I am conscious, too, that there will be a time when a few of the men and women I've met here will write about their experiences. Khaing Lin still composes poetry sometimes, in the evening, and occasionally jots down her thoughts on her life, as it is now, as it was before she left her country. "But I am often tired," she tells me. "There is . . . how do you call it, when something is missing?"

"An absence?"

"Yes, but another word. A lock. A lock on inspiration?"

"A lack! You mean a lack of. A lock is on a door, to keep it closed."

"Hmm. The lack of, yes. Also the lock on. I would like to write, but it is hard. When I was in Rangoon before the strikes and nothing ever happened to me, I wrote pages and pages. Now so much happens, but it is painful to write, and tiring. Sometimes too hard." She physically shakes herself—her head, her shoulders, even her arms, which loosen and lift off her lap as she attempts to rid herself of an encumbrance.

I spend long hours with Khaing Lin, December, the other women and children in the camp. Each bird-filled green morning burns into a silent, hazy afternoon, the heat so thick that it's hard to breathe, especially when the water-boiling fires are going. During these hours, of sweat and thirst and physical discomfort, I repeat to myself: almost ten years in the jungle.

I consider living this way for one. Could I do it for one year? Doubtful. I think of the rainy season. This far north, the cold season would be bone-chillingly damp. Every morning, I stretch my aching back and hips, wondering how long it takes to get used to sleeping on bamboo. A decade?

One of the hardest things is the smallest, the most trifling. We have to haul the water up from the stream. All right. I do this task on the sly, otherwise Khaing Lin refuses to let me have the buckets, saying a guest shouldn't have to haul water. Frankly, no one should have to haul water up that fucking hill. The first time I attempted to ascend the kicked-in steps with the full buckets, I fell on my ass—twice. I lost so much water that I had to go down to the stream and refill. But it's not the hauling, or even the falling, that bothers me so much.

It's the drinking. The stream water has to be boiled long and hard. In this heat, forty to forty-five degrees Celsius, the water never cools. I don't like freezing-cold water; I don't need ice. But it's dispiriting to drink bath-temperature water when you are sweating and thirsty at midday.

As our cauldron comes to the boil, I offhandedly mention this to Khaing Lin, trying to frame it as an observation. She laughs at me. "You are suffering with the hot water. Oh, me too. We are used to it, but it is still bad. I went to Chiang Mai a couple months ago. With December. She was scared of ice cream! She didn't know anything could be so cold. It is a strange life in the jungle."

"Do you ever wonder what might have happened if you had stayed in Burma? Do you think it might be better?"

"You mean more easy?"

Is that what I'm asking? I nod.

"Inside Burma the people are less free. If you want to do political work, even if you don't go to prison, you are a prisoner. The country is still closed, though tourists can visit. I might have been sent back to prison if I had stayed."

"You were in prison?"

"Not for so long. Just two years."

Just two. Only two. "I didn't know." A bolt of shame drills through me. I am such a suck!

"Decembaa!" Khaing Lin jumps up and grabs the little girl, who is too close to the fire. She reprimands her sternly, then sends her off to play. "I worry she will fall into the fire. Aie! What a disaster, so far from a hospital."

Danger aside, cooking on the open fires is a time-consuming, physically draining task, like washing clothes by hand. Those clothes, I discover, also include the rags women use during menstruation.

"That's the way it is in the jungle." Khaing Lin shrugs. "Simple living."

We're washing clothes in the stream, which runs shallow at the edges, as streams will, and deep in the center, where we bathe in the evenings. Midmorning, it's already too hot; we sprinkle our faces and heads with water. Thump-thump, thump-thump-thump: bunched cloth beaten against flat stone, fistful after fistful. When Khaing Lin sees my ocher-and-black sarong, with its design of peacock-like birds, she takes the material in her hands and examines the unprinted side. "It's from Burma, isn't it?"

"Yeah. I bought it in Rangoon."

"At a big market?"

"No. Just a little shop on the street near my guesthouse. A tailor. But he had some nice material. His wife sewed the waist for me."

She looks carefully at the broad tube of black fabric at the top of the sarong. "It's well done. Two stitches, everything sewn inside."

"Hemmed."

"Yes. I forgot the word." She hands the cloth back to me. "We all need new clothes. We get clothes from the charities. From Europe, from the United States. Sometimes very nice. Sometimes . . ." Her voice trails off.

"Sometimes," I venture, "unbelievably ugly! So ugly no one wants to wear them, I bet."

Her eyes flash mischievously. "You are naughty."

"I'm just honest!"

"Naughty." For good measure, she says it in Burmese, too.

For a while we wash in silence. Even though we've wet our hair, our heads are baking under the sun. But it's lovely down here, by the water. Light refracts shreds of rainbow through the spray. "It's hard work," I say, and stretch my back.

"Yes. I like it, though. I love to have the clean clothes." She dunks a lime-green shirt into the water, pushes it up and down, wrings it out. "That was my most difficult thing, with living in the prison. So dirty. We never had enough water for washing. There are more bugs in prison than in the jungle."

"Where were you?"

"Insein. When I got out, I knew I couldn't stay in Burma. I was too angry. I was a strike organizer at the university. When the MI picked me up, they wanted to know all the student-union names I knew. Four different groups of men interrogated me, tortured me over two weeks."

The most common form of torture in Burma's prisons is beating. I have had so many different kinds of beatings described to me, in such careful detail, that I sometimes dream of them. I am in the cell, watching, unable to say anything, unable to stop what happens. But such a dream is not really a dream. It is the hidden truth made visible by the imagination.

Beatings with the fists, with boots, with sticks, with leather belts. Beatings standing up, beatings squatting down naked with hands clasped behind the head. Beatings tied or handcuffed to a chair. Beatings until the individual's face and body are bruised and swollen beyond recognition. Beatings until the kidney or the liver or the spleen or the intestine is irreparably damaged; beatings that cause permanent paralysis. Beatings with a black hood over the head. As though the victim in the interrogation cell, through her actions and her voice, has become her own executioner.

Khaing Lin wore such a hood through several days of torture. It made everything worse, which was the point.

The water flows past us. I look at the long-limbed trees; their green leaves point to the red mud. Her words are sometimes inaudible, drawn away by the murmuring current. "Eventually, I told them. The names of the other students." She is still ashamed. "But they had those names already. So they kept torturing me."

They didn't care about the names. I've learned that through my other interviews. This is a fact I wish I did not know. I would like to believe that people are tortured to some purpose. A purpose would not make the torture less criminal, but it would make it nominally less senseless. I would like it to be more like a Hollywood film, where the hero, through his brave silence, keeps safe the secret formula or the secret name or the secret whereabouts of the treasure.

But in the real world of interrogation there is rarely a secret. The acquisition of information is almost never the point. In the drama of torture, confession resembles the climax, but it is not the climax. The drama affirms only one resolution, the same one it begins with: that the regime will use absolute violence to wield absolute power. The individual represents her whole society. What can be done to that sentient representation, the human being? She can be beaten, cut, electrocuted, prodded, forced, forced against herself so that, finally, there is no language left, only moaning, weeping, crying out. Then silence.

Forged through brutality, through destruction of flesh and spirit, the climax is silence.

Khaing Lin stares at her hands under the water.

We sit beside the stones black with wetness, electric-blue and ocher and lime-green whorls of fabric piled beside us. We're so far away from that time. Yet it is here, in her voice, in her lit eyes. "What they do is unbelievable. But you have to believe it, don't you?

"They hit me on the very top of the head. Over and over, until they got tired. Then someone else would come. They did it softly at first, like water torture, then harder and harder, until I was about to fall down. But I was not allowed to fall down. Eventually, I lost my consciousness. After, I can't remember what happened. There is a hole. In my memory. There is a hole right here." She taps her head and laughs.

Someone calls out to us. We look downstream toward the sound of the voice. But no one is there. It's just the water, talking. Khaing Lin does that distinctive body wave again—head, arms, long slender torso—as though she were shaking herself out like a carpet. Then she pulls another piece of longyi through the funnel of her fist and begins to pound the cloth against stone.

CHAPTER 39

LOVE IN THE MOONSHINE

. . . .

The Bodyguard comes to get me from Khaing Lin's hut. We walk across the center of the camp and down the little hillock, along the path. I'm relieved to feel the first cool breath of evening on my arms.

There are visitors at the cook shelter, some Karen officers from the post upriver. Maung, sitting among them, grins at me with uncharacteristic goofy pride. Small yellow candles light the table, which is scattered with bundles of cheroots and little bowls, mostly empty of peanuts. I smell roasting meat. We've eaten soy and rice since we got here; the decadence of cooked flesh makes me lift my head and peer at the charcoal grill on the other side of the table. "Is it chicken?"

Maung rubs his hands together. "It's monkey." He's been telling me since we got here that monkey meat is sweet and delicious. I don't think I want to eat a monkey. It would be too much like eating a second cousin I've never met.

I turn to the radio operator, who blinks at me with owl eyes. "Is it really monkey?"

"Ma di boo." I don't know. He adds, also in Burmese, that the Karen officers brought the meat. Odd: he's always keen to practice his English with me.

As soon as I sit down beside one of the gregarious visitors, he picks up the bottle on the table and asks, "Are you thirsty? This will defeat your thirst!"

Why didn't I see it immediately? They're all drunk. The clear stuff in the plastic bottle isn't water, it's hooch, presumably the famous Karen moonshine I've heard stories about. So strong it could knock over a bull elephant. So strong it'll make you see triple. Stronger than the strongest vodka. Paint thinner, essentially, but without the utility of that worthy poison.

I smile back at Maung, handsomely rakish in the candlelight, and glance around at the rest of the men. Then I laugh out loud and smack my little glass on the bamboo tabletop.

Three hours later, the camp is asleep and we've just managed to send the Karens stumbling away to bed, giggling and burping, with Gorky's champion. Now there is just me and my lover left, touching each other under the table and breathing in the drug of sweaty flesh.

Praise the Lord for Karen moonshine! It's the aphrodisiac the world has been searching for. Or, at least, the only love potion Maung needs to forget his duty, his example, his important moral codes. We're horny as hell and alone for the first time in two weeks. He wriggles his hand under my longyi, between my legs, and—

Wait—

What's that, the shadow falling across the path near the shelter's entrance?

Oh. Of course. It's just me and my beloved and his bodyguard.

Fine. Who cares, really? He's just doing his job. Ubiquitous yet unobtrusive, like a butler in an old English manor. I want you to fuck me. I think I just said that out loud. To Maung, not the bodyguard, who is a stone's throw away.

Just to make sure Maung knows—maybe I only thought it last time—I slur, "I want you to fuck me."

He murmurs something back in Burmese. Then, still in Burmese, "Let's go down."

At first I don't know what he means. For a few gleeful seconds, I think he's going to go down on me! Oh, I love Karen moonshine, I love it. Why haven't we been drinking it since we got here?

But the translation is wrong, because he's not going down at all, he's getting up, up; he's so much taller when he's standing. Does he want me to give him a blow job? In the cook shelter?

"Come on," he whispers, pulling on my hand. "Stand up!"

I didn't think so.

My body floats off the hard bench like a helium-filled inflatable doll. My genitals rise (oh, the swell and the burn, oh-oh-oh) and my arms reach out for him, all the pieces ascending of their own accord, because it can't be my legs doing the work. I can't feel my legs. Fascinating, really. I thought it was hyperbole when scandalously drunk people said, "I can't feel my legs."

I can't feel my legs, but my pussy pulsates wonderfully between them. I've never wanted someone to fuck me so badly. Let's do it here, on the communal table. *Vive la révolution!* Impregnate me tonight. I grab onto his shoulders (because I've lost my balance and am about to fall down), and he props me up. "Are you all right? Can you walk?"

Walk? Are you kidding? Look at me, I can fly! I lean into him again and whisper a series of loving obscenities in his ear. He kisses me quickly, refusing to get too involved, then places his hands on my hips and spins me around. "Go." He nudges my butt. Forward, march!

We stumble out of the kitchen shelter. Oh, how beautiful. It must be very late, because the no-longer-full moon is up again, whitewashing the

bamboo and the rocks and Maung's hair with mercury. Glimmer, glimmer everywhere. I think I said that out loud. I make sure I did by repeating it. "Glimmer, glimmer. Where are we going?"

"Let's go down to take a bath."

"A bath?"

"In the stream. We'll go swimming."

When viewed late at night from the top rather than the bottom, the hill
is actually a cliff. I notice this as I fall from one kicked-in step to the next
on my heels, my flip-flops splayed away from the bottom of my feet so that
I step into the mud. How slippery it is. There are *nats* in the forest, those
benign Burmese spirits in the trees—no, really, there are. They keep me
from tumbling down and breaking a significant bone, or a couple of ver-
tebrae in my neck.

Suddenly, here are the stones, there, steps away, the stream, cricket
song in the water rush, water full of silverware, a thousand polished forks
and spoons. . . . No, that's just the moonlight. Maung drops his bag—
what's in there? a towel? his gun?—on the bank and takes my hand. We
walk right into the water and sit down, roll like otters. I can't believe how
cold the water is, and I don't care. We fumble with our longyis, the cloth
suddenly heavy in the cold water. I lift mine up, he unknots and lowers his.
We press against each other's warm flesh.

Trying to get a better purchase on the stones, I shift position, lift my
head, and see a red light glowing in the bushes on the bank, maybe twenty
feet away. "What's that?" I ask, knowing exactly what it is: the bodyguard's
cheroot. Now, on the brink of the Act, as ass-bruising as it may be, I no
longer feel inclusive of the bodyguard. A wave of sober clarity hits me.
Such a shame, that wave, when I'm still so lustfully drunk.

"Maung, tell him to go away. He should just go back up the hill. It's
not like anyone is going to try to assassinate you right now." I hope.

"You tell him. He will listen to you right now better than he will listen to me."

"Fuck off!"

"No, he will, I promise. A woman is more powerful than a man in a moment like this."

So I shout at the bushes, in Burmese, "Go away now." The bushes respond with a deep murmur that I cannot understand. "What did he say?"

"He says he doesn't want to leave me alone here."

"You're not alone!" I shout again, "Go away!" rising clumsily to a squatting position.

The cheroot burns redder: he's taking a drag. Then I gasp and squint. There are two cheroots in those bushes!

"Maung, look. There are two men down here, watching us! Two of them! It's not just your guy."

"Karen, never mind. Let's just take a bath. We'll enjoy the water. Come."

He pulls me from the shallows into the deeper current. We half float, our feet pulled downstream. Thirty seconds later, we are entwined like sea creatures and newly inspired, inside the protective shadow of a tree, our wet clothes more or less out of the way.

Maung pushes me down, crushing my cold naked ass against a pointy chunk of rock. I shift, but the new spot is too slick with algae, so I wriggle back to the chunk, doing my best to remain open to his thrusts. It works, ahh! It doesn't work, shit. It works, ahh! It doesn't work, damn. What's wrong? He keeps missing the mark. We kiss, we splash, we groan. An image flashes into my mind: the flayed red backs of desperate salmon, spawning themselves to death. I want to cry. Maung starts laughing.

"What's so funny?"

He laughs again, and kisses my cheek. "Sorry."

He's lost his erection. The wave of clarity crests again and knocks me in the face. If it weren't for the stupid bodyguard, we wouldn't be here in the deeper water, struggling to fuck. We're in the jungle, for Christ's sake! Couldn't we just have had sex in the trees?

"Do you have a gun in that bag you left on the shore?"

"Why?" Maung asks.

"Because I want to shoot your bodyguard!"

He laughs harder, rolls off me, and splashes into the water on his back. "You can't shoot him," he says, giggling. "He loves me!"

I stand up, slapping my hands on the water. Then I start to shiver. It's unnerving, in the hot season, to feel so cold. The second we emerge from the stream, clothes dragging with water, our hair plastered to our faces, the bodyguard and his fellow voyeur beat it through the brush. We hear them tramping all the way up the hill, their hysterical laughter hushed but audible. As Maung and I ascend, my teeth begin to chatter. I start crying, primarily out of sexual frustration. It's a new kind of crying for me, I must admit—tearless, jaw-clenched, hiccuping.

Maung and I are alone, finally, when we reach Khaing Lin's hut.

"Are you all right?" he asks.

"I'm great," I say, wiping my nose on my arm.

He embraces me tenderly. Our bodies touch, which makes me aware of something clinging to my leg. I wonder vaguely if it's a leech. Maung wipes the hair away from my eyes. He has a sweet, serious expression on his face. "Sometime, maybe tomorrow, I have to ask you about irony."

"What? Irony?"

"Yes. Because I know you are not feeling 'great,' but you said you were. Is this irony?"

I let out a dry sob, which sounds like the bark of a large dog.

"Oh, Karen, I'm sorry. This was not a romantic evening." When I say nothing in response, he whispers, "Yee Yee Cho, I'll see you in the morning, okay?"

"Okay. Good night."

I watch him walk away until the darkness swallows him up. The moon is long gone now, dropped behind the trees. Shivering, dripping, I consider the cacophony of crickets and other night insects. They are so loud, yet no one even hears them anymore. But if I have a well-deserved crying jag I'll wake up fifty people and have the whole camp gossiping. I can't cry inside the hut; that would be too disruptive. I can't cry here, right outside; the walls are too thin. Wandering off into the black trees does not appeal.

A match strikes inside the little house, then the glow of flame shines through the woven wall. Khaing Lin comes out blinking, sleep-addled, curly hair sprung off her head. She holds up the candle and appraises the situation. "Oh, Yee Yee Cho! Wait a minute." She slips back inside, returns with a towel and a longyi. "There is some water in the pot, on the fire." She takes my hand and leads me to the cooking area behind the hut. I dry myself and step into the clean longyi without falling down. She restarts the fire and we sit on our usual perches. A moment later, she hands me a steaming enamel cup.

"Burmese men," she intones sagaciously. Then can't help herself and starts to laugh.

I smile miserably and sip my water.

Hot water. How sweet it is, how delicious.

CHAPTER 40

WOMEN'S WORK

. . . .

Someone comes to fetch me in the morning. How kind of Maung not to send the bodyguard. My beloved and I greet each other bashfully and drink our tea on the veranda of the hut where he's staying. Other men move around inside; we say nothing to each other about our aborted lovemaking. We commiserate about our hangovers and take aspirin together.

After the first pot of tea is finished, I lower my voice. "Maung, I need to talk to you about something." It pisses me off that I have to confide in him; after last night I want to be cool and independent. But I'm not. I need him.

"What's wrong?"

"It's been days since I've had a bowel movement." The change of location, the stress of living among strangers, the low-fiber diet: I know the reasons. But still, constipation is supposed to be temporary.

"Hmm." He ducks into the hut and consults at length with the other men. I cringe, listening to this manly discussion about my inability to shit.

I am to have no secrets, not one. One of the men reappears, smiles at me, and rushes off.

Ten minutes later, he returns to the hut with a little brown bottle and hands it to Maung, who gives it to me. I twist off the cap. The thick liquid is also brown, and smells like a combination of fermented tree bark, molasses, and lemon. "Tamarind," Maung explains. "And other herbs. A jungle cure. It will work fast, so be careful."

I hope it's not poisonous. I swallow two teaspoons right away, and say goodbye to Maung. He's off to check out the latest camp improvement: a water pump. Hurrah, I think; a pump will save the women from hauling water up from the stream every day. I return to Khaing Lin's and play with December, carefully observing my bowels for signs. Will the laxative work in an hour?

No. In two?

Nothing.

Khaing Lin, December, and a few other women eat noodles for lunch. My appetite on the wane, I decline the noodles and opt for three more teaspoons of the laxative. So far, it has had no discernible effect. So much for jungle cures.

Later in the afternoon, when the first coolness slips, amphibious, out of the shade, Khaing Lin tells me the women are going down to the stream. "Isn't it too early to bathe?" I ask.

"It's not for bathing. We help with the pump. You can come with us. To watch."

In a clearing at the top of the hill, men are tearing open bags of cement. Maung stands beside the impressive-looking water pump. The men will lay a cement foundation for this new machine and the generator necessary to power it. The leveled-out patch of ground is twelve or fourteen feet square. Maung comes over and chats with the women, slowly working his way closer to me.

He turns to me with a smile and explains in English that they're going to build a shelter around the pump and generator and possibly add on a new latrine as well. "A new latrine is a good idea," I say, without complaining about the one they have now: a filthy hole in a rickety shack. Very buggy, too. I don't mind bugs, generally, but the resident centipede gave me a start the first time I saw it. Longer than my foot and lightning quick, I initially thought it was a snake.

Maung's hand brushes the back of mine. *Zing!* Amazing how well the electrical connection between us still works, despite moonlit fiascoes, constipation, centipedes. As he turns to say something else to the women, his shoulder grazes mine. He moves past the group, walks back over to the water pump, and looks at me. We stand there staring at each other. I would like to have sex with this man for the rest of my life. (Or, for that matter, even just once or twice more, please God.) Is that a good-enough reason to get married?

What am I thinking?

He looks down at the prepared ground. "It will take us until dinnertime to finish pouring the cement. We didn't want to start earlier in the day because the work would be too hot for the women."

"What are the women going to do?" I ask.

Khaing Lin answers, "We're going to bring the stones for the foundation up the hill."

"Stones from the stream?" I ask. It's not easy to mix cement by hand, but carrying stones up that hill is not a simple operation, either. That's a lot of river rocks.

She holds up the bucket she has in her hand. "In here. On our heads."

"Really? That's an interesting division of labor," I observe. "The women do the heaviest work."

No one responds. The women are already filing down the hill, each one carrying an aluminum bucket. I pick one up. I have no intention of standing around to watch communal work. Khaing Lin leads the way down the steep path. The women below are a milling rainbow in their bright longyis and T-shirts. Halfway there, she glances over her shoulder. "Yee Yee Cho, we do not want you to help."

"That's too bad," I mutter under my breath.

"*Sa-yeh sehyama* doesn't need to do this work."

"But you are also a *sa-yeh sehyama* and you can do this work." She protests, but I won't let her get away with it. "It's true, Khaing Lin. You write poetry. You make notes for a book about your life in the jungle. You're a writer. But you're also going to carry stones up this hill in a bucket."

She cocks her head charmingly and raises her eyebrows. "But you are a guest."

"I'm also strong." I hold up my arm, muscleman style, and flex my biceps. She rolls her eyes. "I've come to the camp to see how people live here. How will I know if I don't do the same work?"

"Yee Yee Cho, you are very naughty."

We join the other women.

There is the huge banyan tree; the wide stony beach stretches beyond it. I arrived here almost two weeks ago in the back of a pickup truck, on the other side of the stream. That moment in time seems distant—months ago, years.

Khaing Lin and I kneel down. The stones in the stream will be easier to collect than the ones packed tight on the beach. Rippling large, they rise up smaller and gleaming as my cupped hands lift from the water. They're dappled grays and blacks, with an occasional flash of dark red. Unlike the flat chunks of slate downstream, these are mostly round; they roll and rumble against one another, then clatter into the aluminum bucket. A group of women return, ready to carry up more stones. There are at least twelve of us loading up, making a tremendous racket.

Khaing Lin shows me how to wrap a rag around my hand and place the flat coil of it on the top of my head. The first time, she helps me hoist the bucket up onto the small round pad. It's a shock—I thought I was stronger. How much does a large bucketful of stones weigh? Twenty pounds? More. Wobbling slightly, I begin to walk.

The ascent of the hill is no laughing matter, though the women filing up and down sometimes laugh and call out encouragement or advice. Water drips through our hair onto our faces and necks. Within four trips of dumping loads into the growing batter of cement, our shirts and longyis are soaked. After I've dumped six loads at the worksite, every return trip to the edge of the stream brings with it an irresistible desire: I want to lower my mouth and drink—for the first time in two weeks—cool water.

Within fifteen minutes, we are transformed from women into a carrying factory. A pause in the work breaks the rhythm of the machine. Unless a woman loses her balance and needs help, we work on our own, together, scooping, loading, carrying, dropping the load into the pile up the hill. The cloth coil on the head is a crucial aid, but for me it's an exercise in good posture and balance to keep it there. Each time I've filled up with stones, I have to lower my body far enough to get hold of the bucket's handle, then heave it straight up to keep the cloth from sliding off my head.

Physical labor relaxes the mind. The laboring body becomes its own purpose, expressing its own rhythm and wisdom as it forges on through aches, pains, exhaustion. And hangovers. The only thing that's left of the Karen Moonshine Mistake is a ferocious thirst. Half a dozen of us stop at the foot of the hill to rest. A water bottle is passed around. I take a small gulp and pass it on to the next woman, knowing I could have drunk the whole thing. Wishing. Then it's time to put our buckets on our heads again.

I linger, rubbing my left shoulder, where an old injury howls, "Why are you doing this to me?" I dig my fingers into the muscle under my scapula and watch the women ascend in tandem, their shoulders and hips swaying in opposite directions each time they lift a foot to find purchase on the water-slick path and rise one step higher.

How I love the human body. I love it for precisely this, my torn old muscle and Khaing Lin's graceful neck and head balancing a freight of rock. Vulnerability and tremendous power. Contradiction is made human by our flesh.

She is almost at the top of the hill. I pick up my bucket, settle it on my headcloth, and begin to walk. My eyes scan from the wet clay to the woman a few steps ahead of me. The passage of so many feet has worn away the kicked-in footholds, so we walk with extra caution. I glance up. A woman carrying a hoe is on her way down. Wherever there's a break in the work line, she digs new steps out of the clay. Whenever a water carrier reaches her, she steps away onto the sheer incline so we can pass. Each one of us mutters a breathy thank-you when we reach the new footholds.

I dump my rocks onto the pile. A few more women arrive, upend their loads. We can see that the foundation is almost laid now. The man overseeing the work claps his hands and announces, "You're finished!" We let out a cheer. Khaing Lin hands around a bottle of a neon-pink, warm liquid. We gulp down the flat sweetness and grin at the square of wet cement, at the water pump, at the cluster of camp children who have attended this show all afternoon. Tree shadows fall long across the messy building site and our sweaty faces.

Khaing Lin smooths back her damp hair, drops her bucket with an unapologetic clank, and says, "Let's go take a bath." We fetch shampoo, soap, clean clothes, then head back down to the water wearing our bathing longyis pulled chest-high and tucked under our arms. Trees and boulders, bushes and red-clay banks form a cool tunnel around us. We recline in the water, lathering soap over our grimy skin, into our hair, letting all the dirt flow away in the steady current. Most of us stay for a long time in the stream, talking, resting, shedding the day. Our bodies, which have been so loaded down, float up almost weightless to the surface.

Much later, after we've eaten dinner in the falling dark and put December to bed, Khaing Lin turns on her little shortwave radio to listen to Voice of America's Burmese programming. Everyone in the camp listens to the VOA and the BBC. Those without radios go to their neighbors' to listen. After news of Burma—the generals' latest development projects, the newly arrested NLD members—come the English lessons, dictated in a haughty British accent. Listening intently to every word, Khaing Lin sits in front of a mirror the size of her palm and brushes her clean hair by candlelight.

"I'm going to look at the stars," I tell her, and step outside. I walk toward the center of the camp and turn around slowly, surveying the huts. Each one is lit by candles and dotted here and there with the red embers of cheroots.

The call-and-answer part of the English lesson has begun. The women are the most determined and the least embarrassed to respond to the radio as though it were a living teacher. "Would you like to go to the library tomorrow?"

"Yes," respond voices high and low, lighthearted and solemn. "I would like to go to the library tomorrow." Plates clatter on the other side of the camp; a toddler complains loudly and is hushed. I make out the singsong pitch of Khaing Lin's voice among the others and walk toward it. Crickets fall silent around my feet. My friend's words grow distinct in the darkness.

The radio asks, "Would you like to go to the university tomorrow?"

"Yes, I would like to go to the university tomorrow," Khaing Lin answers, the irony that so puzzles my lover complicating her tone. Then, eclipsing the next question, she breaks into the irreverent laughter of a rebellious student.

CHAPTER 41

IN THE JUNGLE, NOT FAR AWAY

. . . .

We're walking through the jungle. When I ask the word for *jungle,* the bodyguard tosses his hand toward the leaves and shadows. "This is not really jungle. Just many trees with a path." Six of us travel the incline single file. Breathing hard, Maung, too, asserts that these trees and vines are "close," whereas the real jungle is still "far away."

"Close to what?"

"Roads. Thai villages. On this trip, you will not see the deep jungle." This feels like a failing on my part. I glance from my feet to the extensive-layered, thick, variously green, complexly viny foliage. Then I glance back down at the path. Hot season usually means dry, but here the red earth is wet and raw.

Like my feet. My expensive sports sandals are useless because we repeatedly trudge through streams. It's too time-consuming to peel the Velcro straps apart and stick them together again for the water crossings, so I leave them on, not wanting to hold the group up; the wet straps rub and rub. Wherever the one-inch bands of high-tech material touch my feet— the loop just below my ankles, the edge of my toes, the band around the heel—the skin burns. Within an hour or two, I will have strap lines of blisters on both feet.

Ostensibly, I chat with the bodyguard to practice my Burmese, relearning the words for spider, tree, snake. In actuality, I am preparing to make a deal. I ask the word for blister. A minute later, he's thrilled to give me his orange flip-flops in exchange for my sandals. Good riddance—he can have them. He steps into the cushioned rubber soles, adjusts the Velcro, waves off my (insincere) concern that they're slightly too small. "Let's go," he says, and we do.

An hour later, we pause to rest. I ask how he's doing. Loves the sandals, they're very good! He bends to admire the stupid North American things. I stare at his sweat-rimmed baseball cap, conscious of the large blisters between my toes—new blisters, from his loose flip-flops, which match the hot little geysers rising elsewhere on my feet.

We will get there soon enough. I will not complain. It's just a few hours' walk. I remind myself of how many dissidents used to live middle-class lives in Burma, until violence and politics brought them here. I think of good-looking blond Charlie, who sometimes wears high heels, slogging for miles through the monsoon jungle with a battalion of Karen soldiers, puking up her malaria pill only to dig through vomit to find it again.

I will not complain.

How mortifying, to want to complain so badly, especially about small patches of irritated skin. It's not like I've been shot, is it? If I lived here as long as Khaing Lin and Aye Aye and the other women, I would toughen up like them. I would learn to fold my longyi so that it wouldn't loosen and slide down all the time. (Why am I wearing a long skirt on a hiking trip? Because everyone else is. I am walking with five men; they wear longyis. Carrying stones uphill for three hours, the women wore longyis; they laughed whenever mine started to drop down my waist.) If I stayed here for a year or two, I would learn to endure more stoically.

I consider this claim as we trudge across another stream. It's bullshit. Not because I would be physically incapable of living here but because I would not want to stay. To be held here by history, by fate, even by passion-ate conviction, would suffocate me. I would rather sell deep-fried grass-hoppers in the Mae Sot market than live in a jungle camp for a year, never mind a decade.

After another stream-crossing, I furtively carry the flip-flops pressed against my leg. The path has narrowed again. We return to walking single file, Maung ahead of me. He can't see my bare feet. Painless bliss!

I'm impressed that he moves so quickly. His shining head angles down, his arms barely swing. He doesn't lead a physical life in the cities and towns of his exile, but the rapid pace returns to him with ease. Bare-foot, I can match his speed. Just when I'm starting to enjoy the feel of my toes digging into the earth, the bodyguard loudly asks, "Where are your shoes?"

I flick them, twinned flippers, at my side. He grunts (consternation), then adds, "It's dangerous to walk without shoes." A pair of overlarge flip-flops is not going to protect me from anything, but I say nothing, know-ing it's the lack of civility that rankles. Without breaking stride, Maung shoots a look over his shoulder. "We may be in the jungle, but we do wear shoes."

Yes, my love. It's not deep jungle, though, is it?

"If you go barefoot and step on a . . ." He searches for the word, the an-tennae of his mind waving around like those of the ants on the tree we just passed. " . . . a thorn . . . no one will carry you." The man in front of him asks him what he said. He translates. The man glances at me.

I keep walking barefoot. Just a few more minutes. I'm too embarrassed to tell Maung how much my feet hurt.

The oval of sweat on his back lengthens. I listen to the musical voices of the guides ahead of me, talking. Around us is more intricate music, lay-ers of birdsong rising as the heat lessens. A few steps along, when a brown shadow with a streak of red plumage torpedoes across the path, I find my-self wishing I could walk after it. I ask the men what the bird is called, but they don't know.

Other animals are here, too, hiding in the hollow trunks of old trees and the rotting stumps, in the dense undergrowth. Some watch as we walk, their eyes on our strange bare arms. Macaques. Snakes. A cobra or two. Gibbons. There are panthers in this jungle, but not very many. Not as many as before. War takes up land, and land is the animals' single need.

The Karen people eschew the human-destroying trade of opium smuggling, but they've financed their side of the war by cutting down the last old-growth Dahat Teak forests on earth. They sell this precious contraband to the Thais, who sell it to Japan, Europe, North America. The Burmese military government also auctions off timber, gems, oil, and fish to various multinationals, polluting the country's rivers and seas in the process. The Canadian government does exactly the same thing. What government doesn't pimp its territory to the highest bidder?

Humans have always waged war against the wilderness. And animals have always been civilians, ignorant of bombs. A young man in Chiang Mai who does environmental work told me that sometimes wild elephants step on land mines, then wander, bleeding and disoriented, or furious with pain, into villages. He believes that wild elephants, and Asian tapirs, and the capped langur monkey, and a little deer called Fea's muntjac will become extinct in our lifetime. "We're killing them. Forever," he told me. "But no one cares. No one even notices."

I stop to rest, and notice. Even the trees ask for that. Since I was a child, I've liked to stand among trees. Being upright like me but taller, they often had some wisdom to impart. They still do.

Say nothing. Breathe. Bend.

The men have passed me. I stand alone on the path, listening to their fading footsteps. Bend. I will have to change. Beyond putting on my flip-flops. Maung and I will have a child—an alteration I can't fathom at the moment, with my muddy feet and bounding mind. Really, I should say I will have a baby, because who knows where Maung will be when I give birth?

Not long after I arrived in Burma, I thought the place would alter me somehow. And it did—in the sense that we are always altered by powerful experience. Only now, though, with this difficult love, do I sense my self changing. Breaking open. This is what I am—these are my elements, scattered. After breakage comes . . . what?

Less self. And less certainty. But the spirit augmented.

"Yee Yee Cho!" Maung yells. "Where are you?"

"I'm in the jungle. But not far away," I yell back, and keep walking. Barefoot.

I wake up with the gun pressing against my anklebone. Like a finger. At first I think it is a finger, attached to the tattooed hand of the soldier who sat here beside me, reading a Burmese paperback while I dozed. But he's gone now. The paperback lies facedown on the stool where he sat. He left the gun on the sleeping platform beside me.

I presume that the safety catch is on. Nothing untoward would have happened if I accidentally knocked the gun to the dirt floor. When I was still awake, I asked him what kind of gun it was. "M16." I made a mental note of the relatively short barrel.

"Where does it come from?"

"Cambodia." But I thought M16s were American-made.

I rise up on one arm, nudging the M16 with my foot. Like the other guns I've seen on the border, it looks well used. Old. Could it have killed people during Pol Pot's reign of terror? Though the Khmer Rouge did not favor bullets. Too expensive. Maybe it killed people in Vietnam.

My face, where it pressed against my elbow as I slept, is marked with lines from my cotton sleeve. I can feel them like thin scars, from the top of my cheek to the place where my ear begins. How long was I out? I don't usually fall asleep in the presence of strangers with guns on their laps. I sit up and rub my eyes.

This is where I am to bunk for a week or two. Maung and his bodyguard will stay in a similar hut slightly farther down the slope. Despite the thatch and the dirt floor, the room feels clinical. Usually these places are stuffed with personal belongings—Burmese calendars of popular singers, Thai posters of fruit and waterfalls, photos, little mirrors. Talismans that ward off no-one-ness.

In contrast, this hut is full of anonymity. The view through the doorway is straight down the narrow valley we switchbacked up—when? Two hours ago? Three? Above the mass of trees, the sky glows magenta. The trees are already black. Voices filter down the hillside. From below, I hear a guitar. It's not a tape deck because the player misses the same chord twice and picks up the phrase again, repeats, repeats, faintly and patiently melodic, like a child practicing piano scales. The sound brings tears to my eyes.

CHAPTER 42

RAGE AGAINST THE MACHINE

.   .   .   .

This place is a lively village, with many Karen families living and working alongside the ABSDF members. Small clusters of huts spread over the thickly forested hillside. I take a walk on my own through the heart of the camp—Maung doesn't want me to go too far away without a guide—and marvel at the elegant system of irrigation. Long pieces of bamboo channel water to a dozen gardens at different levels. In the morning and the evening, the bell-like music of fast-falling water fills the clearings.

In one of those clearings, people keep rabbits. A Karen woman explains that they've had mixed success with rabbit breeding. Too many other animals besides humans are interested in the easy pickings, and disease occasionally wipes out entire litters and breeder pairs. Nevertheless, the rabbits continue to be amorous, and the men keep getting better at building snakeproof hutches.

Glancing over my shoulder, I quickly slip away on a path that leads to a less inhabited area at the edge of the camp. A brand-new meetinghouse stands there, with a view across the river into Burma. I lean out the big window, wondering how far the range of a rocket launcher is. The river is wide, but not that wide.

My eyes are in Burma, my feet in Thailand. How strange borders are. Even the obvious demarcation of the river seems an arbitrary line to distinguish one stretch of land from another. It wouldn't be that hard to swim across it. The trees, the animals, the mud, the nature of pain and of suffering, the way people die: it's all the same across the water. But for everyone in this industrious, well-run camp full of children and guns and military fatigues the far bank is dangerous, enemy territory as well as homeland.

Considering the work that has gone into this structure—the fresh yellow weave of the walls, the carved beams, the bamboo-strip floor—I wonder how long it and the rest of the outpost will last. Three years? Five? Maybe six months, if the Burmese military infiltrates that porous emerald wall across the water. The KNU base of Manerplaw was like a small city, a bastion for both the Karen people and the democratic movement. But the Burmese military overran it in January 1995, looting and burning everything.

I know only the basic facts about Manerplaw, but when people discuss the loss of that stronghold their eyes tear up, their voices tremble. Even Maung, who is so matter-of-fact about everything, including losses, doesn't like to talk about it. "After Manerplaw, we have to do revolution differently. That is what we learned. The Burmese army is more powerful than our forces. We accept that. But there are other ways to be powerful. That is what we learn now, slowly."

When he talks this way, measured, sure of himself, I feel sure of him also. English is a recent second language; in Burmese, his voice and his words are more incisive and weighted. For a politician—isn't a dissident a politician without an expense account?—he has the rare diamond quality: he inspires trust. At least among some. It surprises me how much I trust him, not just with my safety here but with my safety in general. My heart.

Yet he has been dishonest with me, and he is often far away, inaccessible. That is my future with him. I say it to myself over and over, attempting to muster . . . anger? rejection? acceptance?

I'm testing them all out. I dig through my emotions, trying to find what I am, unbury my private nature. But, more and more often, the big primordial Nature takes me by the shoulders, gives me a good shake, and says, "Child. Baby. Dig that, honey."

For the first time in my lustful life, lust has a purpose beyond its own fulfillment. I want him to fuck me because I want to get pregnant. A shocking admission. It makes me think of my mother, who often says, "Be careful what you wish for." A baby is a squalling, shitting, utterly needy concept. Not a concept. A human being. A mongrel boy or girl born whole out of this fragmented world we find ourselves in. Is that profound love? Or my ovaries on overdrive?

I am a maze. Or treacherous. I worry about trusting him, but can he trust me? Half an hour after fantasizing about the lovemaking moment of conception (a simultaneous orgasm, of course), I busily compare one kind of life with another. I examine the life I have had in Greece. Short flights from Athens to London, Paris, Amsterdam, San Sebastián. Friends in each city. I miss the great calm Europe of the mind, the long conversations over food and good wine, in languages that are easier than Burmese. Where will I be able to become myself?

That the self changes constantly is a tenet of Buddhism and a fact of life. With motherhood, everything changes. First the body stretches, then the heart, then the whole shape of one's existence. Love and selflessness become a function of biology.

But I didn't need to have a baby to figure that out. Burmese people have taught me a similar lesson. To care is the essential human act. A long time ago, as an infant, my life depended upon such care. That little one grew and thrived. But she didn't grasp until recently that nurture is the crucial template of all human life.

Is it a twist of the poetic mind that after the word *nurture* the next one that comes to me is *torture*? Or is it because we're in the jungle?

I finally asked Maung about the executions. He came to see me at my guesthouse in Mae Sarieng the day before we left for the ABSDF camp. "Other officers made that decision. It happened in the North. I wasn't there. They found evidence of treason. There was no place to imprison traitors." He started to light a cigarette, then stopped. "We've had to do things that, in the other life, we would never do." He turned his face away. My will failed me. I didn't ask him about the allegations of torture, the woman. How many. The names.

I watch him among the people here. Do they trust him? They obviously respect him. Most everyone defers to him subtly or overtly. Demure smiles from the girls. Indulgent, motherly nods from older women. Young men gaze admiringly as he passes. I don't think I've really believed it until now. That he is a leader. He has power over people's lives.

Is that why I trust him? Not because he is trustworthy but because he has power? A narrow power in strained circumstances, but that only makes his life, and therefore my own, more intense. Any man who is powerful in his world exerts a magnetism, drawing many toward him, repelling others just as strongly.

When he walks around the camp, he could be any famous leader. He cuts a far more arresting figure than Clinton, not as tall but much better-looking. He even stands with an air of utter self-possession. I study him. There is no doubt about it: that wholeness and self-confidence is attractive. Still, I question myself about the cliché of women falling in love with powerful men. Observing the swagger, I try to be critical. Sometimes I hear, or sense, the patrician affection. Yes, my children, I have arrived. I will try to ensure that all is running smoothly. Yes, it is good to see you, too. I wish I could be among you more often.

But I'm being unfair. He is affectionate with people, and kind, but he doesn't hold forth or talk down to them. He is their leader; they give way to him. That's part of the culture as well as part of his position. As far as I can tell, their regard for him is genuine. And many Burmese men swagger, ceremoniously tying and retying the knotting fold of their longyis.

I've heard the joke, several times. Why are so many white women hooked up with Burmese dissidents? It's all in the wraparound skirt.

Two men interrupt these thoughts. They wear jogging shorts, not longyis, but they immediately command my attention. I watch from above as they come up the path, Karen men, muscular as triathletes, quick-footed despite the incline and their impressive cargo. Between them, strapped to a bamboo pole, is a monitor lizard, gray-and-yellow-scaled, almost four feet long. Many coils of rope fasten the living animal to the pole, testifying to the lizard's strength.

Monitors are powerful carnivores. While not normally a threat to large animals—like us—they can be dangerous if provoked. I'm sure being tied up like that is extremely provoking. A thinner nylon twine binds its jaws shut. I step closer, my hand out. The javelin-blade head hangs down at an awkward angle, eyes open but resigned.

The hunters have climbed higher up the path. They stare at me harder than I stare at the lizard, surprised to find me alone in the beautiful empty building. "I wonder if it's thirsty," I say to the man in front.

He immediately responds, "We are also thirsty." The other man, younger, wearing a Rage Against the Machine T-shirt, laughs loudly. He wipes the sweat from his face and gives me a disarming smile. Rage against the machine, indeed.

"I have some water." I hold out my water bottle to the thirsty man, but he refuses. I insist. I point at the lizard. "Or I will give it to him." He smiles and takes the bottle.

"We've been walking for a couple hours," Rage Against the Machine says as his friend gulps audibly.

"Drink all of it. I'm going back up to the camp in a few minutes." I have to return soon or Maung will send out a search party. I don't know the words in Burmese, so I try in Thai. *"Tukouwad sia-jai,"* I say. I'm sorry for the lizard. Literally, the phrase means, The lizard breaks my heart.

The men laugh again. "Are you Buddhist?"

"A little. Enough." But do you need to be a Buddhist to feel sorry for a lizard? "Will you give him some water when you get home?"

Neither man responds, though Rage Against the Machine says "Thank you" and hands me the bottle. As though in a dance, they change carrying arms at the same time, stepping around either end of the pole. Just as they lift it back up to their fresh shoulders, a ripple shudders through their arms and down their bodies. The quaking radiates from the lizard, who undulates his long, roped-up self in slow motion. The hunters shout, dance an involuntary jig, and grasp the ends of the carrying pole with both hands.

Then it's over. The animal is motionless once more, defeated.

"Will you give him some water?" I repeat.

"Yes, yes," says the man in front impatiently. They begin to walk again, slowly—the gravelly path past the new building is steep. The tip of the dinosaur tail pokes over the man's shoulder. I watch them go, wanting to run after the monitor lizard with my water bottle.

I hope they kill the animal soon, but they probably won't. The point of a living reptile is that it can survive for days on end, fresh meat at the ready in a place without refrigeration.

CHAPTER 43

SPARROW HANDS

· · · ·

I tilt my head back and open my mouth. Starlight pours down my throat.

I hope it's a laxative. Nine days and counting. What a grave insult it is to assert that someone is full of shit. I've eaten almost nothing for two days. I don't want to drink water. But I must, and I do, and I've been peeing a lot in the past twenty-four hours because a particular stinging sensation informed me yesterday morning that I also have a bladder infection. Cystitis. No doubt from that stupid erotic wrestling in the stream. This is karma all right, a Buddhist lesson in cause and effect.

"What are you doing out there?" Maung's voice, from the war office. It may be a bamboo hut, but they still call it a war office. It holds radio equipment, guns, maps, important papers, good cheroots. I stand a few feet away, at the beginning of the long path that skirts the side of the small mountain. This path will lead us back down to the camp proper.

"Waiting for you." What else would I be doing? "I'm looking at the stars."

"We're just going over a few more things. We're almost done."

"There's no hurry." I am calm and dignified, almost obedient. It's the new me. I can wait for him for an hour or two at a time, meditating, or making notes. Scribbling thoughts toward my deathless prose. My time is endless. No, let me be more grandiose. I am endless, like the stars. Who believes that most of them are already dead?

Maung comes out a few minutes later and, before the others join us, kisses me quickly and well, a wet-tongued probe of significant innuendo—he's so damn good at that, the bastard—then darts ahead of me with the flashlight. We walk carefully down the hillside, on our way to a dinner of dried fish and curry.

We eat in a group, as we always do, discussing the day, sharing stories. Several people notice me pushing the food around on my plate and suggest that I eat more. I satisfy the dinner table with a few bites. The attention moves elsewhere. Voices murmur, crickets fiddle away, fifty other kinds of insects whir and hum in the invisible trees.

And then we hear . . . yodeling? Sort of. People stop chewing. Between the long, loud notes we also hear words, men talking and hooting in the dark. They must be coming up from the Salween. I can't understand what they're saying, but one of them sings a few high-pitched lines in an overdone, plaintive voice, which sends his companions into paroxyms of laughter. Everyone at the bamboo table listens intently now, amused. In the candlelight, the grooves and wrinkles made by our smiles become exaggerated, theatrical.

Maung is smiling with the rest of us, but I see something else beneath the handsome mask. I recognize this expression now. It's something like well-held sadness, but not exactly. It's evidence of the separation between himself and the men and women he loves. He thinks as they do; he feels as they do. Then he thinks something else, beyond them. He is always a step away. Is that the nature of leadership? Does the apartness come first, giving someone the aptitude to lead, or does it come after assuming the role, a toll to be paid for power?

He sees me watching him. "Soldiers back from the front line," he explains. The English words sound angular, almost crude. The yodeling singer raises his faux-feminine voice again.

"Sparrow," someone says with a grin, and gives a comical salute.

That is my introduction to the man.

The next morning, Maung and I walk down toward the river, following the stream as it tumbles fast over fallen trees and boulders as big as the backs of elephants. Here, close to the water, the well-used track widens. To celebrate our stolen moment of solitude, we walk side by side, holding hands. My happiness erases my doubts. I am deeply in love. I will marry this man, have children with him. My life will change forever, as it is changing now, and I will know joy and suffer and hate my days sometimes, as I have known joy and suffered and hated the solitude of being unmoored, completely free. An hour. Five warm fingers laced through mine. This is all I need from him to feel certain again.

Past a thick stand of bamboo, we come upon three children, frozen by our approach, each one standing on a great round rock above the small pool of water. Two boys and a girl, they are gleaming wet, their threadbare underwear hanging off their little round butts. To me they are like a sweet Greek-Asian tableau: satyrs with chocolate skin, wood nymphs cavorting in the jungle. They stare from me to Maung, back to me again. Their gazes take in our joined hands, which allow them to understand everything instantaneously. The girl, whose height suggests that she is the eldest, formally greets us. One after the other, the two boys yell, *"Hla-deh!"* like a war cry, and leap into the waiting pool of green water.

Hla-deh. That deep, soft word. My first. More than a year later, I know that in Burmese *beautiful* is a verb, not an adjective. Maung and I immediately drop hands, smile at the kids. Then we wave goodbye. He can't be away too long. The path narrows again; he walks in front. "The languages are so different," I observe, knowing that he is not usually interested in this sort of thing. "In Burmese, to be beautiful is an act. In English, it describes a state."

But he surprises me. "That is why, in Burma, and in Burmese, a woman doesn't have to be so pretty to be beautiful. The real beautiful is not the face, not the body. It happens in the heart."

I suspect that he's practicing some good old Western irony on me. But when I touch his shoulder to make him turn around his face is grave. We stare at each other for a few seconds. He steps close to me, touches his lips to my lips. Breathes "I love you" into my slightly open mouth. Then he turns away again. We keep walking.

Returning to the camp, Maung and I approach a hut where two of last night's yodeling guerrilla soldiers on leave are staying. We see that they're busy with lunch, bent over their enameled Chinese bowls like old men, clawed fingers scooping rice into their mouths. This visceral, unapologetic way of eating brings to mind my friend Barba Andreas, a seventy-five-year-old Greek shepherd whose olive grove borders mine. Like these skinny guerillas, Barba Andreas always eats as if he were starving. It's a habit learned from a time when he *was* hungry, when the young, and old, and unlucky did starve in Greece, during the Second World War, after the Germans stripped the land of food for their troops.

There's another reason that one of the men reminds me of the shepherd, though I'm not sure what it is. I look at his thick black hair; Andreas's head is pure white now. When Maung and I stop in front of the small veranda, the dark little man looks up from his bowl and asks us the polite question of greeting, "Have you eaten rice?"

Then I understand. He has a big, near-handlebar mustache very similar to Andreas's—though black and fringed here and there with grains of rice. On a Southeast Asian man, this abundant growth of facial hair is striking. He also wears a full beard. Maung introduces me as Ma Yee Yee Cho.

The mustachioed man puts his hand over his heart and sighs. "Pleased to meet you. Sweet to meet you! My name is Sparrow. I am little bird. I love to sing." He starts collecting the rice from his mustache with his tongue and his lower teeth. I smile inwardly: Andreas does the same thing. How curious to be the connective tissue between the most distant, most unlikely relations.

Sparrow asks his companion if he has finished eating from the communal plate of food. Yes, the man replies. There is nothing left but fish bones. Sparrow picks up the deep-fried fish head with his fingers and carefully fits it into his mouth. One cheek bulges out in a fish-nosed triangle as he chews. Stretched lips, stretched mustache, stretched face. He ramps up the absurdity by batting his eyelashes like Betty Boop.

A Karen man stops to say hello to Maung and the two guerrillas. Then a young woman joins us, cradling her woven shoulder bag to her stomach. "What's inside?" Maung asks. She holds the mouth of the bag open and we take turns peering down the rabbit hole at a sleeping, ears-back white bunny. "Is something wrong with it?"

Maung translates her answer. It's the second smallest of the litter, but the runt died and its territorial brothers and sisters seem to have taken a dislike to this one. They won't let it near the doe to drink any more milk. "But with some help it should be fine. The litter is already eating solid food."

Sparrow, finished with the fish head, sticks his hand into the bag and pulls the creature out. We exclaim at how cute it is. Sparrow licks his lips and belches. We laugh indulgently, though the woman barely hides her irritation. He lifts the white, soft-furred creature up close to his thick mustache. "Hello, Mr. Rabbit. I am Mr. Sparrow. We live together in the jungle and we are brothers. Mr. Sparrow is very hungry." The young woman mutters something under her breath. Sparrow looks up, black-water eyes shining with innocence. "What?" The young woman takes the bunny from him.

Five minutes later, while Maung and the Karen man are talking on the veranda, Sparrow says to me, "Give me your hand." He once was a fortune-teller who read palms at the Sule Pagoda in Rangoon. I don't ask him about his long journey from there to here. Nor will I ask the other man how he lost the thumb and index finger of his right hand. The closed-over wound is a purple, C-shaped line of bumps and clumps, suggesting a surgery that was at best utilitarian. The shark bite of shrapnel. Or a land mine that mostly missed. I don't want to ask either of these men depressing questions. Let them take their brief vacation from active combat. Let them drink themselves into as sweet an oblivion as they can manage on Karen moonshine. Maybe it'll work for them better than it worked for me.

I give Sparrow my hand. He closes his eyes and begins to massage my palm. His brown thumbs knead the pads of flesh that meet to form the love line and the fortune line. His nails are long, broken, black with dirt. Thirty seconds pass. Forty. After a minute has gone by, I ask, "What do you see?"

"Dark."

I guess that's what you get when you're not a paying customer. "Just darkness? Are you joking?"

His head is canted back, suggesting rapture. He's missing a couple of molars. "Ma Yee Yee Cho, I not joking. My eyes closed. All dark. Can't see nothing. But I feel. I feel! You have so soft hand." His fingers massage in rhythm to his singsong words. "I like very much. Lovely hand." Eyes still closed, he lifts his eyebrows and gasps audibly—whether in mock or actual ecstasy it's hard to tell. How long has it been since he touched a woman?

Maung laughs and gives him a good shove in the shoulder. Sparrow squeezes my hand before he releases it and falls over sideways, trilling drunken laughter. This morning I saw satyrs. And here is Pan, their love-starved older brother, using humor to manage his miserable change in status from woodland god to guerrilla soldier.

.   .   .

Until now, most of the ABSDF and DPNS members I know have had a level of rank, education, or skill that has brought them out of the jungle for protracted periods of time. Those who live in the towns and cities, like Maung and his closest men, are too well padded with flesh to be mistaken for working soldiers. Cheap Thai noodles and deep-fried snacks have served them well. Before we left Mae Sarieng, I asked one of these officers, who is almost chubby, if he was worried about getting fat. He shrugged. "Since living in camp, the only thing I worry about is being hungry all the time."

I've seen documentary footage of Maung taken when he still lived full-time in the jungle. At first I didn't recognize him; I knew him only through the steady baritone of his voice. But for his somber, intelligent expression, he resembled a malnourished teenage runaway. His limbs and neck were elongated—an optical illusion arranged by the same thinness that made his eyes seem so large. The young men and women posed with machine guns in their arms resembled one another: skinny, displaced, stunned. And heartrendingly brave.

But those early images of Maung and his student comrades—many of them taken by Charlie—have not prepared me for the guerrillas I meet here at headquarters camp. In these men, the early malaria and malnourishment of 1988 and 1989 have been multiplied to the power of ten: a decade of deprivation. Sparrow's mustache and beard are disguises that give his face substance but cannot hide the fact that the world is in close contact with his skeleton. The skin is thin, the muscles long and beaten out, like scalloped meat. There is no reserve of flesh, not the finest marbling of fat. He has become his namesake, the little bird as light as a handful of feathers.

I meet him again the next night, along with half a dozen other men on leave, all front-liners. Maung and a few other people are here, too, men and two other women, which is a blessing. Sometimes, when men without women suddenly come into contact with one female of the species, the air feels charged. With just a couple of other women here, that tension dissipates. At ease with one another, in a good mood, we sit around a fire. Maung and two of the guerrillas take turns playing a warped guitar. It looks beat-up enough to be the same instrument he played the night I met him. But the A string doesn't break.

One of the front-liners, sick with malaria, is wrapped and shivering in a gray blanket. He laughs at Sparrow's rapid-fire jokes; he chats with his fellows. Yet he could easily play the part of a zombie in a Hollywood film—his cheekbones jut out, eyeholes burn under a pronounced forehead, teeth look large for his mouth. Suddenly declaring that he's very hot, he throws the blanket off his shoulders. The expensive long-sleeved dress shirt he's wearing is a gift I gave to Maung before he went to America. I feel insulted for just a moment. Or two. Obviously the man needs the shirt more than Maung does. The expense of it, here, is revealed as a waste of money. If only it were medicine. If only he could eat the excellent cotton.

When I quietly comment on the soldier's unhealthy pallor, Maung says, "Maybe he'll stay in camp longer than the others." But, maybe, in a week, he'll go back to his rocket launcher. Maung's head is angled down, but his eyes look up at me sheepishly. "I'm sorry about the shirt. I wanted to give him something. I like to give the men gifts."

"It's okay." I would like to give them something myself, say, twenty pounds of fat. I am thinner than I've ever been, but I still feel plump beside these war-whittled men. I don't know if Maung also feels embarrassed by his sleek-seal health. Does he make pacts with himself, when he goes back to the city, to not eat so much curry? Or does he, too, eat only with the memory of the malnourishment he has already experienced?

For the past five minutes, Sparrow has been busy fashioning a stick into a skewer. Through the fire, I watch his stained hands do their work, wielding the sharp knife dexterously. His skinny body hunches over. His energy channels down his arms, pours into his fingers. Once again I think of Andreas, whose powerful, slow-moving hands are the callused record of his life. Sparrow's hands are that, too, but speedy, twisting and tearing like weasels. He scrapes down two knots and then further sharpens the point of the switch.

Beside him is a bowl I haven't noticed, and in the bowl is a plastic bag, from which he withdraws a glistening red slab. In the wavering light, I can't make out any limbs, just a small head. It might be a bird, but it looks too meaty. Is it . . . the fetus of a larger animal? As I suck in a shocked breath, the fire crackles and leaps. Maybe it's not a fetus; it's just a little dead animal. He pokes the stick through its anus, up through its center, and out through its throat. The little head swings down. Then he centers the skinned animal in the hot tremble over the fire.

What a small snack for this large company. We've all had dinner, but the roasting flesh reawakens appetites. I hope he and his sick comrade eat the animal, just the two of them, but I know that once the morsel is cooked the stick will be passed around, a bite offered to everyone. I venture a question in Burmese. "Is it a bird?" I ask this first because I know the word for bird.

His eyes glitter in my direction. Sparrow is one of those people who, with a glance, makes you aware of both how much you don't know and how amusing your ignorance is. Rather than being insulted, you can't help smiling with him. I lean away from the fire to enter directly the small, bright province of his eyes.

"It is not a bird," he answers in the voice of a riddle-teller. "I would not eat my own brother." Everyone laughs.

"Is it a rat?"

"It is not a rat." His mustache lengthens with his smile.

"Is it a . . . ?" My vocabulary remains paltry. How do you say "guinea pig"?

Sparrow flips his heavy mat of hair off his face and grins lecherously. He is drunk again; I don't hold it against him. "*Ya-ba-deh,* Ma Yee Yee Cho." Never mind. "It is meat. Meat!"

We stare at the sizzling animal. It will be ready soon. I feel grateful that I've forgotten the word for bunny.

CHAPTER 44

CHASM

. . . .

We sit on the small veranda of a hut close to the war office. Two men are inside working. I've come up to see Maung, who isn't feeling well. "Diarrhea," he says with a sigh.

"A Greek word."

"Another one? Really?"

"From the verb 'to flow.' "

"Ah. Right."

"Well, I envy you. I wish I had diarrhea. I haven't shat in twelve days."

"That many? Why didn't you tell me?"

"I did tell you."

"The special syrup never helped?"

"Maung, I told you, I drank the whole bottle. Nothing happened. Don't you remember?"

"You will get sick if you don't shit."

"I feel sick." I'm not in the best of moods this morning. "I'm pretty sure I have cystitis, too. Even peeing is difficult."

While fiddling with his not quite wrapped areca nut on the table, he mulls over this new information. "It's from the stream, no?"

"I suppose." He smiles with such idiotic pride—why, I have no idea—that I have to resist the urge to slug him. "It's not funny."

"I agree, I agree. It's bad for your kidneys."

"Which? Constipation or the bladder infection?"

"Both. Some antibiotics will clear up the cystitis. But you really have to shit."

"It's not like I don't try! I try every day. It's not easy to spend half an hour in the latrine down there, hoping for the best." The outhouse close to my hut is not nearly as high-tech and tidy as the one close to the war office. I sometimes walk ten minutes up the mountain to make my great attempt on the porcelain squat toilet set in cement—the equivalent of luxury—but mostly I can't be bothered. I brave the smelly, maggoty depths; I'm used to them now. "The only thing I've got for all my efforts is hemorrhoids. At least, I think they're hemorrhoids."

He nods thoughtfully and fits the betel-wrapped areca nut into his cheek, which distorts his answer. "Ung. We au haff hemorrhoids. Fac of jungle liffing."

I laugh at the philosophical tone, apparent despite the wad in his cheek. He shrugs. I put my tea down on the narrow table in front of us. He reaches out and brushes my fingers. "Lovely hand," he says, imitating Sparrow. I laugh again.

I look at the little box of areca and betel paraphernalia. "Maybe I should try betel nut for the constipation. One of the women at the stream was saying it might work. It's a stimulant."

"Really? I've never heard of it being used to treat constipation. Maybe you should drink a strong coffee and smoke a big cheroot. That usually works for me."

He's about to laugh but winces instead, then grimaces, as though the skin of his face has been yanked from the inside. His color goes. Before my eyes, his skin turns gray-brown. He's no longer looking at me, but down the hill. "I have to go to the toilet. Excuse me." He stands, quickly reknots his longyi, and stumbles to the path.

A few minutes later, one of the officers comes out of the hut, bleary-eyed, blinking against the daylight. He pours a cup of tea from the aluminum pot, looks at the areca nuts, and says, "You chewing betel now?"

"I'm thinking about it."

We talk about what is worse for your health: chewing betel or smoking cheroots. Neither, apparently. "Cheroots are not bad like cigarettes, and chewing betel is good for you. It makes you strong. On long marches we all chew betel." But he dislikes the peppery, bitter taste of it. "Here, this is a very nice cheroot, try."

He hands me a newly lit khaki-green cigar. I inhale, exhale, and almost fall off my chair from the head rush.

"Very good, no?"

"Strong."

My stomach flips over, gurgles. Maybe I should try cheroots. I look down at the latrine. "Maung's been in the toilet for a while."

"Don't worry, he will come back soon." I can hear the amusement in his voice, and imagine his thoughts. She's so lovesick she can't even let the man take a dump.

I follow his gaze away from the outhouse, farther down the trail into the valley, scattered with huts and communal gardens. The fresh hours are almost finished. Soon the day's heat will settle into the mountainside. We keep talking, but I mostly nod and watch the outhouse door. How long has Maung been in there? Fifteen minutes? "I think you better go check the latrine. He wasn't feeling well." I stand up. If he doesn't go, I will.

"Okay, okay," he responds. It takes a minute for him to walk down the slope to the little building. He taps lightly on the door. Then knocks properly. No response. His face flashes in my direction as he pulls open the door. He shouts.

The other officer inside the hut emerges and runs down the path.

Maung has passed out. It's a struggle for the two of them to get him out of the latrine. The first man runs back up to the hut and radios for help.

I try to stay out of the way. There are too many of us inside the little hut, but I don't want to leave him. Men talk among themselves as I watch Maung's sweating face. His eyelids lift; I think he's waking up, but it's just that his head is sliding back over the rolled towel. One of the men shifts Maung's body rather roughly, to make his eyes close again. How can someone get so sick so quickly? Is there no medic? Can't anyone check him? I look around me, asking questions into the air. Vomiting, diarrhea, fever, unconsciousness. Is it dysentery?

Men and women sit around him, their faces sullen with concern but accepting, too, acquiescent. No, that can't be. They're just not showing their emotions as I am, fear in my voice as I ask questions to which no one responds. I catch some of the Burmese back-and-forth, but most of it is beyond me.

"We will take him out. Back to Mae Sarieng."

"It's hard to know what is wrong."

I ask, "If you think we should leave, shouldn't we go right away?"

Several people look at me blankly. Another fifteen minutes pass, filled with murmuring around the feverish man. The women who've come want to nurse him, too; they ask me to move so they can hold cold cloths on his face. We compete, briefly, at hovering. They win.

I step into the sunlight. The valley, which I have thought beautiful, has been transformed into a burning, hazy trap, far from civilization, too far from doctors and hospitals. Someone hands me a cheroot and I take a deep drag, steadying myself against the side of the hut.

Maung's bodyguard calls me into the dim room. Maung's eyes are open, but he's on his side, moaning, clenching his stomach with both hands. He looks at me, speaks English. "I think, dysentery. But I don't know why—" The words are sucked into a gasp. "I don't know why it's so bad.

The pain." We hold each other's gaze for two, three, four seconds. That's it. Five seconds, the moan that comes erupts into a hoarse roar. Then a cry. Like a woman in labor, I think, never having heard a woman in labor. My shoulders involuntarily rise toward my ears against the sound.

Then we all have to leave the hut, because he can't hold his bowels. Two of the men have to get him up again; they will hold him over the waiting bucket. Once most of us are outside, we stare at the dark rectangle of the doorway and listen to the violent sound of Maung vomiting.

His bodyguard comes out and says, "We're going soon. You should get your bag." When I turn, he follows me down through the camp, past the gardens, the rabbit hutches, the little houses. The people must be there, leaning on their small verandas, working, chatting, but I see no one. I feel only the bodyguard walking behind me as he has so often shadowed Maung. In the empty hut where I have lived this past week, I quickly gather up my things, erase my traces, making the place as unpeopled as it was before I arrived. It's always a shock, isn't it, how quickly a person can disappear.

The journey out is a dream, hyperreal as well as illogical. Time speeds up, hours pass more quickly, yet it often seems as though we ourselves are traveling faster. How is that possible when we have to hike more slowly? Our shirts become damp and then heavy with sweat. For an hour, two hours, I rarely take my eyes off Maung's hand and wrist hanging over the side of the stretcher. I think of another hand loosened like that, attached to a child's arm dangling from a bed in Rangoon.

One of the men loses his sweaty grip on one of the stretcher poles and it drops precipitously, throwing the other man off balance, upsetting the sick one who lies there. I listen to him moan. Sometimes I listen to him not moan, which is worse.

The sounds we make—his moaning, the men's murmuring, my swears when I stumble—are absorbed into the foliage, a detail that I found intriguing when we walked in but which is only threatening now. The jungle, too, is parasitic, predatory, it will swallow us alive. The colors of the trees and the red earth and the vines and one bush with small yellow flowers are too vivid, poisonous with brilliance. I walk too closely behind the men, annoying them, especially when we go through streams and they need to slow down.

What's wrong with Maung? How many parasites are there in the camp? How many cysts and spores and microscopic creatures pass over our dirty hands, or survive in a pot of insufficiently boiled water, or lie in wait on contaminated vegetables, in meat? Every living thing needs to eat other living things, either by consuming them whole or by living in guts or tissue or burrowing into skin. Is Maung sleeping or is he unconscious? What is the medical difference between the two states?

The stretcher-bearers get tired. They switch with the other men who are walking behind me. Then I watch those two get tired, too, and turn their wills as well as their strength to carrying the sick man. The body is so heavy in sleep, in sickness, and its fabulous appendages useless.

But awake and able it is a persistent wonder. The men's toes spread and grip at rocks through the flip-flop rubber. I take my eyes away from Maung's hand and watch their ankles, their ropy calf muscles, their flanks like those of spooked horses, bunched and straining. I feel grateful for their strength, their sweat. I encourage them in my mind, yet I say nothing. I ask nothing. I don't want to waste my energy speaking, trying to be understood.

The blisters re-form on the tops of my feet, between my toes. How could I have complained of blisters! The word hisses out of my mouth like a curse.

When we reach the ABSDF camp, I'm so happy I want to cry. The little village at the top of the hill, which we don't ascend, is blessed, blessed. Why? Because of what exists at the bottom of the hill: the track that will metamorphose into a road that will become asphalt that will take us into Mae Sarieng, Mae Sarieng, Mae Sarieng, Mae Sarieng. A hospital, doctors.

We walk faster along the stream. When we come around the last bend before those always-slippery steps kicked into the clay earth, we don't even notice the steps, because the red Toyota is there on the bank, a bizarre anachronism, an impossible machine from the future, and from the past, too, the same truck that brought us here. The one-eyed Thai man sits against the front bumper, smoking, watching our approach. A few people have come down from the camp at the top of the hill; they will return with us to the town. We load the bags up first, then the men count one two three and carefully lift Maung and slide him in. The women maneuver him off the stretcher onto a blanket.

We climb in, the driver gets into the cab, guns the engine. The truck crashes over the rocks as it crosses the stream. Maung's head is thrown around, his body jostled. Several of us move at the same time to steady him, to hold him. How far is it, again, to Mae Sarieng?

I've forgotten the interminable length of three hours. The hike out seemed fast because our bodies worked hard, crossing distance. But the truck, racing along the parched track, forces us to sit here and makes everything slow. We stare at a man who gets sicker under our eyes. I hold a blanket over Maung's dehydrated, drawn face. We move a bag under his head to make sure it's up when we try to give him water; we hold his jaw closed after he drinks. But he barely takes in anything, and he is heavy, his head like a big stone, rolling between us as the truck dives into and leaps out of potholes, over tree roots and rocks. I crouch beside him, trying to brace his body with my own. Sometimes he gasps or his body jerks and stiffens, but there is nothing we can do but stay close to him, as if we could absorb his pain through touch.

I start appealing to gods, God, the old Karen and Karenni gods of the river, the mountain, the trees—the god of that tall banyan tree on the edge of the stream. I suggest deals that would not interest them because they would have nothing to gain. Let him live, I think, and I will marry him. Marriage, children, work all my life for Burma, for the Burmese people. But gods don't care about countries, they're not interested in borders, which tribe gets what territory, puny human sacrifices. They roam the whole world at will, and smile at us when we are desperate enough to try to barter with them.

All this talk of gods, as if I'm in a myth or a fairy tale, when I'm just terrified of death. More precisely, I am terrified of losing this one, this one I love, to the chasm in time that shatters the past and swallows the future. As I hold the blanket over him and stare into his slack face, a weight presses against my throat. This, too, is love. I reach out to touch his beautiful warm body, flesh of my flesh, but it's cold, he's cold, in this heat, he's no longer there.

CHAPTER 45

MAI PEN LAI

. . . .

Death is close in the poor towns of Southeast Asia. It crowds the hallways of this country hospital, which is not antiseptic, not even clean, definitely not white. The walls are filthy. Maung is sleeping the sleep of the profoundly ill, his body invaded and conquered by some parasite that has not, so far, appeared under the microscope. He lies sweating on a gurney in the hallway, an IV dripping saline into his arm. By the time we reached Mae Sarieng, even the men were mute with fear that he might actually, unbelievably, die. After hours of vomiting and diarrhea, he was unable to keep down any water.

A sick woman ahead of him groans on her gray sheet and stares out of eyes thick with a yellow, suppurating infection. Ten minutes ago the doctor said to me, "We don't know exactly"—his raised eyebrows pushed one deep wrinkle into his otherwise smooth forehead—"what the problem is. But his vital signs are stable now. *Mai pen lai.*"

Never mind, he said. *Mai pen lai.* Just another sick Burmese refugee. When the doctor first spoke with us—an anxious knot of six people—he turned to me and asked if I had money to pay for Maung's care, insulting the men, who drew themselves up taller, proud, and answered him, "Yes, yes, we have money."

I glance around the cramped waiting room, up and down the hallways, trying to find a place to rest my eyes. So much for "the land of smiles," that long-standing slogan bandied about by the Tourist Authority of Thailand. There is no hint of a smile here; you can smell the cloying brine of sick people. Death's messengers hang out, death's siblings and cousins and old friends fraternize with the dozens of people on benches, on the floor, slumped against the walls. Little Asian tiger, Thailand, here is the underside of your economic miracle.

The clinic doors are open wide, but the waiting room is airless. The people are sanguine about the oozing skin conditions, the swollen necks, the infected wounds, the eyes glued shut with pus, the parasites, the bronchial coughs. I doubt they were ever horrified by their bad luck—"horrified" is too histrionic, and implies surprise, that such bad things could happen to them—and they are not horrified now. They are listless, sapped of energy, their hands fallen open on their laps. They stare perplexed at my white skin. What is she doing here?

When I stand beside Maung, it is obvious what I'm doing here. Too obvious. I forget that I'm not supposed to touch him. I lay my hand on his shoulder, his bare hot arm; though he was cold on the drive in, he has a fever now. I cannot help standing over him, staying near him. But this annoys the women who have come from the camp and from the ABSDF Mae Sarieng house. They glower at me. They call me away from him for a moment, to ask about this or that. When I return to him, a line of his women comrades have closed around him. They wipe his face with wet towels, they hover and whisper with one another. Stretched as though on a hammock between illness and sleep, he belongs to them. I see this, and I understand it in the simplest way: his life is their life.

After the deposit is paid, a slovenly attendant pushes the gurney into a small private room. Half an hour later, when Maung wakes up, I elbow my way between the women with a cup of water. It is my petty triumph that I react to his thirst before they do. I hold the plastic to his lips, I lift his heavy head off the pillow, he drinks. I would like to kiss the top of his head, but I refrain. He smiles at me like a drunken man, noticeably disoriented, still untangling himself from an underworld. But, as he slowly drinks, his eyes change. They focus in a discernible way. He has seen the three women and two men standing beyond me, also at the bedside, watching him, watching us. He takes the cup in his own hand, finishes drinking, and addresses them.

I don't understand what he says. It's a joke. Of course, he would make a joke. They smile, the men laugh, I laugh, but there is no hiding it, from myself or from them: I do not understand. More words, discussion, and I step away; he needs to talk with everyone, acknowledge each person. We have all been sick with worry.

I know what a quick study he is, what a precise reader of inflection, inference, pointed glance. Part of me wishes he were still sleeping—vital signs stabilized—so that I could have him to myself. Within minutes he apprehends the tension: how the women want to care for him, how my presence here is problematic.

What am I but an intruder? What do I know of his life with them, the struggle they have lived through together? Nothing. Or only words. I can see and feel the edges, the hardness of this, another life, a more rigorous life than I have ever imagined living, an existence that requires sacrifice and love and *stopping,* too, a diminishment of the self. A silencing of the self. It has not been thrust upon me as it has been thrust upon them. I have to choose it.

I sit on the single chair in the room. The people crowd around their leader—I find it so difficult to use that word—and I observe their expressions of concern, the women's hands busy folding towels, giving water, lifting to check the saline drip. The low tones of Burmese resonate in the small space.

If I back away emotionally, get myself out of it, I am able to appreciate their love for him. It makes me ask, What do I know of his love for *them*? I can only think of our love. I want love to be all of a piece—good big love, one size fits all—but it isn't like that. There are many kinds of love, and sometimes it divides people, makes us jealously face each other down.

In Buddhism, jealousy and envy are called defilements. They do defile the more noble emotions, the more generous heart. It's all right. I don't have to hold his hand or touch him. I'll get a room at the guesthouse and visit him early, or late. There is no such thing as visiting hours in a hospital like this. When I'm not here, I'll go to the local temple and meditate. I will use this; I will work with my defilements in meditation practice. Oh, I am so good!

A few minutes later, everyone leaves. I am confused, then touched—he has asked them to give us a moment. We look at each other. I am flooded with happiness and a pure gratitude to see him awake, fully conscious, though he looks like hell. I go to his bed, lean down, and kiss his cheek.

"I am so glad to see you. We were afraid for you."

"Me, too. I was wishing that I could die because the pain was so bad."

"I'm glad you didn't get your wish."

He nods. "I know it's been hard. I'm sorry. But I think you should go back to Bangkok."

"Maung! You're sick. They still don't even know exactly what's wrong. I want to stay here."

"There are lots of people to take care of me now."

I am burned right to the core. It would be a strategic error to cry, but that's what I want to do. Cry until my nose runs. Then blow my nose noisily. He doesn't want me close to him.

I do not cry. My sensitivity is the problem. To be Burmese, one has to absorb the sadness into the already sadness-saturated body. The Thais are this way, too; I've seen it in my Thai friends. What is the first truth of Buddhism? The first truth is that life is full of suffering. Certainly one sees that plain fact right here, and in the waiting room fifty steps away. The ability to endure, then, is a necessity. You must absorb disaster, loss, death, a host of other minor disappointments. There is no need to wave any of these around like gaudy flags; you furl them up tightly, inside. If you are a Burmese dissident, a fighter, a revolutionary, you can also plant them in the cause. A profound political cause can absorb human suffering for decades.

That is another part of my problem. I do not have a cause. Not really. I am not like Nola and Charlie, or the other women who are married to Burmese dissidents. I observe, I listen and gather stories. But I am suspicious, still, of joining. I am joined to Maung, to the people in the waiting room, even to the women with whom I compete. I am joined to people. And a few valuable ideas, ideals, fiercely held, upheld. But not to causes. Not to the cause. This is my shortcoming. He must feel it.

I blink, absorbing the tears back into my eyes. "You want me to go away?"

"I think it is better for now."

I stare at him. The brown skin has regained much of its vitality, its brightness, but his face is noticeably thinner. We can change in the space of hours. I look at his broad cheeks, his lips. There. I'll have to be satisfied with that, looking at but not kissing them.

I don't know what else to say.

Goodbye, I suppose.

They are sending me home on the bus, like a child who has misbehaved at camp.

Does the whisper begin as I walk away from the hospital? No, it began before, quietly. It's louder now. *I don't know if I can do this.*

But you love him.

Yes. But I don't know if I can be what he needs. I am too spoiled and childish. I want him and I will never have him.

Well. You will grow up. You will get tougher, like the other women, you'll become less selfish.

What about my work? Didn't you just say, Writer, that to be with Maung and to live this life I have to silence myself? Where the fuck have I heard that before?

I'm sure you're going to tell me.

In a hard chair at church, that's where, as a twelve-year-old who had fig- ured out the censorial nature of a maniac god.

I think you should calm down and get yourself some dinner. It's been hours since you've eaten. A whole day.

I have no desire to eat. There is no room in my stuck guts for food.

CHAPTER 46

THE NEED FOR PROPAGANDA

AND PARASITES

. . . .

At least in Bangkok I am able to shit.

The system starts to work again the morning I get back to my dusty apartment, after spending a cramped night on the bus. Maybe it was the congee that cured me. All-nighter buses in Thailand invariably stop halfway through their nocturnal journeys and eject their passengers into the lurid fluorescent half-dream of the *cow-tom* experience. Stumbling, purblind with exhaustion, familiar with but always mesmerized by this travel ritual, I, too, took my seat at the table (one of dozens) and ate my bowl of cow-tom, the Thai equivalent of Chinese congee, or boiled rice soup. I was invited to this meal by the lecherous old Thai man seated behind me on the bus, who slid his hand under my ass—ostensibly to wake me up—and offered to buy my soup.

To which I responded, "Don't touch me, you bad man. I will buy my own cow-tom."

And I did, stopping myself from having a second bowl because the driver was ready to go.

Ah, Bangkok! You diesel-belching, blemished monster of a city, I am pleased to breathe in your smog from the filthy balcony. I step back inside and admire the shining parquet floor, this room's most attractive feature, though the coily mattress also seems the height of luxury. Sleep knocks me down for a few blind hours.

Upon waking, I get up and visit the VD clinic at the corner of Soi Dang, hoping the som-tam seller doesn't see me. The good doctor listens to my symptoms and prescribes the right penicillin for non-honeymoon cystitis. He also looks at me with concern and says, "You are very tired. That's why the infection is bad. Now take the medicine, and drink lots of water, and rest. Then you will be happy again."

What a sharp clinical eye. Will it work? Will I be happy again? Am I unhappy? Best not to think about it too much. I drink cold water. I make some ice in the small freezer. Popping it out of the plastic tray, I revel in the cold transparent edges, the white heart. Ice, after weeks of drinking warm water. *Ice*. It's like a new word.

I dust off the companionable Buddha postcard. I genuflect, sit, breathe in and out. An ice cube melts in my mouth. I meditate long after the cold water is in my stomach. My weariness asks for nothing but stillness. On the exhalation, I release, again, the besieged mind. In. Out. In. Out. Why don't we learn this in grade school?

Over the next week, I return to my novel, but when I reread the work it's false. The characters are doing romantic things; they are predictable, they are flat. I've started writing about a white woman, an Anglo-Burmese man. They are more graceful and better-looking versions of me and Maung. Nauseating. The people I had before have receded. When I'm not writing the Harlequin romance of Burma, I'm writing political-tract crap.

I stand on the balcony, careful not to put my elbows in the pigeon shit, and light up a cheroot. Both romantic and political self-indulgence involve oversimplification, which is the dullest, most effective form of lying; but political self-indulgence is the worse crime. I don't want to write *propaganda.*

"What's wrong with propaganda?" Maung asks. He's no longer in the hospital, though he's still in bed in the Mae Sarieng house. "We need as much good propaganda as we can get."

"The movement needs *support,* but that's not the same as propaganda."

Silence. I fill it by asking, "Are you feeling better?"

"No. I'm still sick. I haven't had an attack like this for a long time." As the dysentery subsided, a virulent recurrence of malaria knocked Maung off his feet again.

"I hope you're not smoking too much. Can you eat anything?"

"I don't have much of an appetite. It's all right. I've lost all my Bangkok weight. How are you?"

"Just meditating a lot. And writing shit."

He laughs. We say goodbye without mentioning when we might see each other again.

Two days later, I wake to a lightly thudding skull. The headache sinks down until the same monkey banging its nasty drum swings high and low through my bones. An exotic flu. Picked up at the VD clinic, perhaps.

It's malaria, of course. A dozen or more people have described this pounding achiness as one of the earliest symptoms. Yet it's relatively uncommon to contract malaria during the dry season, especially when one has Deeted one's skin to carcinogenic levels. I heave myself up, make a cup of tea, and dismiss the self-diagnosis as melodramatic.

The next day: dengue fever?

Evening of the next day: brain tumor?

The morning after that, in forty-two-degree-Celsius heat, my teeth begin to chatter. I put on my sweater and my windbreaker and lie down under the hitherto unused blanket. I get up and unfold the big clean towel on top of that and get back into bed. I'm still freezing. Child of Canadian skating rinks, veteran of a poor winter in Montreal without good boots, I've never been so cold in my life. When I wash my hands under the cold bathroom tap, it's like rubbing ice on blistered skin. My brain is curious about the physical manifestations of illness, but I don't take them too personally. At first I think this is a consequence of my week's successful meditation practice: I have attained a certain level of detachment from the self. Though no Bodhisattva, I am at least on the long road to enlightenment.

This causes me to feel self-congratulatory until the late afternoon, when, *poof,* just like that, the chills vanish. A few minutes later a fever sparks, catches, and burns across the plains. A state of arduous panic begins under my skin. Something besides fever happens, some other event. I can't describe how the sensations are communicated to me, but I feel flesh, fasciae, muscle, organs—all of these surge into action, trying to protect the whole. It reminds me of the useless mobilization ants undertake when someone is burning their nest. But the illness—which is unlike any flu I've experienced—is taking over. That's what makes being sick such a perpetual surprise to the healthy person. The illness doesn't win, necessarily. But it cannot be resisted.

I want to get up and phone someone. My Thai brother and good friend Goong, who stayed with my family when I first lived in Thailand, is out of town. Aye Aye Lwin is on a training course. Chit Hlaing and Ma Tu live more than an hour away by bus, and their schedules are so busy that I don't want to disturb them. I am shy about calling my journalist friends; months ago we quarreled over white entitlement and Asian politics and I dropped out of the documentary project we were doing together. We've seen each other since, but we are no longer close. I don't know Nola well enough. Besides, she might tell me to pull up my bootstraps and take my quinine. Not that I have any quinine. I sneer at the phone on the floor. Why doesn't it ring? I don't want to phone Maung in desperation. I want *him* to call *me*.

I resist the one person who might be able to comfort me as the afternoon becomes evening and the fever breaks hard into chills again, then the chills simmer back into fever and morph half an hour later into worse chills, making me shiver so hard that I no longer have the strength to call anyone. I don't want to get out of bed or talk. It's enough to lie here, sipping water. Sleep will come soon.

The next morning, I am sicker. I take my temperature: 39.5 degrees Celsius. Which is 103 degrees Fahrenheit. How bad is that? I call Maung, finally, because at least he's a doctor. "Why haven't you phoned me?"

"The house is very full of people right now. It's hard to use the phone or have any privacy. I'm sorry. How are you?"

Grumpily, I describe my symptoms.

"That is malaria. It usually takes a couple weeks for the first symptoms to develop after infection. You probably got it in the first camp."

I bet I know the night, too, and the place from which the mosquito sucked my hot, dumb blood.

"Take some paracetamol for the fever. Wait until tomorrow, then take a cab to the Tropical Diseases Hospital on Ratchawithi Road. It's close to your place. They will test you and then maybe give you some drugs." Maybe. He likes that word. It's a prophylactic against being wrong.

"Why should I wait?"

"So that more parasites build up in your bloodstream."

"Oh. What are they doing in there?"

"What? Where?"

"The parasites, in my body."

With galling cheerfulness he responds, "They are eating your red blood cells."

"Oh."

"Not exactly eating. Destroying. They already spent some days in your liver, and now they're in your blood. Then they might affect your spleen. That's the only thing you have to worry about. If your spleen gets too big. Spleen helps get rid of old red blood cells, so many parasites end up there."

To this impressive lecture, I say nothing. I feel a lot of spleen, though.

Because I'm not talking much, Maung observes, "You sound sick."

"Hmm. I don't feel so well."

"I'm sorry that I can't come to you. There's too much work here, and I'm still sick."

"That's fine. I didn't expect you to come. I just . . ." I clench the phone, chest caving inward, body seized by some unexpected force. What is this? Heart failure? No. I've started to cry. I quickly let go of my monumental disappointment. I didn't expect him to come to see me. I sniffle for a minute. He says he knows how hard it is (which he does). There is no need to overwhelm him, no need to be overwhelmed. Very Buddhist. I dry it up.

"Soon Aye Aye Lwin will be back. She will come to see you."

"I know. I just . . ." I cannot believe that I've made a vocation of being a writer when words are often so useless.

"I know. I miss you, too. I love you, Yee Yee Cho."

At the end of the day, tens of thousands of parasites are munching away in the back of my neck, in the major arteries in my thighs, in the veins in my hands. I slowly get dressed and go outside, carrying with me a plastic bag, because I'm not sure how much longer I can resist throwing up. There are two kinds of people in this world: those who can abide vomiting and those who cannot. I belong to the latter tribe. Swallowing, I step into the elevator. Swallowing, I step out. I don't have the strength to walk down the soi and catch a real cab on Phaholyothin, so one of the motorcycle boys gives me a lift to the Tropical Diseases Hospital. I see nothing of the near-accidents and mad weavings; my head rests heavily between his red-vested shoulder blades.

Soon enough, I enter a waiting room full of sick people on wooden benches and plastic chairs. Rather than being depressed by this familiar scene, I'm happy to be among fellow sufferers, out of my empty room. Most of the folks here don't look as poor or as dejected as the ones in the Mae Sarieng community hospital. A young male attendant takes me to someone who pricks my skin with a needle, then ushers me back to my bench.

Either I doze for half an hour or the results come fast. A commanding female voice bellows out my name. I approach the desk, behind which sits a stalwart woman with an old-fashioned nurse's cap mysteriously affixed, as though by glue, to her bouffant hairdo. She glares up at me over her reading glasses. "Go back home." She sounds exasperated, as if I'm wasting her time when she could be helping real sick people.

My lower lip trembles. I'm so raw with illness and the gut-wrench of self-pity that I want only to lie down on a hospital bed and have a nurse— a gentle, loving one, not this sergeant major—bring me water and pat my hand. She sees how upset I am and softens her tone by a quarter of a degree. "Whatever is making you sick, we don't know. Dengue fever? Maybe. Malaria?" She raises her hands in that seemingly universal "Who knows?" gesture. "There's not enough of it in your blood yet. *Mai pen lai.* Go back home and come here again when you are sicker. We need more parasites."

I should have listened to Maung and waited until tomorrow.

The next morning, the paracetamol doesn't seem to be controlling the fever very well and nothing controls the chills. I take three more tablets and look at the clock. Ten. My temperature is 104.

At four in the afternoon, sicker, nauseated and newly afflicted with diarrhea, I return to the hospital on the back of another motorcycle-taxi. What am I thinking? I am thinking that it's much faster to get there on a motorcycle; all I want to do is arrive and be placed in a hospital bed.

Once more the blood test shows nothing conclusive. "Have you thrown up yet?" the sergeant-major nurse asks.

"I hate throwing up."

Her eyes needle me mercilessly. "Come back tomorrow, after you puke." I don't think to check myself in and get sicker in the hospital. I don't even know if that's an option. It's not a hotel. I return to the apartment, where I keep a bucket by my head.

I shiver under the blanket and towel; I burn in my underwear on the cool floor. The rising throb of invasion marches into my joints and muscles, lays siege to the viscera behind my eyeballs. It occurs to me that this is how dying begins. Tennyson spat out the words, "This is how our children die." Yes, I remember now. This is the disease of the border. This suffering is the ritual, the rite of passage that should marry me to the cause as effectively as a wedding.

I cry for a long time—for myself and beyond myself, for the people who have described their small roles in Burma's history, their lives in the camps and the prisons and the interrogation centers. Why do I know these stories? Why do I know how the world becomes inverted, wrong, transforms into hell, less and more than hell, because hell implies some awesome rendering of justice, whereas the tortured students, the terrorized villages, the starving slave porters are savaged for . . . what? To what purpose—the regime's twin addiction to violent power and greed?

I cry because I have learned not only the horror of evil but also its oppressive stupidity—the sheer waste, the way it takes promise, intelligence, youth, all human rightness and possibility, and destroys them, consciously, tears them apart and swallows them down like Saturn devouring his children. What can I wield against such a force? Scratches on paper. My good intentions are laughable. Such powerlessness makes me angry, and beyond my anger is despair, a grief that cracks open my rib cage and pins me to the bed.

It's the same feeling I had on the phone with Maung but managed to swallow down. It has returned in full force. I can't howl, because I'm too sick, but at last I permit myself the relief of weeping, the freedom of being sad. What is inside me? A fracture, from my left shoulder across my chest. Invisible traces of Burma and the border. Parasites the doctors cannot see.

Is this not what I wanted, what I have always craved—to be transformed? The change I sought when I first went to Burma is complete. It is an irrevocable alteration: the fever has seared something into me, burned something out. She is gone, the one who could go forth so easily, so readily, wishing to enter another world and opening herself to it completely, like a door or a flower.

CHAPTER 47

WHEN I FIRST

GAVE MY HEART TO ASIA

· · · ·

The next day, I almost fall off the motorcycle. I swoon and the machine dips and swerves dangerously. This rips the dizziness right out of my head and makes me yelp with a fear so high-pitched it sounds like laughter. Luckily, the car beside us is not too close. The skinny motorcycle boy somehow rights the bike and swears with Thai words I've never heard before.

A minute later, we joke with each other, he shouting into the diesel fumes, I whispering in his ear, "It would be funny to die on the way to the hospital."

Three times lucky. A new nurse calls me to the desk and tells me, "You have malaria. Do you want to stay at the hospital?"

"Yes."

"Do you have money?"

"Yes." Is it because I am white that she doesn't ask me for a deposit?

An attendant brings an old wheelchair. As soon as I'm sitting down in it, I ask for a bag and throw up, wretchedly but triumphantly, too. I'm in the hospital! It's as if I've won the lottery.

I see a doctor whose name I immediately forget. I don't even know what he does to me. Checks my reflexes? Asks me if I'm allergic to drugs? He drifts out of the room like a ghost wearing large glasses. Then I am helped into a hospital gown by a woman with warm hands. She tucks me into one of the two beds in an empty room. Someone else—a nurse, presumably—gives me pills. I sleep.

They give me a lot of pills, several times a day. Though normally I'm suspicious of the medical establishment and leery of pharmaceuticals, sickness has made me acquiescent. I take the drugs without asking a single question. The nurses are the kind nurses of my dreams, bearing trays of water that I drink and food that I do not touch. Something about the side effects of the drugs—they kill the appetite.

I spoil myself. After the first couple of days, I could just buy the pills and go home. But the malaria has frightened me. I don't want to be alone in the apartment; I want to be taken care of. The day after I'm admitted, I call Maung on the pay phone down the hall, to tell him where I am and that I'm all right. I run out of change before we can say goodbye.

Since I first became ill, the flesh has been melting off my hips, my belly. My breasts deflate; the double ladder of ribs shows under my skin. The invisible diminishment of self is a more gradual process. As I get skinnier, my heart swells with self-pity. Am I allowed to feel sorry for myself? *You don't have to tell anyone.* I stare at the fingerprints on the wall at the end of my bed, imagining the crowd of people who were here before, like the ones who hovered at Maung's side in Mae Sarieng.

Give your heart to Asia. I have thought often of those words. My mind walks around them, turns them over. What is on the other side of that moving request? I sometimes say it out loud. "Give your heart to Asia." Curiously, the words have lost their original incantatory effect. I stare at the fingerprints and ask myself why.

Because I understand them. I realize that Maung was asking me to do something I'd already done. That first weekend by the lake, when he said,

"I hope you give your heart to Asia," the words didn't express only romantic longing to me and for me. They had the import of prayer because they also described an act of grace from my past. They explained the small miracle that launched my adult life. I gave my heart to Asia when I was seventeen years old, a wide-eyed, serious, brash girl from Calgary adopted into a Thai family, a Thai town, a Thai school, and made to feel, for the first time, despite the initial culture shock and language barrier, like a normal teenager, doing normal teenager things. I had never experienced family life so rooted in calm dailiness, in peace. To my surprise and complete delight, it was not too late.

That is why I will always be a great advocate of the wisdom of physical escape. It's not always appropriate, though sometimes it's imperative. It can save you from yourself, or from them. Leaving Canada for Thailand allowed me to depart physically from many things: my father's alcoholism, my brothers' increasing violence and delinquency, my sister's suicide (she died one year before I left for Asia), my mother's long-standing faith that religious fanaticism might help our family alleviate some of these problems. Physical departure is not enough, I know, but it is a crucial part of a long disentanglement. It would be easy to leave fucked-up families behind if we did not love them. We want to keep what we love, rightly. Distance has helped me learn how to do that.

I had already started packing my bags to leave the country when I discovered that I was pregnant: knocked up at seventeen, like my grandmother and my mother and my sister before me. Such is the power of a family pattern, and of that octopus dysfunction, stretching out its tentacles to drag me back into the fray, that I briefly considered canceling my plans to depart for Thailand, ceding my last chance for a taste of peaceful childhood to the child I would bear.

My mother was profoundly against abortion as a crime against God, but she counseled me to get one as soon as possible and leave the country. She told me that, besides all the other problems it would bring, having a baby at seventeen would undermine my dream of becoming a writer. My mother! I love her utterly. She has done the best she could do through years of recurrent disaster. She has always taught her children the value of generosity, humor, and gratitude. Only now do I begin to comprehend her bravery. Her love for us has always been more important than her obedience to a wrathful God.

I was still bleeding when I arrived in Denchai. But all that other unpleasantness disappeared. I shed my family the way a snake sheds its skin, and, as with a newly molted reptile, my eyes were brighter, my aspect gleaming. I saw the world clearly, in all its rawness, brutal and beautiful and, for me, replete with kindness, for I was protected from the brutality by my vigilant Thai fathers, the members of the Denchai Rotary Club. They showed me the beauty of temples, silk, Japanese electronics, large rice cookers, low mountains, tall waterfalls, well-made badminton rackets. And the most they wanted from me in terms of religious faith was to sit still in a temple for a few minutes and have my fortune read by a good-humored old monk with three teeth in his head, one of them so pointed and gold that I couldn't take my eyes off it. The sitting still was harder than it looked, but no god threatened to kill me when I failed.

I came to love the very air of Denchai, the red dust of the roads into the countryside, dust I would draw my hands through, delighted with the smooth transfer of earth to skin. I wanted to lick it off my fingers, leave prints of it on my clothes and skin. I loved, too, the sleepy faces in the marketplace at seven in the morning, when the gaggle of us schoolchildren— I was a school *child!*—would hop in a songtow to go to school in Prae, half an hour away. Once there, I walked with my friends through the gates and past the light green buildings of Nareerat School to my classroom, which overlooked grounds full of roses and indigo morning glories. What power had brought me here, to these flower-bedecked buildings of colonial architecture and the village with ghosts under the bridge and Chinese soap opera and horned bugs the size of golf balls and lizards everywhere? It had to be a kind of magic. Thai friends said that my good karma delivered me to a Buddhist country.

Concentrated in the space of one year, I received the unexpected gift of a happy childhood, for as soon as I realized that I could be a teenager, I reverted, I went farther back, and became a little girl. My Thai parents and teachers accepted my behavior, perhaps assuming it was peculiar to Canadian adolescents. I was naughty occasionally; I misbehaved grandly a couple of times. One time they wondered if they shouldn't send me back to Canada. This threat saw me become diligent, self-sacrificing, winning: a traditional Asian daughter. Like my Thai mother, I would have got down on my knees and given my Thai father a pedicure if he had asked me to—or anything else, for that matter. But no one asked anything outrageous of me, or dirty, or wrong. I stayed for the rest of the year. How could I not have given my heart to Asia?

I get out of bed and rummage through my knapsack to find the photograph of Maung. It's from the roll of film I shot when he came to see me at the lakeside resort, where he said those words that were part of the charmed dialogue new lovers employ to bind themselves closer together. I must have said similar things, seeking to draw him in, hold him.

I hope you give your heart to Asia. What a powerful, encompassing request. I look at his face in the photograph and know beyond a doubt that I love the man I see. His smile in this photo makes him look touchingly young. He's loose-limbed, relaxed in a way I've rarely seen him, his mouth open to the camera—he was in the midst of saying something when I pressed the shutter button.

The whisper comes again. I write it out in my notebook, as one should write a whisper, in a narrow script: *I do love him. But is love enough? (Doesn't love have to be enough?) To whom can we ever give our heart, really? I need my heart. I need to keep my heart.* The metaphor works only in the abstract, on a grand scale. I can give my heart to Asia even while it pumps my replenished blood and powers my limbs.

But Maung's was a veiled request, and a natural one, the desire of the man newly in love. What he really meant was "Give your heart to *me.*"

CHAPTER 48

THE GIFT

· · · ·

I push down the window and let in the hot, filthy wind of Bangkok. We are what we are: complicated, fretful, endlessly involved humans. We are not much. The megacities teach this without concern for their pupils, the men burning garbage, the women collecting newspapers from soiled bins, the girls selling green mangoes, the dozens of children who live with their families in shanties on the tracks' edges. They stare at me staring at them, and sometimes they laugh, and often they wave as if we were friends. I wave back, our eyes touching until we can no longer see each other.

The very fact that humans are so compelled to look at each other contains a mystery, evidence of a pact that goes beyond language or culture. What is exchanged through the eyes? A lifetime condensed in a meaningful glance. Some primordial form of love no one has named. A map, in every iris, of a corresponding galaxy of stars.

Of course, it's easy to stare into the eyes of poor people when one is being borne away from them on a train. The wisdom of escape can also look like an appetite for adventure, or a need for open-ended freedom. But is it simply cowardice?

When we rush past a fish pond, a white egret wheels up from shimmering green into blue sky. I have booked a flight to Greece. I think about this as much as I think about my current destination, Chiang Mai, still some several hundred kilometers north, where Maung is waiting for me.

I wonder if he is waiting. He has work to do in the northern city. But he has asked me to come and see him, and I am glad. We will look different, and feel different in each other's arms, because both of us are skinnier than we were in April. I begin to understand the monks, why the wisest among them grow thin. It's easier to meditate when you eat lightly. Successful meditation facilitates right thinking, and I'm trying to think rightly about leaving. For months I've wanted to go back to the island to write and rest, but I've repeatedly put it off. Maung can't understand why I'm still second-guessing my decision.

That's not hard to explain. I feel guilty about leaving him, guiltier about leaving *at all,* when so many other people are trapped. When I try to explain my discomfort over the phone, he chuckles and says, "Don't worry! It's all right for you to go. You are a global person." Translation: Other white people deal with their white guilt and they manage just fine.

Perhaps my lack of appetite has nothing to do with the getting of Buddhist detachment. *Anorexia blameworthia:* hunger as penance for hailing from the fat midriff of the world. But that seems so unlike me, and unsuitable for a Grecophile. Guilt usually cannot restrain me from a good piece of roast lamb. But since the antimalarial drugs—no, since the jungle—I'm rarely interested in food. Not eating is a novel experience. Life becomes sparer and sharper, somehow . . . detached. I carry it around in my mouth like a bone.

We pass from irrigated to non-irrigated fields, whisked from jade and emerald to the semidesert in the space of minutes, zebu cattle in the distant yellow lowlands like a vision out of the African savanna. I'm riding third-class to save money; there's no air-conditioning. The rocking motion of the train lulls me into a sweaty doze.

A face peers over the seat in front of me, startling me awake. I raise my eyebrows at the boy. He raises his eyebrows back, unsmiling. Then he sinks into his own seat again. We are mirrors of each other.

And sometimes caricatures of ourselves.

Escape. The train approaches Denchai, the little town I lived in when I first left Canada. In the outlying fields there are no water buffaloes standing under shade trees. I don't see a single buffalo-driven cart. The dusty red tracks have trails of smoke rising from them, the fumes of small trucks and two-stroke motorcycle engines. As we come closer to the town, I see the new development wrought by rapid industrialization, fancy cement houses painted white, with red tile roofs and Italianate balconies: Thailand's response to the West's large, wasteful suburbia. Middle-class Thais build them but often still live as they have for decades, on the floors above their narrow shops in the hearts of their towns and cities. The houses are for parties, for weddings, for show. When I returned to Denchai earlier this year, several of my Thai fathers took me to see these new trappings of their hard-earned wealth. But we talked and gossiped back at the liquor store, or the electronics shop, where the families, the business, and the outdoor kitchens remained, humming with liveliness.

Denchai's train station remains unchanged. Simple elegance and mild squalor fit together companionably—fine wood details darkened by varnish and dirt, plastic bags hooked and fluttering in the rafters. We take on several new passengers who have come from Prae to catch the train— young people on a weekend outing, backpacks slung lightly over their shoulders.

Through the open window comes the smell of creosote and sun-warmed dust: a reminder of my seventeen-year-old self. I gaze at the platform and its old benches. I used to sit on the left one, scribbling in my journal or studying Thai. I was also waiting to hear the train whistle that would tell me it was past six, which meant that I had to go home for dinner. Now, when we pull away from the station, I stretch out the window and wave back at no one, at the town, at the huge tree by the crossroads, at the white girl sitting cross-legged on the bench, writing in her notebook, staying too late just to have the pleasure of watching the train pass through Denchai.

You can know a thing for years but not have the language for it. Then an event, or the ferment of years, acts as a catalyst and crystallizes the knowledge of the flesh into words. Until I went to the hospital two weeks ago, I'd never thought of that first year in Thailand as a reclaimed childhood. I thought of it unequivocally as a gift, but I wasn't old enough to grasp the depth of the gift's meaning.

I'm old enough now. Time promises us we'll age, and time delivers promptly, but illness speeds up the process. When I was alone in my room in Bangkok, sick but not sick enough, alone and afraid of getting sicker, four words looped through my mind, mantra-like: *I am not endless.* I was not meditating, but the words are a variation on the truth of *annica,* the Buddhist concept of impermanence. Animals know it. Molecules know it. Atoms know it. Even subatomic particles know it. Unceasing change is a condition of existence. Why does human consciousness make it so hard to grasp this until it smacks us in the face?

I watch the young people in the seats ahead of me, preening, chattering away, taking photographs of one another. Three girls and two boys. The boys have a lithe, androgynous quality that suggests homosexuality but may not be. All five are specimens of human perfection, including the one with a rash of acne on her cheeks. I have no idea how old they are. Late teens? Early twenties? They respond enthusiastically to one another's jokes. The girl with the most beautiful long hair swings it around like a loose black fan.

Simultaneously unaware of itself and morbidly self-conscious, youth crows endlessness and beauty while it busily fears being ugly. I think of the young girl I was, surrounded by other girls and boys, most of us variously plagued by mirrors and magazines and one another. Do these young people, too, wish they were taller or smoother or thinner when they are already lovely, yet dumb to their loveliness and good luck? Life hummed inside me, as sweet as a beehive, and whirred out of me like bees disturbed. Yet I never fell on my knees in gratitude for my functioning limbs, my thumping heart.

When I got back to my room on Phaholyothin last week, that's exactly what I did. Am I so old, then? No, I just feel older. After a few months on the border, standing at the edges of a war, I know I am not endless. I, too, will die. As my sister died. As the child in Maw Ker died. Fragile human, think of the border. Burma. Across the other border, Cambodia, and farther east, Vietnam. Millions of dead, battalions of ghosts more abundant than the armies that felled them.

Every army is in love with death. The men in the camps carried their guns proudly. They relished the roles they had been given, or had been forced to take: killer, destroyer, wielder of the blasting weapons, sower of mines, captain of the rocket launcher. To embrace those roles is a human's only chance of surviving them. How could I have compared Sparrow to the god Pan? Like every soldier, on any side—like Maung, too—he is a child of murderous Ares.

Is it wrong that I crave peace? If it is not wrong, then why is it shameful? I feel ashamed of returning to Greece, embarrassed by my wish to plant a garden and watch life reassert itself in a small, fundamental way.

When I first came to Southeast Asia a decade ago, my experiences here were a healing balm. Now I want to return to an Aegean island to partake of the same good medicine in Greek form. Is this the template I have chosen for my life? In response to brutal realities, I get on a plane and flee toward Eden?

This formulation is too reductive; I dismiss it as soon as I've made it. But it comes back in more complex forms, like a virus mutating in order to cause new damage. Marla's self-righteous criticisms return to me: "Not

every experience is for the artist's palette. You are not allowed to use everything." Maybe she wasn't being self-righteous. She simply recognized my
treacherous, inconstant nature.

*Please! Soon you're going to quote some old inquisitor on the inherent
wickedness of women. Get a grip. You're going back to Greece for a while. Big
fucking deal. You've been planning to leave for months, and soon you will leave.
You need a break.*

But I'm afraid that Greece will make me fat and happy again and I
won't want to come back here.

*You're afraid of that, are you? Better to be afraid of another parasite. Or get-
ting pregnant. But aren't they the same thing? Remember the high-school
teacher who always used to say that pregnancy was parasitism made good?*

I've brought condoms.

*I know this may be hard for you to believe, but they won't work in your toi-
letries bag.*

This contrary voice goes on and on, bossily, with crass humor. It's no
longer whispering.

CHAPTER 49

DRAGON MEDITATION

. . . .

~~Maung comes to~~ see me in the little apartment I've rented near Chiang Mai University. This is the neighborhood where I first met him at the drunken Christmas party. I look down from the window of the apartment and see not only trees but the confounding maze of streets and houses that complicates the hillside. At the top of the hill is an old monastery and, outside its grounds, a mostly unused pagoda. Optimistically, I plan to meditate there every morning.

When I come down from my rooms, Maung is waiting for me in the atrium of the apartment building. We stand looking at each other; we don't touch. The sight of him moves and unsettles me. I take deep, slow breaths, willing myself to produce no tears. Why cry? Here he is, in the flesh, wearing his blue shirt, smiling with a mixture of hesitation (not showing his teeth) and expectancy (his eyebrows lifted slightly). This is the face in the photograph that I carry around, but it is the real face, older, more closed. More handsome, too, though he looks tired.

We don't embrace in the plant-filled foyer. We approach each other slowly. Hello. How are you. We link hands and walk up the stairs. There is a space between us. Or is it the missing flesh? Between the two of us we've lost twenty pounds or more. We need to be in each other's company for a few hours. The closeness will return, settle back into and between us.

Upstairs, in an apartment twice the size of my room in Bangkok, with tall windows filling one wall, we leap from conversation into hungry lovemaking. We do everything gluttonously, too quickly, until the food of delight is devoured in record time and we lie spent on the bed, panting, covered in a sheen of sweat. Maung hops up and goes to the bathroom, runs the shower. After a few seconds, he calls out, "There's hot water!"

"Only the best for you, my dear," I respond lightly, though I'm listening to the shower spray on tile as if it's some kind of warning. I don't know why. Fucking like animals made the separation between us wider than before. I'm angry at the sex itself. It didn't work. It cinched us together but didn't release us into each other. Vexed, confused, I yank the anonymous sheet over my naked body and tuck it under my arms. Back against the wall, I stare out at the splendid, rounded treetops that float beyond the fourth floor.

Maung emerges from the bathroom with a threadbare white towel wrapped around his waist. I can tell by the careful way he walks toward the bed that he has something unpleasant to tell me.

But I'm wrong. He has two unpleasant things to tell me.

The first is, "I have to leave soon. I have a meeting to go to." He watches the disappointment freeze my face. I look out the window. Why don't I know the names of those trees? "Please don't be upset, Karen. I can't help it. I'll have dinner with you tomorrow. And the next day."

My voice is toneless, unfamiliar to both of us. "I don't know what I was thinking, to expect to have dinner with the man who's just fucked me. Honestly. What was I thinking? How long has it been since I've seen you alone?" He's confused for a moment, unsure whether or not he's supposed to answer my rhetorical questions. I clarify by adding, "It's all right, Maung. I understand. Go. Just get dressed and go." This makes it sound as if I'm ordering him to do something that he will do regardless.

But he doesn't move. I stare out the window, my mind reeling. I'm so angry that I don't know what to do. My jawbone could crack because my mouth is shut so hard; my throat is closing up.

What is this? A fantasy, fed on absence. A fleeting world created by two lonely bodies.

But it is also love. I love him. We do love each other.

What kind of love is it? A starving love stretched thin by political exigency. And bad manners. Whatever it is, it is not enough. It will never be enough.

Don't be so melodramatic. What does "never" mean? The political situation will be different next year; Maung might not have to travel so much.

Don't refer to the future. What about this moment?

I am frozen. My mind hisses away, back and forth, like a whip. I'm grinding my teeth. Will I be able to grate a few words out of my mouth? He hasn't left yet. In fact, he has sat down on the bed. Scent rushes into my nose: tangy green soap on warm skin, clean-cotton-towel smell. His hair is slicked back like the pelt of an otter, thick and gleaming. I want him to embrace me, comfort me. I hate him.

He has used me for sex. I cannot speak. What is there to say? If he'd told me that he was going to leave after making love, I never would have undressed. He knew this. I want him to go. Then I will take my own god-damn hot shower.

He sits on the edge of the bed, his hands in his lap, his gaze soft, a fake penitent. But gradually I realize that's not it. He isn't asking forgiveness. He's sitting there blocking my view of the trees because he has something else to say. I force myself to look at him. The obvious regret on his face makes me think that he'll tell me something hopeful. Make it better. Or change his mind and stay with me.

"I am sorry. Truly sorry."

Well, that's something, an apology. Then I learn what else he is apologizing for.

"But I have to leave Chiang Mai in a few days. I'm going to meet with a military group in China. An important meeting. I wanted to tell you before, but you were so sick, and I knew the news would upset you. When you got out of the hospital and said you would come here, I thought it would be best to wait and tell you in person."

I laugh—a violent spasm in the throat—and shake my head. Again he doesn't know what to say. Am I really laughing, or barking out a dry sob? I'm not sure, but I will not shed a single tear in front of him. "It's fine, Maung. I'll see you later. You need to go, don't you?"

"Yes," he says, relieved to be able to answer a simple question.

I don't watch him dress. I take a long shower. To my surprise, I don't cry. Fuck crying, it just gives you wrinkles. I get ready to go out by myself. Fury has wakened something unexpected in me: an appetite. For the first time in more than a month, I'm ravenously hungry.

Over the next few days, Maung and I return to each other. We make love with concentrated tenderness, as though we're holding our breath. I don't bring up his speedy postcoital departure. *Why bother,* says the voice, *it's part of your job description, and his.* We eat together. We are close again because we have to be; he will leave soon. Lying in bed, I ask the inevitable question: "How long will you be on the border?" The Chinese border, not the Thai or Indian one. I know the answer, but I want to hear him say it with that familiar tone of regret that has become, for me, an expression of affection.

"Almost a month."

As I thought. He will be in China when I leave for Greece. These are the last days we'll spend together until I return from Europe. By silent agreement, we will not discuss the date of my return. Also by silent agreement, we decide we mustn't waste our last week together. We must love each other now. I make him use the condoms. A barrier method, yes. Little border. I regret it every time. While I crave and relish the lovemaking, I deny its greater purpose. I deny our deeper longing, which feels like a betrayal of us both. But I don't want to leave Thailand attached to Maung by an unborn baby.

One evening, after making love, we lie in bed listening to the warring street dogs. After a particularly vicious brawl I ask, "Does it ever feel like you're failing?"

I don't need to explain the question. He looks at me with endearing condescension, and smiles. "You are so new to this. Failure has nothing to do with it. When you are on the losing side, the struggle is not about winning or losing. It's about . . . continuing. The one who keeps going will triumph."

"Perseverance. Endurance."

"Yes."

I don't necessarily believe this, but I hold my tongue.

He pulls out of our embrace to look me in the eye. "It is not about my life. The struggle may be longer than my life. I hope not. But I don't know when I will die. I might not see Burma become democratic. But it will happen. Maybe for the next generation. I do what I can. Of course, I have my ego, my selfish desires. But I understand they aren't important, they are the normal imperfections. I am just a man. You cannot be a good leader if you don't understand your weaknesses."

I wait for him to say, "What about you, what are your weaknesses?" because I want to unburden myself, I want to confide in him, tell him that I love him but am not his match, not his equal. He has some steel alloy in him where I have none. I am made of nothing but flesh, and words.

But he doesn't ask me, and I don't offer. Never mind giving my heart—I can't even bear to reveal its workings, because I don't want to hurt him. I'm afraid of making my reservations irrevocable by giving voice to them.

In the middle of the night, he wakes me up, shouting incoherently, striking the air with his hands. "Maung, wake up!" Still half asleep, he pulls me close and nestles his head against my chest like a child. "What's wrong?" I whisper.

"I dreamed I'd been stabbed five times. I was dying."

I kiss the top of his head. "Go back to sleep. I love you." I love you. Despite the failings of love, it is such a balm to say and to hear those words. He falls asleep again almost immediately, and in the morning barely remembers his nightmare.

How will I leave for Europe without promising the date of my return? He reads the *Bangkok Post* out loud and we laugh about some ridiculous news items. He walks into the apartment and guesses what I am thinking in five seconds. After we drink a good bottle of wine, he announces that he has an important question. I raise one eyebrow, half curious, half cringing. He asks, "Why does every bottle of wine have such a complicated name?" We go swimming at a swank hotel pool and we are like young lovers—we *are* young lovers—playing in the water just as we did those first days at the lake. I must try to be patient. To see what happens.

By a daily act of will, I calm my anger. More accurately, I dismantle it and put it away, as a soldier might take apart his gun and place it in a case, each chunk snug in its separate compartment. The tool I use to accomplish this tidy sorting-out is meditation, for I am true to my aim and walk up the hill almost every morning to the dusty, ant-tracked pagoda, where I sit and breathe out fury like a dragon. Meditation proves instructive, in that it allows me to realize just how furious I am, about how many things.

Being inveigled into sex by a revolutionary has made me think about all the ways in which women are used. The revolution uses men, certainly, but it uses women in ways that rarely allow them to be celebrated as heroines. What have I been doing here? Why have I spoken to so many men? Why are my notebooks full of the words of men?

I think of the stoic faces of the women from the jungle and the refugee camps. Some of them I spoke to, through men. Why didn't I have a woman translator? I remember how many of their husbands were away, busy fighting battles in a war they will not win. The women raise children alone, without proper health care, without resources. When the men return on leave from their fruitless war, they impregnate their wives again.

Why is Khaing Lin in a jungle camp carrying stones uphill on her head? Why has it taken so much longer for a few of the women to get out of the camps? This is the good revolution. These are the good men. But many of them scoffed openly when they found out that a large sum of NGO money from abroad was earmarked for women's projects: sewing and weaving workshops, ventures in education, family planning—the most basic networks of communication for women to share their common concerns and to help one another. From women I have learned that domestic abuse is a serious problem in the refugee camps, but not one in more than a hundred men I've interviewed ever brought this subject up—even when we talked specifically about camp life. Maung says it's all a matter of education, but he always says that.

At Dr. Cynthia's clinic in the town of Mae Sot, I saw a strange exhibit of small twigs and bits of metal. Some were straight, some jagged or fashioned into hooks. They formed a display that might have come from an ancient culture, a collection of mysterious tools whose uses were lost in time. Except that the young assistant who showed me around the clinic explained that they were all objects found embedded in the cervixes and uteruses of poor Burmese women desperate to have abortions. Performed by "herb women," the abortions are sometimes successful, sometimes not. It depends on one's definition of success. The abortion usually works. But many women suffer from life-threatening bacterial infections and too many of them die.

These and other thoughts arise when I meditate on the hill in the disused pagoda. I join them, as the sages recommend, to my practice, releasing one image after another on the out breath. But when I breathe in they come back, the curved bits of wood and metal, the faces and bodies of women. I have missed too many of their voices. And I'm leaving soon. Just as I learn that their breath is also my breath, I realize that it's too late to know them.

CHAPTER 50

THE SHINING SEPARATION

· · · ·

Maung leaves Chiang Mai today. He's coming to pick me up; we'll say goodbye at the airport—a first for us. An airport farewell promises a heady combination of formality and romance. I will be graceful and movie-star-like. Sad movie-star-like. But strong. Glistening eyes, no spillage. Ingrid Bergmanesque. Though she was the one who got on the plane in Casablanca and flew away.

I won't see him for at least two months, more likely three or four. Like most significant departures, the impending one feels unreal, a shape with no substance, which may be why I keep thinking of Hollywood. His cell phone will not work in China, and he's not sure what kind of land-line access there will be. In Greece, I won't have a telephone, either.

Whom is he meeting with on the Chinese border? The Kachin Independence Army? No. The KIA signed a cease-fire with the Burmese junta a couple of years ago. Underground agents? Doubtful. Old school buddies? I have no idea.

The phone jangles, makes me jump. Maung is here, waiting down in the atrium.

I am careful not to trip on the last flight of stairs. My beloved stands there in a suit jacket and pressed trousers. I'm surprised he's so dressed up. He could pass as a businessman. I suppose that's the idea. Or maybe he's meeting someone from the Chinese government? I wish I'd worn a skirt.

We smile and walk out into the afternoon sunlight. I've forgotten my sunglasses, but there's no time to fetch them. Maung steers me by the elbow toward a large black truck parked in the road. None of the dissidents I've met own a black truck. None of the foreign NGO workers, either. The passenger's and driver's doors open at the same time; two men step out and turn toward us. Just as I wonder where the perfunctory smiles are, they appear. They're in their late forties, early fifties, a charming couple— one slight and gentle-looking, the other, according to the international cliché of pairing the good with the bad, meaty and brutish, his big head bristly with crew cut.

I take in their nice clothes, their relaxed yet faintly demanding demeanor, that massive black machine still purring exhaust behind them: they are Thai. They have power. Resisting Maung's hand on my elbow, I slow our pace and whisper, "Who are they?" Why aren't we going to the airport in a hired car, or even a songtow? Why are we going to the airport with two Thai men? We stop walking. To the Thai men, we might be having a tender moment. Maung does his best, looking with round, liquid eyes into my narrowed slits. "They will help me if I need help." I frown harder. "So that I can pass security." I tilt my head. "Because I'm traveling with a fake passport."

They are Thai military intelligence agents. I've met other Thai MI before, in Mae Sot.

"Why didn't you tell me they were coming with us? Or, more accurately, that we are going with them?" I swear under my breath. I don't mind, I just wish he would tell me. A few details. Occasionally.

"Because I wasn't sure they would be available." The relief in his voice makes it sound as though he's smiling. He is happy to have them with us. For their airport-security powers as well as for the monster truck. What man doesn't want to be sent to the airport in a gleaming black machine with tinted windows? If it makes his passage safer and easier, then I am glad they are here. So much for our romantic goodbye.

After brief introductions, I step up on the running board and duck down. Spacious back seats, tan leather. Maung follows me. Alone, we turn to each other in the freezing air. I'm covered in goosebumps. Maung runs his hand over my forearm and whispers, in Burmese, "It's very cold, isn't it?" Neither of us is used to air-conditioning.

The skinny man throws his cigarette down in the parking lot; the bigger one takes Maung's bag to the back of the truck. Then we're on our way through the lively streets of Chiang Mai and the sunstruck landscape that will lead us to the airport. Through the smoky glass, everything is tinged a shade of gray or purple. It's such a realistic way to see the world, perpetually bruised.

When will I meet Maung again? That is the question I ask myself as our odd little company goes through the motions of his departure. We approach the flight desk, smile at the Thai service attendant, take in her dazzling gold jewelery and purple eyeshadow. Maung's hand, I see as he passes over his ticket, is shaking slightly. Probably just too many cigarettes. Nicotine and coffee overdose.

We have said goodbye already, standing in the diesely air of a loading zone as people hurried past. Farther out, bougainvillea burned in the flower beds, vivid in the stark light of midafternoon. The Thai agents had gone to talk on their separate phones. I realized this would be it, my last moment alone with him, standing in the public blur and clamor. His face was close to mine, though we did not think of kissing. He was talking. I breathed in words with the scent of tobacco from his mouth.

"You know, there is a place I hold people," he said. "A place inside where the ones I love stay with me. They never go away. There are my parents, and a few others. I need to care for many people, but that isn't the same as this feeling, this place inside. You are there. I will hold you in my heart forever."

His declaration left me speechless. I wished he had made it earlier, so that I would have had more time to respond. We are not in the habit of making declarations. I gripped his hand and closed my eyes, unprepared for the onslaught of my own tears. No Kleenex, as usual. He gave me a handkerchief. "I knew I had to bring two," he said, laughing, his fingers on the small of my back as we reentered the terminal building, where the Thai agents stood waiting for us.

What a demanding job they have! Watching over Burma's busy political population in Thailand, dissidents, activists, revolutionaries of various ethnicities, NGO workers. Keeping their Burmese MI-agent counterparts happy. Managing their own finicky relationship with the Thai democratic government. Playing to every side, trying to amass as much information about everyone as they can, keeping tabs, doing damage control, being everyone's friend. They are the ultimate diplomats, really. The Burmese acronyms alone must drive them crazy, as well as the fact that almost everyone has at least two different names, a real name and an activist name.

The big guy is respectful to Maung and solicitous with me, politely running through the beloved questions that all Thais must ask foreigners: Where do you come from? Do you like Thailand? Can you eat hot food?

In turn, I would like to ask him, How far do your earthly powers extend? To China? Will you make sure he gets on the return plane? Will you protect him even when you cannot see him?

Suddenly I am afraid something will happen to Maung: an accident, a violent incident in the rough border town where he will stay. Though he forgot his own nightmare of being stabbed, it has remained with me like a bad omen.

But this is not the time to worry about portents and dreams. He's leaving. We stand outside the security gates for a few minutes, but he's anxious to go through, in case the false passport holds him up. That's when our in-

fluential escorts will become involved. Maung and I talked about his papers last night, while he sat drinking a beer and smoking and I lay on the
bed examining the signature binding of his passport. I held the coveted
little book up to the light and flipped its pages. "An excellent job," he said
of the forgery.

It's increasingly difficult to travel on these documents. Airport security
is getting wiser; there is talk of installing cameras at ticket counters. Soon
there won't be any anonymous travelers. The very best forged passports
that cost thousands of dollars will be identifiable and traceable. "But I prefer not to think about that right now," Maung told me. "One trip at a
time."

The Thais stand a few feet away to let us say goodbye. We kiss each
other quickly, lightly. A hug. Remember this: his body fits so easily into
my own, the hollows to curves, bones nestled into flesh. Underneath the
light suit jacket, I feel his shirt damp with sweat. The airport, too, is air-
conditioned. He's sweating because he's nervous, though it doesn't show on
his calm face.

"I have to go," he whispers against my cheek, and I release him immediately. He pulls me close again and murmurs so quietly in my ear that I
scarcely catch all the words; I have to piece them together by rhythm: "I
take strength from knowing you are alive on this earth."

I, the writer, have nothing so profound to say to him.

We stand and watch him join the queue of people. Two men check tick-
ets and passports. Maung approaches them and hands his passport to the
younger one. Because he's Burmese, there is the usual scrutiny accompanied by the suspicious sidelong glances. The men squint at his ticket, then
slowly turn the pages of the passport. In their hands, as opposed to my own
last night, it seems insubstantial, not a document at all, just small squares
of paper. The older attendant asks Maung to stand off to the side, while the

younger one takes the passport away. Maung stands there, handsome, dignified. He smiles at us once, then lets his eyes rest elsewhere.

The Thai agents standing with me are also experts at dissimulation. They chat with each other distractedly, littering the air with words. When my eyes flutter over the slender man's face, he gives me such a fatherly smile that I have to look away. The three of us watch the scene unfold just inside the security gate.

But it's undramatic. No intervention is required. The young man returns with the small red book and hands it to Maung, who thanks him. We can see the round sweat stain on his back when he removes his jacket for the X-ray machine, but he walks through it without incident and slips the fine jacket back on. Like any traveling businessman, he refastens his watch and returns his documents to his breast pocket.

It's done. He's going to China.

Maung and I meet at the glass wall between the terminal and the departure hall. We wave and smile like children through the shining separation. He puts his hand on the glass. I place my hand there also, fingers against fingers. But of course I cannot feel him.

A moment later, the Thai agents appear. The burly one with the crew cut says, "We need to go now. We'll take you back to your apartment." Maung inclines his head to them, and to me, then turns away and joins the other travelers.

EPILOGUE

. . . .

A Day Later, Maung called me from China and said, "I'm afraid you will leave me and not come back." We had never spoken of ending our relationship. My upcoming sojourn in Greece was only a trip away from the center of the world, to which I would return, to continue life with the man I loved and the people who had befriended me. Aye Aye Lwin, Ma Tu, Chit Hlaing, and dissident friends referred to the time when I would live in Thailand, not on the actual border, not in a camp in the jungle, but in Bangkok or Chiang Mai or Mae Sot, on the border of the mind inhabited by so many people who work for Burma. My return was a given. I believed in it as much as they did.

But Maung had undone me. "Are you still there?" he asked.

I finally replied, "I can't do it, Maung. I can't be the wife of the dissident, the revolutionary. I'm not strong enough. I'm sorry."

"It's because I couldn't come to you when you were sick, isn't it?" he asked. "It's because I can't take care of you."

Yes. That was it, partly. But it was also the surreal walk I had taken with the Thai MI agents, through the airport parking lot, each of them grilling me about my mate and my choice of a mate.

The agents had monitored our final touches, our last glance. Then they monitored me some more as they took me back to my apartment. It was a brief, profound lesson, as well as a teeth-rattling shake. By necessity, my life with Maung would involve his people, his supporters, his comrades, his men, his women. I had accepted that, somehow; it was a work-in-progress. But I hadn't thought of these others. Also by necessity, my life with a Burmese political figure would involve them, Maung's watchers and observers, both friend and foe.

They were kind to me, the Thai MI agents. But they were not subtle. "Your boyfriend has many problems," said the slender one, turning in his seat to look at me. He had two moles in the places where dimples would be, which gave him an almost clownish smile. The beefy one was driving, but glanced often in the rearview mirror.

"They have a military government." I stared back at the smiling man. "You know how difficult the military can be."

He laughed outright. "I do, I do. But when we are with such people we also have their problems."

"Who doesn't have problems? I'm sure you do, too. But your wife loves you, doesn't she?"

"Of course," he replied with an impatient wave of his hand. "But my problems are not like *his*." A new thought passed as a frown over his face. "You're not *married* to him, are you?"

I sighed. "No."

He shook his head. "I don't understand." In Thai, the literal translation of that phrase is "It doesn't enter my heart." "What are you doing?"

"I'm doing what I have to do," I replied, my voice grave with real emotion. But I was also acting. I wanted my Ingrid Bergman line, and I got it.

The bristle-headed driver ruined the moment with a deep belly laugh. I met his merry eyes in the mirror. "But you can do anything you want! You are beautiful, and free."

More questions came. The slender man covered the territory: what I was doing in Thailand, when I planned to leave, when I would return. He asked me repeatedly, in different ways, what Maung was going to do in China. For once, I was pleased to know nothing.

I was trembling by the time the truck pulled up in front of the apartment building. I said goodbye to the agents and hopped out. They waved as they drove away. I waved back, spat on the road, and stared in the direction of their monster machine long after it had disappeared.

Two weeks later, a surprising thing happened.

Maung returned early from China—before I left for Greece. I think he came back to show me that he *could* come back for me; he could act on my behalf, because he loved me. Or perhaps he came back because he finished his work in China early.

It was too late, though. "You've already decided to finish our relationship," he said sadly one evening, after we reached the end of a conversation we'd had several times before. But it wasn't so much that I'd made a decision as that I'd imagined my escape. Escape was still my solution to insoluble problems. I was soon to be disappointed, though, because fleeing from Maung and the border didn't work. That failed escape was, in fact, the beginning of the end of escaping. As a modus operandi that had once saved my life by differentiating me from my family, it had become a habit that had outlived its usefulness. Almost.

I left Maung and arrived on my beloved island, emotionally and physically exhausted. People I'd known there for a decade didn't recognize me. I'd lost too much weight. I looked different. Like a nun in both the Buddhist and the Greek Orthodox Christian traditions, I compounded that difference by shaving my head—an act that Barba Andreas, my old shepherd friend, talked about for years afterward, and never forgave me for. But I was a different woman from the person they had known. I gave away or burned all the strappy, flowery dresses from my early, voluptuous twenties. None of them fit me anymore, in size or in spirit. My hips were too lean, my breasts too small.

The villagers and my friends were not impressed. They fed me and fed me. The island earth fed me. I took to lying in the field at night, under a massive bowl of stars—the same stars I had seen in the jungle, though they looked different from a half-wild olive grove. I let my skeleton settle into the earth. One night, a scorpion scuttled up onto my hip, under my sleeveless shirt. Recognizing its particular double-pronged scurry, I lay motionless, though part of me wanted to move and to be stung. It seemed a way to transform my inward pain into the electric pain of the body, which I could release with a scream and tears. My healthier instincts prevailed; I remained completely still. The scorpion crossed over the hill of a breast, across the top of my bare shoulder. It slid down onto the ground and scrabbled away through the grass. With the still-warm dirt pressed into my flesh, I thought: I might already be buried. Staring up at the Milky Way— *galaxias,* from the Greek word for milk, *gala*—I wondered if I had made the defining error of my life by leaving Asia, abandoning a man I loved so deeply and a purpose I believed in with my whole, fragmented heart.

In that free, fertile kingdom, ribboned by the azure Aegean, I waded into a gulf of loss and treaded water for a long time, mourning the losses of those in Burma and on the border. I mourned my own loss. I still loved Maung. An attempt to love someone else, as a distraction, failed miserably. I loved him; I wanted him still. Yet I had left him purposefully. It was a knot of emotion and circumstance I could not undo. It's unnatural to rupture a profound physical and emotional connection at its zenith; I wished we'd been arguing openly, the relationship cracking at the seams. I knew that the tensions between us had been real, and impossible to ignore. Neither of us had had the time, the peace, or the maturity to attend to them. Why was I still thinking about it, many months later, almost a year? I had betrayed him, willfully, adding to his deprivation. What kind of love was that?

.   .   .

And yet. I knew in my gut that I had made the right choice. To keep my own future safe for my work as a writer, I had to leave both Maung and the border. I had seen my private nature: I would not be able to make the sacrifices that other Western women had made when they married Burmese men. Most of them would not use the word *sacrifice,* at least not openly, and that was the difference between us. I berated myself: *You should have known better all along.* You should never have allowed yourself to fall in love with him. Hadn't Zoë foretold everything, in her way? But I had not listened. I thought further back, to Marla, who had accused me of being a selfish artist. I had proved her right. But if my vocation had become subsumed in Maung's life and in the life of our sure-to-come family and its added responsibilities, who would I be? What was I but a writer?

I could not risk testing that question. My self was, and still is, bound up in my identity as an artist. To endanger the work endangers the self.

So I left Burma and the Thai-Burma border behind. But they did not leave me. In the little stone house in Greece, I put up dozens of the photographs I had taken in Burma and on the border, and I returned to the novel *The Lizard Cage.* It soon became clear that the book had stalled because I was too entangled emotionally, politically, and physically with my material. The closer I had been to the turmoil—witnessing the aftermath of events, absorbing stories directly, receiving that steady stream of faxes outlining the latest disasters in Burma and on the border—the less capable I was of creating art out of it. Now that I was far away, forced to imagine myself back into the world I had left behind, I was able to enter the fictional prison of *The Lizard Cage* and stay there.

Stay there I did, for another eight years, during which time I managed to get a visa to return to Burma once, in 2001. This was a changed and an unchanged Burma, a country that felt more open in some ways: limited Internet access was available, telephone connections were more reliable, foreign NGOs had established or reestablished offices in Rangoon, and were doing important work with street kids, in HIV prevention, maternal health, and education. And Ma Thida was free. She was the young woman writer and doctor whose unjust imprisonment had drawn me to Burma in the first place. Though she had served only seven years of her twenty-year sentence of solitary confinement, the Burmese junta had released her in response to intense lobbying by Amnesty International and PEN.

It was a miracle for me to sit across from her in a tea shop and listen to her stories, which she told without a drop of melodrama. She had contracted pulmonary tuberculosis in Insein Prison, and become so ill that she couldn't walk; fellow prisoners carried her to her parents when they came to visit. Her weight dropped to eighty pounds. She developed such severe endometriosis that she bled copious amounts every day. She was soon suffering from acute liver failure.

The prison authorities eventually took her medications away because they believed she would try to commit suicide. "Can you believe how ridiculous they are? I was trying to live, not to die! I told them that if I died it would be their responsibility, their fault—I would have nothing to do with my own death! And the warden said to me, 'You see, Ma Thida, you are free. You are free in your mind and your heart. But we are government employees, and we are trapped. We have to do what they say.' " Over Burmese tea, we laughed together at this absurd, profound truth.

Like many political prisoners, she credited her survival to daily vipassana meditation. That liberating practice still seemed to sparkle around her and through her clear, forthright voice. In a fearful place, she had come to live beyond fear. She had returned to her medical work and to her writing. I visited her clinic, where she often treated other former political prisoners who had been tortured. We ate meals together, talked books and politics, and laughed a lot, surprised by how much we had in common. She was hopeful about some kind of change within the SPDC, as the ruling junta was now called. (Repeatedly criticized for the Orwellian moniker

SLORC, the generals had changed their name to the State Peace and Development Council.) But she was not banking that change would come too quickly.

A few years later, in 2004, the prominent student activist Min Ko Naing was also released from prison after fifteen years in solitary confinement. His release made many Burma watchers hope for a softening in the regime's policies toward its opponents, in particular toward that other famous political prisoner, Aung San Suu Kyi, who has been under house arrest for much of the past twenty years. Another encouraging shift has been the gradual relaxation on travel restrictions; more Burmese citizens manage to obtain passports for travel abroad.

Tragically, though, Burma today remains closed in the most crucial ways. The junta, led by General Than Shwe, has moved the capital from Rangoon to a new city called Naypyidaw, built literally from the ground up, to the tune of several billion dollars—in a country whose spending on health and education is one of the lowest in the world. This bizarre move several hundred kilometers inland separates the top brass as well as the entire political and civil administration more completely than ever from the people they govern. Alienation is arguably the ruling junta's most serious pathology. Though allied to the many hungry nations and individuals who covet the country's natural and human resources, the generals are increasingly isolated from and ignorant of the sixty million people to whom those resources rightly belong.

In August 2007, the junta dropped all subsidies on oil and natural gas, resulting in a doubling and tripling of fuel prices. This led to a rapid increase in the cost of food. The price of Burmese rice has long been a gauge for measuring unrest in the country; when it goes up, people literally go hungry and get angry. Min Ko Naing and other activists began to protest the SPDC's debilitating fuel-price increases in mid-August. By September, thousands of monks and nuns had joined these protests and marched together in Rangoon and Mandalay. The Sangha is the only large organization left in Burma that still has some freedom of movement, freedom of assembly, freedom of communication. Hundreds of thousands of people across the country joined the Saffron Revolution, as it became known, inspired by the Sangha's peaceful but bold acts of civil disobedience.

The rest of the world was inspired, too. Footage taken by clandestine Burmese video reporters allowed the Saffron Revolution to go global. Aware of the cultural and religious importance of the monks and the nuns, many of us held our breath, thinking that their presence would prevent the junta from ending the protests violently. But we were wrong. Soldiers opened fire on their own people. Dozens were killed, though the exact number of deaths has never been determined. Many people remain missing, disappeared. Min Ko Naing, other political activists, and scores of monks and nuns were arrested and given prison sentences as long as sixty-eight years.

Mourning for those who were murdered in 2007 was not over when Cyclone Nargis hit the Irrawaddy Delta in May 2008. Though official death tolls for the devastation wrought by the high winds, floods, and collapsed buildings are usually placed around 100,000, some NGOs estimate the number of dead to be much higher. The cyclone severely affected between two and three million people.

But the hardest thing about Cyclone Nargis was not the loss of life due to the horrific violence of nature; it was the SPDC's criminal response to the tragedy. Through decades of military rule, the leaders of Burma have systematically damaged their people's ability to communicate, to organize, and to trust. Cyclone Nargis showed that the generals are not immune to the deformations they have wrought upon their citizens. Faced with the biggest natural disaster in Burmese history, the SPDC did not know how to help its own people—it was too accustomed to treating them as enemies. General Than Shwe refused to allow dozens of qualified Western aid workers to enter the country. Unshamed by the rotting bodies of people and animals, the generals dithered away precious days, fearful of who might see the truth. Ever-resourceful citizens from less affected parts of the country did as much as they could to help. Groups of entertainers, young medical students, businessmen, and thousands of members of the Sangha collected funds and mobilized to help feed the people and attend the injured and sick.

After a meeting with the U.N. Secretary-General Ban Ki-moon, General Than Shwe finally relented and opened the door to foreign-aid workers, regardless of nationality. But the damage was done, and, in the words of one Burmese writer, "this was the deepest damage. The people already hated the regime, of course. They were already angry at the regime, yes. But now they became bitter. Such bitterness! It is like our leaders are no longer Burmese people anymore. If they were Burmese people, how could they do this to us?"

On my first visit back to the border in 2001, friends filled me in on the news, and I saw evidence of it myself. One significant development was that international and Burmese NGOs had begun to focus directly on women's issues, and the result was awe-inspiring. Burmese women dissidents had become a force in their own right. Some spoke two or three ethnic languages as well as Thai and English, and they were articulate, impassioned, and fiercely intelligent in every tongue. Maung had fallen in love with and married one of these remarkable women. Friends explained that he had left the ABSDF, formed his own NGO activist group, and made a home in Chiang Mai. Revealing my own unfulfilled longings, I immediately asked whether or not he had children. No, I was told, not yet.

What a hard emptiness opened inside me then. I had no children, either, no husband. Where were those brown-eyed babies we might have had? They were ghosts in my body. His life was different now, more stable. Perhaps I had been too impatient, as usual. I returned to the apartment I was staying in—the same place I'd been staying when Maung left for China—and I lay down on the thin, anonymous sheets and cried. What if . . . ? My yearning made no sense, but yearning doesn't have to adhere to logic. It needs only to yearn.

Later that week, I went to meet a friend at a conference at the University of Chiang Mai and there he was, Maung, walking down a wide set of concrete steps. White cotton shirt, dark trousers. Him. Deep brown skin, hair thick and shining across his forehead. My friend and I were standing with several other people. I saw him seconds before he saw me, but it was no advantage. When he reached the bottom of the steps, he was standing directly in front of me, his mouth open, his eyes on my face. He began to talk, as he would, to my friend, whom he had worked with occasionally. She didn't know who he was to me.

Who was he to me?

I blinked at him, my ears ringing. "How are you?" he said.

"Surprised." Stunned breathless.

He smiled back. Ah, yes, the mouth. "Me, too. I didn't know you were here." Our eyes locked. He looked so familiar, my own kind. It was difficult to believe that we no longer had any claims on each other. No children. No future. Just a time, some years ago. Yet there was in the air, like an invisible cord around us, the possibility of touching.

I mean, the impossibility. We said goodbye. I didn't watch him walk away.

ACKNOWLEDGMENTS

· · · ·

I am grateful to everyone, without exception, who appears in these pages, but I am especially grateful to Burmese friends, colleagues, and strangers who told me their stories and sometimes made me promise to publish them. Thank you, Ler Wah Lobo, for the help with translations. I remain indebted to the journalist Heather Kelly, who invited me back to Thailand in 1996, and who encouraged me to visit Burma. Despite some harsh judgments in this book regarding the Fourth Estate, which reflect my experiences and my thoughts at the time, I am thankful to many journalists, of various nationalities, whose work has provided me with not only facts but also with deeper insight into Burma and the politics of Southeast Asia. Everyone at the magazine *The Irrawaddy,* working in both Thailand and clandestinely in Burma, has my sincere gratitude.

I owe a special thanks to the people who help turn manuscripts into books, and who put up with my extraordinary ability to miss deadlines: Jackie Kaiser, my agent, and my editors Anne Collins, Lorna Owen, and Nan Talese.

The Canada Council and the Ontario Council for the Arts—meaning, the people of Canada and of Ontario—funded some of my early work on this book, at a time when I wasn't sure that I should be writing it. *Tzey-zu-tin-ba-deh:* thank you. I finished a good portion of the manuscript while I was Nonfiction Writer-in-Residence at the Toronto Reference Library, where many good people made being a writer more enjoyable and less solitary. I would also like to acknowledge the publications where some of the chapters first appeared in altered form: *Brick, Outpost, Prairie Fire, The Irrawaddy, This Magazine, Shambhala Sun,* and the travel anthology *AWOL.*

To dear friends and colleagues Anne Bayin, Linda Griffiths, Diana Bryden, Ann Shin, Mireille Katirzoglou, my sincere appreciation. I could not have written *Burmese Lessons* without the work of child-care providers Angeline Ducado and Grace Fernando, to whom I remain obliged for many things, including, perhaps, my sanity.

And to Robert Chang, my husband, thank you for the spacious world we live and work in together. I could not be more blessed.

A NOTE ABOUT THE AUTHOR

Karen Connelly is the author of nine books of nonfiction, fiction, and poetry. *The New York Times Book Review* compared her novel of Burma, *The Lizard Cage,* to the works of Solzhenitsyn, Mandela, and Orwell. It was nominated for the Kiriyama Prize and won Britain's Orange Broadband Prize for New Writers. Raised in Calgary, Connelly has lived for extended periods of time in different parts of Asia and Europe and now has two homes, one in Toronto and one in Greece.

A NOTE ABOUT THE TYPE

The text of this book was set in Granjon, designed for the
English branch of the Linotype Corporation in 1928. Granjon
is a reproduction of a sixteenth-century version of Garamond.
It is considered a beautiful and exceptionally readable
typeface in both text and display sizes.